Dadibaajim

CRITICAL STUDIES IN NATIVE HISTORY

ISSN 1925-5888

Dadibaajim

RETURNING HOME THROUGH NARRATIVE

HELEN OLSEN AGGER

UNIVERSITY OF MANITOBA PRESS

Dadibaajim: Returning Home through Narrative
© Helen Olsen Agger 2021

25 24 23 22 21   1 2 3 4 5

University of Manitoba Press
Winnipeg, Manitoba, Canada
Treaty 1 Territory
uofmpress.ca

Cataloguing data available from Library and Archives Canada
Critical Studies in Native History, ISSN 1925-5888 ; 22
ISBN 978-0-88755-954-9 (PAPER)
ISBN 978-0-88755-958-7 (PDF)
ISBN 978-0-88755-956-3 (EPUB)
ISBN 978-0-88755-960-0 (BOUND)

Cover design by Mike Carroll.
Interior design by Jess Koroscil.
Cover and interior images courtesy of Helen Olsen Agger.
Map design by Weldon Hiebert. Maps contain information
licensed under the Open Government Licence – Canada.

Printed in Canada

This book has been published with the help of a grant from the
Federation for the Humanities and Social Sciences, through the Awards
to Scholarly Publications Program, using funds provided by the
Social Sciences and Humanities Research Council of Canada.

The University of Manitoba Press acknowledges the financial support for
its publication program provided by the Government of Canada through
the Canada Book Fund, the Canada Council for the Arts, the Manitoba
Department of Sport, Culture, and Heritage, the Manitoba Arts Council,
and the Manitoba Book Publishing Tax Credit.

Funded by the Government of Canada | Canadä

Miigwech,	Thank you,
Nimaamaawens,	My dearest Mother,
E'wiiji'ishiyan indanokiiwining,	For supporting my work,
E'miinishiyan gigikendaasowin,	For entrusting me with your
E'gikinô'amawishiyan wenji	Knowledge, for teaching me the
Ishpendaagwak i'i	Value of that
Gigikendaasowin.	Knowledge.
Giin, Nimaamaawens,	To you, my dear Mother,
Gidinin,	I express
Gichi miigwech.	My deepest gratitude.

Contents

Preface

My mother, Dedibaayaanimanook, began to absorb the fundamentals of Anishinaabe philosophy as she listened to the dadibaajim conversations of her elders. From the time of my own birth and early childhood, I had the privilege of hearing her dadibaajim narratives as she spoke them to my siblings and me in Anishinaabemowin. But it was not until much later in life, after many years had passed, that I came to more fully understand the wisdom in her narratives and to realize that they are the iteration of what her elders had taught her as a child. As the means by which Anishinaabe people transmitted their knowledges, insights, and teachings from one generation to the next throughout the ages, dadibaajim, oral narrative, is a critical institution of learning. By listening to dadibaajim, not only can we as Anishinaabe people today learn about our ancestors and homelands, but non-Anishinaabe people may learn to reremember their ancestral places of origin. The language of that learning is Anishinaabemowin.

My extensive use of Anishinaabemowin may at first seem jarring, but the language continues to be the means for centring Anishinaabe thought—just as it animated and gave meaning to the world in which Dedibaayaanimanook and her fellow elders were born and raised. I also use Anishinaabemowin to demonstrate that oral tradition and the Western essay-writing convention can blend together to contribute to both the Anishinaabe and academic communities in ways that decolonize research norms and expectations. Highlighting the importance of telling Anishinaabe history using an Anishinaabe frame of reference,[1] therefore, this work sets out a theoretical approach for colonial and neo-colonial

studies that uses qualitative interdisciplinary research methodologies
for engaging with the Anishinaabemowin language and the Anishinaabe
narrative practice, teachings, and knowledges in the academic domain. It
may even encourage readers to think critically about how researchers have
historically interacted with Indigenous communities by suggesting alternative meanings commonly associated with the notion of inquiry to challenge
settler-colonial histories, discourses, methodologies, and assumptions.

Nearly annihilated by the assault of European colonialism,
Anishinaabemowin is no longer widely spoken today. John Nichols and
Earl Nyholm's work[2] is useful for learning how the language functions and
how its essential characteristics, concepts, and rules apply. Facilitating
the process of translation from Anishinaabemowin to English and vice
versa, the information they supply helps us to avoid erasing or altering
the intended meanings of a dadibaajim speaker. This is of critical importance because an accurate understanding of the dadibaajim[3] narratives
is necessary to grasp not only the principles and philosophies of the
aanikoobidaaganag foreparents but the practices that embodied them.
With Anishinaabemowin being foundational to this work, I have included
a glossary of key words wherever an explanation of their meanings in terms
of the contexts in which I use them is required.

Anishinaabemowin sounds somewhat similar to the English language,
and its written form typically uses roman orthography. In Tables 1 and
2 below, English words indicate the approximately equivalent sounds
of Anishinaabemowin's short and long vowels. There are differences
worth noting, however. One is the long vowel e. More drawn out than
the English short vowel e, it sounds similar to the first part of the diphthong a in the English word "ate" (a diphthong being defined as the sound
formed by a combination of two vowels in a single syllable in which the
sound starts with one vowel and ends with another). Unlike English,
Anishinaabemowin always pronounces the e at the end of a word. "Name"
(sturgeon), for example, is a two-syllable word that sounds somewhat like
nu-meh with the accent on the second syllable. In terms of o, I use ô to
represent the sound that is similar to the first half of the o diphthong in
the word "vote."[4] Some Namegosibii Anishinaabe speakers also pronounce
ô as either waa or wô or both. In such cases, Gichi-jôj (Big George)
would be pronounced and spelled as Gichi Jwaaj or Gichi Jwôj. Elder

Dedibaayaanimanook uses all three pronunciations while others of the Namegosibii Anishinaabe community tend to favour one over the others.

A nasalized vowel is pronounced before ns, nz, and nzh in Anishinaabemowin. Examples are the second e in "ikwezens" (girl), the oo in "moonz" (moose), the ii in "agaashiinzh" (small), and the e in "enha'" (yes). Hence, the n in these types of words is not pronounced as it is in words with non-nasalized vowels such as the n in "enigok" (with energy) and "giinawaa" (you all) and the English "into." It should be noted that many Anishinaabemowin writers do not include the nasalized n in their writings and would thus spell "moonz" (moose) as mooz. It should also be noted that according to how Namegosibii Anishinaabe people use the language, there is no nasalized vowel in the word "oshkazhiin" (someone's fingernail).

According to Nichols and Nyholm,[5] the consonants b, d, g, j, and the zh consonant cluster are often voiced. They occur at the beginning or in the middle of words (with the exception of zh, which becomes sh) and are considered to be "hard." By contrast, the "strong" consonants p, t, k, s, and the ch / sh consonant clusters are voiceless and do not generally occur at the beginning of words. An example of an exception occurs when speakers in regions to the south of Namegosibiing say "chi miigwech" (thank you very much) rather than "gichi miigwech." In Anishinaabemowin, b sounds very similar to p; the d, to t; the g, to k; and the j, to ch. For example, the b in Bejii (Betsy) sounds halfway between a b and a p. However, the b sound in imBejiim (my Betsy) may be heard as a definite b. To illustrate further, when the word "diindiinsi" (blue jay) becomes "indiindiinsim" (my blue jay), the first d is closer to a d sound than a t.

Therefore, the letters b, d, g, and j are used instead of p, t, k, and ch at the beginning of words. This convention maintains consistency in spelling and avoids confusion.[6]

Many words contain both the hard and strong consonants, serving to illustrate pronunciation differences. The d and the t in "Detaginang" (Frank Keesick), the b and the p in "bepegwajizhaagigamiiwan" (the ice on the lake is open here and there), and the g and each k in "gakiiwekana" (portage trail) are examples. Incidentally, some consonant sounds are aspirated, with their pronunciation preceded by a slight expiration of air. The p in "aapiji" (quite) is an example of an aspirated consonant. Conventionally, the letter h, used to show aspiration, is omitted when spelling words with this feature.

The glottal stop, indicated by an apostrophe ('), serves at least three important functions in Namegosibii Anishinaabemowin. It shows the possessive case for certain words ending in a vowel, such as in "oniijaanisa'" (his/her children). It is a means for separating vowel sounds within a word, as in "ma'iingan" (wolf) or "dewe'igan" (drum), thus avoiding the need to insert a w or y between the vowels. For some speakers, the glottal stop affirms past tense, such as in "gii' maajaa" (she/he left) or "gii' nigamowag" (they sang).

These are basic Anishinaabemowin elements of pronunciation and spelling, although there are characteristic ways of speaking the language. Some Namegosibii Anishinaabeg speak the language with little inflection and a slower, more even rate of speech. Today's language learners often use the same intonation and rate with which they speak English as a first language. Another variation is the use of certain verb endings. Some say "gaa-nigamod" (the one singing) with a d while others, including Dedibaayaanimanook, would say "gaa-nigamoj," with a j. Often, these speech distinctions are immediately evident only among fluent speakers. Having just cited these characteristics, I must point out that my use of Anishinaabemowin is based on my understanding of and desire to accurately reflect how Namegosibii Anishinaabeg used the language.

In various places throughout the text, I use Cree writings to illustrate particular arguments that are applicable to Anishinaabe people. For instance, I refer to Louis Bird's community-based story work, Belinda Daniels-Fiss's logic, and Freda Ahenakew's findings on language. Namegosibii Anishinaabe narratives support the use of these Cree examples. According to the oral tradition of the community's most senior elder, Dedibaayaanimanook Sarah Keesick Olsen, for example, her father, Dedibayaash William Keesick, hunted and trapped as far away as Memegweshiwi-zaa'igan Mamakwash Lake, in the territories of the Oji-Cree and Swampy Cree northeast of Namegosibiing. Dedibaayaanimanook has also stated that her uncle Naadowe Robert's wife's name was Omashkiigookwe, which translates as Swampy Cree Woman. According to the historical record, Omashkiigookwe was from the vicinity of Osnaburgh, now known as the Mishkeegogamang First Nation. Dedibaayaanimanook's narratives reflect the commonalities in the culture, territories (in some cases), history, language, and experiences that exist among Cree and Anishinaaabe communities.

Even at the age of ninety-eight, Dedibaayaanimanook continues to provide me with her assistance. Whenever I seek confirmation of the accuracy of a Namegosibii Anishinaabemowin word, for example, I write down my question in syllabics which she reads aloud and then responds to by writing down her answer. Recently, I inquired if dadibaajim was accurate for the act of telling a narrative and she nodded in the affirmative. Use of syllabics works particularly well because Dedibaayaanimanook has difficulty hearing and even enunciating certain words. And she is not particularly fond of hearing aids!

Table 1.
Eight Vowels of Namegosibii Anishinaabemowin.

SHORT VOWELS	ANISHINAABEMOWIN	EQUIVALENT SOUND IN ENGLISH
A	asemaa (tobacco)	Up
I	nisin (three)	Pin
O	opin (potato)	Full
LONG VOWELS	ANISHINAABEMOWIN	EQUIVALENT SOUND IN ENGLISH
Aa	aaniin! (hello!)	Far
E	namegos (trout)	Ere
Ii	giiwe (goes home)	Seem
Oo	oodenaang (in town)	Move
Ô	Gichi-jôj (Big George)	Order

Table 2.
Consonants of Namegosibii Anishinaabemowin.

CONSONANT	ANISHINAABEMOWIN	EQUIVALENT SOUND IN ENGLISH
B	**b**iboon (winter)	**B**acon
Ch	gi**ch**i (large)	**Ch**ild
D	**d**ebinaak (carelessly)	**D**ebt
G	**g**aawiin (no)	**G**irl
H	en**h**a' (yes)	**H**at
J	maamakaa**j** (amazing)	**J**est
K	ma**k**wa (bear)	Pac**k**
M	**m**iinan (blueberries)	**M**ilk
N	**n**igig (otter)	**N**o
P	aa**p**iji (very)	**P**en
S	a**s**in (rock)	**S**oft
T	aabi**t**a (half)	**T**ab
W	**w**iinge (very)	**W**ent
Y	wii**y**aas (meat)	**Y**es
Z	**z**iibiins (creek)	**Z**ebra
Zh	mewin**zh**a (a long time ago)	Mea**s**ure

Dadibaajim

Ninamegosibii Anishinaabewimin

We Are the People of Trout Water

Namegosibiing Trout Lake nudges against the eastern rim of Oshedinaa. Deep in the thickest regions of the lofty ridge, three large depressions known to the Namegosibii Anishinaabeg as Binesiwajiing remain hidden from view. These are the nesting sites of binesiwag Thunderers. Associated with powerful forces that presided over the Namegosibiing region, Oshedinaa is a timeless reminder of how the people's identity is rooted in the homelands. The epistemologies of the wemitigoozhiwag European settler people reckon Oshedinaa to be the Trout Lake terminal moraine.

For sports fishers, Namegosibiing may seem typical of other northwest Ontario lakes because its unique attributes remain largely invisible to visitors unfamiliar with the history of the area. Most do not have knowledge about what was once a sturdy log house, now partly hidden by growths of boreal trees and grasses (see Figure 1). Few are aware of another structure, now in the process of fading into the flora somewhere in the northwest quadrant of Namegosibiing (see Figure 2). Although guests may have noticed the headstone with the 1916 inscription, they probably have no knowledge about the individual whose name appears on it (Figure 3). Who built these cabins and what caused their abandonment? Who are the people lying at rest in the cemetery and are there any living descendants today? Indeed, are these questions of any relevance and, if so, for whom?

Despite the volumes of historical documentation about Indigenous peoples, next to nothing has focused on the Namegosibii Anishinaabeg of northwest Ontario. Mainstream narratives dominated the discursive landscapes of the region, leaving little space for the people to articulate their sense of self, name the aanikoobidaaganag ancestors, and tell their dadibaajim narratives. The political, cultural, social, and economic forces of the colonial state denied, ignored, and effectively erased their essential beingness. With the notion of erasure implying recognition of existence and denial, non-recognition of existence, these forces reduced to nothingness the presence of Anishinaabeg as the people for whom the homelands of Namegosibiing are a rightful inheritance. The latecomers have regarded the Namegosibii Anishinaabeg as little more than another exploitable resource.

This lack of Anishinaabe self-description in the written record historically collaborated to remove them physically from the homelands. The latecomers convinced themselves to view the land as empty of any human presence. Speaking unambiguously, however, eight Namegosibii Anishinaabeg recently agreed to discuss themselves in terms of the deeply rooted sense of connection that they have maintained with Namegosibiing and its surrounding regions, as did their aanikoobidaaganag ancestors across time and generations. These individuals concur that dadibaajim must be disseminated and heard.

An explanation of the name Namegosib(iing) illustrates the linkages that exist between Namegosibii Anishinabeg and their places of home, helping to clarify how the ancestral belief systems and homelands were interlocked. "Nibi," for example, is generic for water, but the "sib" in

Figure 1.
Family residence of Gweyesh Annie Angeconeb. Gweyesh and her family
and relatives lived on what began to be called Trout Lake Lodge Island in
the early 1940s. Located in the northeast quadrant of Namegosibiing, the
island was where Dedibaayaanimanook's uncle Jiiyan and his family resided
before proceding south during the spring.

Figure 2.
One of the Dedibayaash family's winter homes. This was where
Dedibaayaanimanook's first child, Aaliz Alice, was born in 1945.

Figure 3.
Ezhi-bimishinowaaj Namegosibiing, the traditional cemetery of the
Namegosibii Anishinaabeg. Still in use today, the cemetery indicates that the
Namegosibii Anishinaabe izhitwaawin culture was affected by the forces of
European influences.

"Namegosib" specifies the clear, pure quality of one of the lake's most strik-
ing features. "Namegos" being the word for trout, "namegosib" is literally
clear trout water. The inflow of only streams and creeks, rather than rivers,
confirms the defining name of Namegosib as a spring-fed lake with sufficient depths to sustain the refreshingly cool temperatures that namegosag
lake trout prefer. Although the standard word for a lake is "zaaga'igan" or
"zaa'igan," as in Wanamani-zaa'igan for Red Lake or Ikwewi-zaa'igan for
Woman Lake, the aanikoobidaaganag ancestors deemed Namegosib a
more accurate depiction with which to articulate who they were as the
Namegosibii Anishinaabeg—the people of pristine trout water.

Maps are useful for explaining various aspects of the relationship
Namegosibii Anishinaabe people have had with the land. The map in
Figure 4 depicts Namegosibiing's location in northwest Ontario. Next,
Figure 5 shows where the lake is situated in relation to the Wanamani-
zaa'iganing municipality of Red Lake and the route the aanikoobidaaganag grandfathers took for their two and one-half days of travel to town
from Gaa-minitigwashkiigaag. A line traces their approximate course
across the frozen Namegosibiing to the lake's western shores, where they
spent the first night of their journey. Having negotiated snow-covered
Oshedinaa, the Trout Lake Ridge north of the Binesiwajiing residence of
the Thunderers, they reached East Bay on Red Lake as they neared the end
of their second day. The aanikoobidaaganag grandfathers arrived in Red
Lake halfway into the third day of their trek. It was a strenuous journey,
undertaken after the lake had frozen over in late autumn. Originally,
aanikoobidaaganag embarked upon these travels only to sell furs and
purchase manufactured goods. As relatives began moving to Red Lake
in pursuit of work, however, these outings became opportunities to visit
and exchange the latest news. To contrast with today's descendants' travel
style, these same distances are attainable at any time of the year in less
than thirty minutes using a Cessna 180. It is, of course, comparatively less
healthful for both the traveller and the aki. Other places of significance
for Namegosibii Anishinaabeg appear in Figure 6.

Namegosibiing's senior elder Dedibaayaanimanook explains that
she, her mother, and her nephew Gichi-jôj spent several days alone at
Jiibayi-zaagiing (Figure 6) Jackfish Bay while her father and brother
Jiins travelled north to trap and hunt at Memegweshiwi-zaa'igan. This
map also shows the family's winter residence (see Figure 2), close to

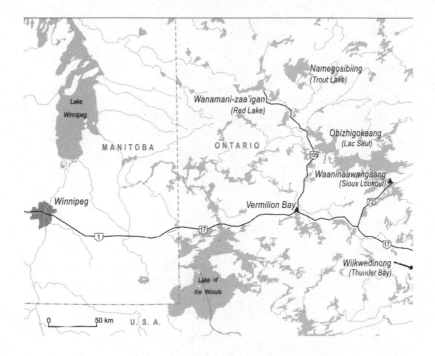

Figure 4
Namegosibiing's location: Northwest of Waaninaawangaang Sioux Lookout
and northeast of Winnipeg.

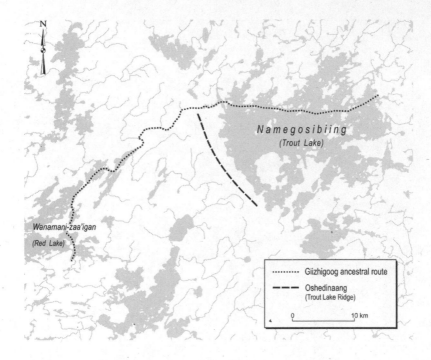

Figure 5
The ancestral route of the Giizhigoog grandfathers to Red Lake.
The dotted line represents the ancestral route from Namegosibiing to
Wanamani-zaa'igan Red Lake. The dashed line indicates the orientation
of Oshedinaang, the Trout Lake Ridge.

Figure 6
Map of Namegosibiing, showing places of significance for Namegosibii
Anishinaabeg. The line marks the Oshedinaang Trout Lake Ridge
terminal moraine.

what is now referred to as Minnow Bay (Figure 6). It is the birth place of Dedibaayaanimanook's first child, Aaliz Alice. Awaiting the arrival of spring, the Giizhig family journeyed to Gaa-minitigwashkiigaag Keesick Bay, where Dedibaayaanimanook herself was born in 1922.

While this portrayal describes only a portion of the Namegosibii Anishinaabe traditional-use lands, it provides a useful backdrop for listening to the speakers' dadibaajim narratives. Their reports about countless cases of unacknowledged responsibilities and accountabilities inject the historical record with greater balance in knowledge production by contributing an Anishinaabe perspective. When, for example, the construction of the Otawagi-baawitig Ear Falls dam flooded Obizhigokaawi-zaa'igan Lac Seul Lake, numerous customary landmarks disappeared. Dedibaayaanimanook and I once drove to Gojijiing, located on Lac Seul Lake where the English River begins its journey westward, to visit the various places of her childhood. Not realizing the island where she and her family often stopped to rest no longer exists, however, Dedibaayaanimanook expressed dismay and sadness to learn it had been submerged when the wemitigoozhiwag latecomers turned the lake into a reservoir. The record of her reaction is an important component of the region's historical narrative.

A more accurate account of the Namegosibiing homelands includes Anishinaabe people's description of their experiences and responses to the activities of the European settlers and their descendants. The documentation of Namegosibii dadibaajim is particulary important now, when there are community members who still recognize and are able to describe historical events from a first-hand Anishinaabe perspective.

What Is Our Dadibaajim?

Eight community members shared the dadibaajim narratives that are the foundation of this book, presenting events, teachings, belief systems, and descriptions of lands that together constitute their sense of distinctiveness as the Namegosibii Anishinaabeg. As a gichi-Anishinaabe senior elder, Dedibaayaanimanook Sarah Keesick Olsen presents her in-depth knowledge about the physical lands of her ancestors where she was born, raised, and lived most of her life. She uses the language of their foreparents when, for example, she refers to Anishinaabe appreciation for the

Figure 7.
The homelands as teacher. The Namegosibiing homeland territories provided people with scenes of inspiration, tranquility, beauty, and the prospects of tomorrow's opportunities on a daily basis.

Figure 8.
The homelands as provider of health. Wild rosehips were a source of
vitamins for the Namegosibii Anishinaabe people as they journeyed home in
late autumn.

aesthetic qualities of the homeland territories—the fresh air, clear water, invigorating activities, and healthy foods that people once enjoyed on a daily basis. She notes that even the seemingly trivial act of brushing against a conifer bough becomes an exquisite gift of healthiness as the tree releases its medicinal fragrances.[1] Having now lived through almost 100 winters, Dedibaayaanimanook has a deep sense of appreciation for the largesse of the ancestral homelands as both instructor and provider of life's many necessities (see, for example, Figures 7 and 8). These are among the qualities and perceptions that characterize gichi-Anishinaabe senior elders.

Oo'oons John Paul Kejick, who passed in 2017, was born on the land of his forebears but had to leave his community as a young child to attend boarding school. Still, he retained his Anishinaabemowin speech. Gwiishkwa'oo Eliza Angeconeb, also born on the noopimakamig boreal territories, experienced the traumas of boarding school attendance but has similarly held onto her ancestral language and many of her parents' teachings. Oo'oons Kejick's younger brother, Niinzhoode Kejick (also now deceased), spent many summers in Namegosibiing with his cousin William King. They too learned Anishinaabemowin, although they grew up during a time when the cultural and economic challenges of displacement kept them from living on the homelands as the ancestors had done. Martha Angeconeb is younger than Niinzhoode. Having kept the language of her ancestors, she cherishes childhood memories of time spent with her paternal grandmother. The two youngest participants, Riel Olsen and Martha's daughter, Janae Fiddler, have early experiences of life in an urban setting, attending public schools where they learned from a Western perspective. They both indicate enthusiasm for and interest in Namegosibii Anishinaabe dadibaajim.

At the core of dadibaajim and experiential knowledge as spoken by the senior elders is debwewin truth.[2] According to Anishinaabe thinker Basil Johnston, the notion of debwewin truth comes about in the following manner: "When a man or woman is said to be speaking to the ends of knowledge and to the ends of language, they are said to be speaking the truth."[3] It is about the "highest degree of accuracy" that a speaker seeks to achieve.[4] Using a combination of Anishinaabemowin and English, Dedibaayaanimanook speaks to the debwewin truth concept when she says, "That's why it's so debwemagak gakina gegoon" in her conversations.

She explains that the land underpins Anishinaabe understanding, that the land and its constituent parts set the standard for the highest order of truth, not humans. Ultimately, the profoundest and most encompassing of truths reveal themselves to those who live in a balanced relationship with the natural world. The veracity and reliability of dadibaajim as an institution of learning derive from this Anishinaabe debwewin principle.

Dadibaajim also incorporates the concept of an Anishinaabe theoretical framework. First, however, it is important to note that Anishinaabe theory and the notion of theory itself exist in the same way other Anishinaabe institutions such as law, teachings, self-governance, and principles of relationship act as underlying components of Anishinaabe identity. Such an assertion confirms the humanness of Anishinaabe people, notwithstanding wemitigoozhi's way of thinking that still gives weight to and privileges only types of cognition that conform to its own concepts of law-making, education, governing, and theorizing.

Theory is "an explanation of a phenomenon," as Anishinaabe scholar and writer Leanne Betasamosake Simpson so succinctly describes.[5] An ever-evolving process in which every member of society has the responsibility of engaging not only intellectually but spiritually, emotionally, experientially, and relationally, theory is the people's way of "finding and generating meaning within their own lives."[6] Anishinaabe theorizing is an ongoing production of ideas that are useful and of everyday local applicability. Flexible and adaptable to its environment, the theorizing takes place over the course of a person's entire lifetime. Namegosibii Anishinaabeg, for example, needed to devise ways for theorizing about the wemitigoozhiwag European arrivals. Anishinaabe people developed theories about the latecomers and their characteristic behaviours as they expanded into the homelands and revealed who they were and how they lived. Using their experiences and observational skills, Anishinaabeg refined their ideas about wemitigoozhi behaviours, methodologies, apparent theories, and ways of thought in order to navigate the changing relational landscape. A critical function of the mawadishiwem practice of visiting one another was, in fact, to create and use dawisijigem spaces that result from clearing away the extraneous for sharing and comparing thoughts and insights about the various realities of wemitigoozhi's presence.

A more specific example of the Anishinaabe theorizing process relates to what appeared to be an inordinate compulsion to acquire zhooniyaa money among most wemitigoozhiwag.[7] Anishinaabe people experienced multiple and ever-changing ways by which the actualities of the zhooniyaa money theory of wemitigoozhiwag began to unfold and impose themselves directly on community and individual lives. When people needed to acquire greater quantities of their own zhooniyaa money in order to survive, for example, they noted the correlation between zhooniyaa and mashkawiziiwin power, influence, and authority. People also knew from experiential evidence that although the drive for money was a prime feature in the world of the wemitigoozhiwag, it did not dominate everyone to the same extent. We begin to see that Anishinaabe theorizing is evident in how they thought about and reacted to Europeans' impositions of racialized colonialism and capitalism—wemitigoozhiiwaadiziwin.

Conceptualizing the historical foreignness of the wemitigoozhi's band council system of leadership is another way of understanding Anishinaabe thought and theorizing. Although compelled to participate by voting chiefs into office, people theorized about the nature of its illogicality. They suffixed "ogimaa" (leader, chief, boss, and so on) with "–kaan," creating the term "ogimaakaan" to signify a fundamentally fallacious system of governance, a fictitious rendition of what to them is true and legitimate leadership. To this day, the term "ogimaakaan" is used in reference to a band chief.

Once a theory proved experientially factual, it became a guide for appropriate conduct. If further observations and experiences proved otherwise, Anishinaabe people expanded upon, refined, or reconfigured the existing hypothesis. They did not generally theorize as a pursuit of knowledge for its own sake. Rather, theoretical engagement generated useful and practicable ways of thinking about, explaining, and living in the world. Gerald Vizenor's notion of survivance illustrates how Anishinaabe people formulated ideas about their survival; hence, ongoing presence, in contexts of wemitigoozhiiwaadiziwin.[8] Demonstrating ongoing processes of creativity, Anishinaabe conceptual frameworks proceeded by means of dadibaajim spoken in Anishinaabemowin by the community's lead theorists and knowledge curators, the elders and grandparents.

Dadibaajim is thus an invaluable resource for understanding Anishinaabe theory and knowledge production. Being a critical part of the people's epistemological system of knowledge conveyance, it produced the compendia of knowledge that allowed people to steward the aki land-earth in a wise and caring manner for millennia—until the wemitigoozhiwag Europeans obfuscated Anishinaabe relationships with and responsibilities to their lands. It is essential for today's Anishinaabe youth who aspire to claim the land-based knowledge of the ancestors and reclaim family and community historicities to actively listen to the dadibaajim of their senior elders. As a primary source of information, their dadibaajim has the power to remedy the ills of exclusionism that have come to characterize today's way of life.

The gichi-Anishinaabeg senior elders combine dadibaajim's custom of oral documentation with other epistemological methods to teach and preserve Anishinaabe historical self-identity. Community-ensconced Cree elder, lecturer, and historian Louis Bird offers an example of how people were able to document their history narratives without having to acquire accreditation as historians, anthropologists, ethnographers, and other academically learned professions of the Western tradition.[9] Senior educators obtained their credentials through years of living and sharing their insights, knowledge, and experiences in ways they enacted along various levels of engagement. Gathering medicine plants and wild rice, lecturing and teaching, producing beadwork, maintaining political awareness, creating birchbark patterns, and speaking in and listening to Anishinaabemowin are all methods they used for anchoring their selves within the ontologies of the aanikoobidaaganag forebears. These are ways for expressing aweneniwiyang our Anishinaabe selves from an Anishinaabe perspective.

Etically generated sources of information serve a supplementary function for the work of exploring Namegosibii Anishinaabe self-identity through dadibaajim. These include the izhibii'igem written record of Hudson's Bay Company (H B C) reports, treaty annuity pay lists (1876 to 1897 and 1910), Canada 1901 census data, and Gary Butikofer's fieldwork.[10] Particularly while one is working with these records, continuing to infuse the text with Anishinaabemowin terms becomes a perspectival reminder about the diversity of human thought, conceptualization, and world views.

The dadibaajim narratives of the gichi-Anishinaabe senior elders, with added information from the written record, are able to delineate a genealogical framework that spans approximately 200 years. For example, one of the earliest written records about Jiiyaan, born in the late eighteenth

Figure 9.
Treaty 3 territory.

or early nineteenth century, describes him as Geean, who traded at the
Hudson's Bay Company Lac Seul post in the early nineteenth century.[11]
Jiiyaan, as will become evident, was Dedibaayaanimanook's paternal
great-grandfather; hence, my maternal great-great-grandfather.

In terms of political context, much of the senior elders' dadibaajim
relates to a time when wemitigoozhi European economic, political, educational, social, and religious institutions were still relatively non-intrusive
in the everyday affairs of the Namegosibii Anishinaabeg. For the most
part people exercised their autonomy to choose the extent to which
they participated in the latecomers' systems of political economy by
holding onto traditional ontologies. During the period when the older
of Dedibaayaanimanook's paternal uncles (Giizhig's sons) were born, the
wemitigoozhi latecomers were still referring to the Anishinaabe historical
lands as Rupert's Land and North-Western Territory.[12] Upon the signing
of Treaty 3's adhesion in June 1874, however, the homeland territories
of the Namegosibii Anishinaabeg along with those of Obizhigokaang
and Sturgeon Lake transmuted into 55,000 square miles (14,244,935
hectares) of Crown land (see Figure 9). An adhesion had been necessary to bring the Namegosibii Anishinaabeg and the Anishinaabeg of
Obizhigokaang—those who had already left the region for their winter
residences the previous autumn—into the arrangement.

The early part of the twentieth century was a time of flux, with multiple
jurisdictional overlaps requiring resolution. Soon after the establishment
of Ontario's western boundaries in 1912, rumours of onzaawizhooni-
yaawasin yellow money-rock incited a massive influx of wemitigoozhiwag
into the ancestral territories of the Anishinaabe people in search of instant
wealth. Most, however, would realize that gold brings material riches to
only a few and is rarely a source of lasting contentment. Many of these
individuals settled in the Red Lake area.

Officially, the Namegosibii Anishinaabeg became residents of territories claimed by Canada and Ontario, and were now living and travelling
as interlopers across what were their ancestral homelands for millennia.
They had become the trespassers! People noted that these realities sprang
from how wemitigoozhiwag formed governments and bureaucracies
and conceptualized and organized Indigenous lands in terms of control,
ownership, and the principles and values of wemitigoozhiiwaadiziwin

capitalism. But the Namegosibii Anishinaabeg did not see themselves or their places of home in those terms.

Treaty-negotiated "permission" to continue with the ancient land-based rights to activities such as fishing, gathering, hunting, trapping, and pursuing ceremony came with sufficient conditions to substantially undermine Anishinaabe autonomy. Due to governments' political imperatives to begin regulating and collecting taxes from the Anishinaabe lands as quickly as possible, commercial fishers and tourist lodge entrepreneurs were able to acquire licences to use Namegosibiing beginning in 1939 and the 1940s. But the province saw few opportunities for collecting taxes from the Anishinaabe people's traditional activities and began to recast them as unlawful competitors for resources. Fishers and lodge owners were now the legal occupiers of Namegosibiing while the Namegosibii Anishinaabeg were left as a people without a home.

Throughout the latter half of the twentieth century, what is now the Ontario Ministry of Natural Resources and Forestry (MNRF) proceeded to convert the places of home into conservation and nature reserves. The Ministry enacted ever stricter regulations, making tree cutting and other construction-related activities illegal without a permit. As game wardens appeared on the landscape and their planes flew overhead in search of illegitimate presences, the MNRF seemed to design and enforce rules and regulations specifically to remove Namegosibii Anishinaabeg from their ancestral homes. There were few dispensations for Anishinaabe people, and in a prevailing atmosphere of uncertainty and fear, they had already noted that Indian agents were not actively concerned with protecting their treaty entitlements to the land and its resources. By so completely reneging on their obligations to treaty people, Indian Affairs' decision makers played a major role in creating the circumstances that made living on the land as the aanikoobidaaganag ancestors had done virtually impossible. The close-knit Anishinaabe community disbanded and dispersed, as members sought wage labour that was, more often than not, steeped in racialized thinking.

At this point, it is important to note the usual ways in which settler latecomers thought about the boreal lands and resources of the Anishinaabe people. Archivist and historian John Richthammer's work captures the essence of these characterizations as follows:

Who were the thousands of people who swarmed into such
forbidding, dangerous terrain. . . .

They realized that the names, memories and deeds of the
pioneers who braved the wilds of a desolate hinterland. . . .

When they deserted and fled to their wilderness homes. . . .

The next time he prospected the northern wilds, Howey
became dangerously ill.[13]

The frame of reference indicated by these phrases strongly suggests
that the lands were so dangerous and forbidding and so desolate and wild
that they were heretofore uninhabitable and, in fact, never inhabited. This
line of logic opened the ancestors' home spaces and even Anishinaabe
dwellers to exploitation unrestrained by protocols of ethical or respectful
conduct. Importantly, it should be noted here that these portrayals reflect
prevailing attitudes and are not Richthammer's own sentiments about
the Anishinaabe people or their lands. In all of his work as an academic
and archivist-historian, Richthammer has steadfastly remained an advocate and friend of the Anishinaabeg, while never attempting to speak
on their behalf.

Only after many years of land claims litigation at the band level would
a slow process of limited redress begin. By then, most of the elders who
experienced the full force of wemitigoozhiiwaadiziwin's initial effects had
passed. Today's off-reserve treaty people have largely adjusted to more
urban ways of life while maintaining their Anishinaabe identity and seeking
to live in ways that honour the ancestors and remember their courage.
Through the elders' dadibaajim, people still seek to listen to what the
aanikoobidaaganag forebears tell us about our Namegosibii Anishinaabe
identity—over and above what wemitigoozhiiwaadiziwin teaches.

As a metaphor for conceptualizing the processes of clearing away
wemitigoozhiiwaadiziwin's clutter of myths, dawisijigem is concerned
with reclaiming the spaces that once occupied Anishinaabe people's
minds, beliefs, and emotions. Dawisijigem, therefore, enables the pursuit
of inter-ontological meanings to bring about greater diversity and a more
inclusive, accurate body of knowledge. As a creative process, it operates

simultaneously along several dimensions and in varying ways. From my own childhood experiences, for example, the word itself evokes vivid memories of what transpired upon my mother's standard pre-meal iteration, "Daga sa dawisijigedaa!" Our kitchen table was the only available place for doing schoolwork, reading, writing, studying, working on art projects, sewing, and so on. Hence, mealtime was very much a time for dawisijigem, or, as my mother would say, "Let's clear away some space!"

When the eight mentor-participants showed a willingness to participate in this project by allocating their time and mental energies to sharing their dadibaajim, they too were involved with dawisijigem. And when Gwiishkwa'oo agreed to speak her dadibaajim, she engaged with both temporal and spatial dawisijigem by choosing the subjects to discuss, rearranging her schedule of activities, and ensuring a physical place for our visits. When my mother and I removed or repositioned objects on her kitchen table to allow a place for her, Oo'oons, and me to converse, we were similarly enacting dawisijigem.

As a device in the performance of the research work necessary for this book, dawisijigem created spaces that were specific to the design, participants' requirements, knowledge sharing, and data analysis required to hear and form understandings of Anishinaabe thought and narration. Dawisijigem allows us to position knowledges, debwewin truths, experiences, and self-identities emerging from Anishinaabe research into the central regions of our consciousness where we are able to hear the voices of dadibaajim above the overbearingness of izhibii'igem historical texts.

Dadibaajim history narratives occupy these cognitive spaces of dawisijigem's activities where they are able to reformulate dominant systems of knowledge production by contesting exclusivities that have controlled, regulated, and distorted Anishinaabe people's origin and self-describing narratives since before Confederation. The reasons for historical misrepresentation reside where and how power imbalances originate.[14] To counter the erasure and denial of Anishinaabe presences by incorporating dadibaajim into the record is to speak to forms and expressions of power. These activities require us to listen to the content of dadibaajim and the nature of its closely linked concepts.

Why Dadibaajim?

Our aspirations to explore, describe, and write down our aweneniwi-yang who we are narratives as individuals and communities are attain-able by using dadibaajim as a guide. Such a set of undertakings would have appeared strange to the aanikoobidaaganag ancestors, whose dadibaajim and odoodemiwin totem systems of genealogical record keeping ensured that all community members understood their lineal origins. These systems for maintaining Anishinaabe histories, however, are no longer intact. With information lost, destroyed, or fragmented, unawareness of the extent to which Anishinaabe voices are absent in dominant discourse reinforces the denial and erasure of the Namegosibii Anishinaabe people's existence, identity, and rightful inheritance. The lack of consciousness that effectively prevents the physical presence of Namegosibii Anishinaabeg in the noopimakamig aki homelands is a function of wemitigoozhiiwaadiziwin. Investigating the identity narra-tives of the gichi-Anishinaabe elders within these historical and ongoing contexts is critical for those of us who wish to restore family histories, learn about our progenitors and how they lived, and gain a better under-standing about aweneniwiyang who we are as a people.

The contexts of the wemitigoozhiwag Europeans' arrival into Anishinaabe lands are an important feature of Namegosibii Anishinaabe dadibaajim. By delineating the Anishinaabe territories; naming the Namegosibii Anishinaabe aanikoobidaaganag ancestors; and speaking directly to experiences of physical removal, displacement from homes and traditional lands, and the tacit denial of their rights as human people, dadi-baajim unequivocally answers questions about historical identities. Hence, the practice of dadibaajim has the capacity to provide a more balanced record of the region's history. In so doing, it calls our attention to the responsibility of all European-descended, settler nation citizens to inter-rogate the colonial mythologies on which dominant societies are founded. Replacing long-standing oversights, erasures, and falsifications about the region, dadibaajim narration is a major contributor to the formalization of the Namegosibii Anishinaabe people's own defined identity.

A more truthful and accurate version of Canada's self-narrative as a colonially settled nation-state calls for the competency of settler descen-dants to self-identify in genealogical terms. I once posed the question of ancestry to an academic who has authored several textbooks that include those on Canadian Indigenous history. Although he was able to state that he was originally from Wisconsin, he actually exemplified the anthropological observation—made by, for example, Emily Schultz, Robert Lavenda, and Roberta Dods—that lineages "endure as long as people remember the descent lines, usually about five generations"[15] by seeming to be largely unfamiliar with his ancestry beyond the third generation. However, upon further consideration, he was able to clarify that he is not of Indigenous lineage. This example suggests that when members of dominant society forget the facts of their ancestors' origins or those of themselves as immigrants, they too easily lapse into a process of negation that erases the histories, pre-existing self-identities, languages, and rights of Indigenous nations, thus vanishing them from the landscape of Canadian consciousness.[16]

The Namegosibii Anishinaabe people, as an oral society, retained knowledge about who they were by using time-honoured devices such as dadibaajim narratives and the odoodemiwin system that anchored their identities to the homelands. When members of the dominant society are able to definitively recognize that their ancestors were settlers, pioneers, homesteaders, frontiersmen, and colonizers—squatters, as some have stated—from the agaamakiing places across the oceans, they may more readily recognize and accept meanings about identity with the original inhabitants of this land.

Wenji Gikendamang

How We Know

There are several interconnecting devices in the Anishinaabe tradition that facilitate exploration, understanding, and transmission of meaning in the journey to investigate Namegosibii Anishinaabe identity. Among these are the institutions of dadibaajim oral narration, the mawadishiwem custom of visiting and conversing with one another, principles of respect and ethicalness, and use of the Namegosibii Anishinaabemowin heritage language. Principles of respect and a strong sense of ethics, for example, are important features of how the dadibaajim oral tradition and the mawadishiwem custom work together when Anishinaabemowin is the spoken language. A discussion about the one necessitates a discussion about the others.

Often, the dadibaajim oral narrative is didactic in nature, replete with listener-speaker relationships and responsibilities. Particularly when the dadibaajim narrator is a gichi-Anishinaabe senior elder, the listener-learner is responsible for having some familiarity with the context of the narrative in order to arrive at the elder's intended meaning. Having an understanding of how the speaker uses Anishinaabemowin to express nuanced meanings facilitates this obligation by supporting a good grasp of the special significances to which the the speaker alludes.

Understanding the concept of dadibaajim is arguably most effective when it takes place within a mawadishiwem setting. Concerning itself with subjectivity, relationship, and community well-being, mawadishiwem was a discursive venue in which two or more people could get together to talk over and share various theories, thoughts, or events by means of dadibaajim. Mawadishiwem, in the traditional sense, was how community members socialized, kept each other informed, shared material goods such as food or clothing, and generally took care of one another. To illustrate the custom from my own childhood, it was deeply gratifying to have a visitor arrive, particularly during winter when mawadishiwem entailed a lengthy journey across the frozen lake. Whenever our aunt Gweyesh visited us on a wintery afternoon, my mother spread out a blanket near the stove for an extended session of cards, conversation, and Anishinaabe cuisine into the late hours. The mawadishiwem host would offer the most comfortable seat in the house and serve tea, bannock, or a full meal accompanied by an invitation to stay the night. Elder Naawi-giizis Jim Clark's insightful description of the custom underscores the critical role of mawadishiwem in how Anishinaabe people attended to one another. He relates as follows:

Mii go mawadishiwed ingoji. Aanawi go ogikendaan ingoji ji nibe'ind. Mewinzha ko wiinawaa giidadibaajimotaadiwag akina gegoo ezhiwebadinig.[1]

So he goes visiting somewhere. Anyway, he knows he'll be offered a place to sleep somewhere. Long ago they used to talk to one another about everything that was going on.

Figure 10 illustrates one way that Namegosibii Anishinaabe mawadishiwem took place in early spring.

Figure 10.
Namegosibii Anishinaabe mawadishiwem. Family members and relatives
came to visit Dedibaayaanimanook (third adult from the right) when
her brother Jiins (fifth adult from the right) shot a bear in early spring.
On Dedibaayaanimanook's right is her nephew, Gichi-jôj, who also
participated in the hunt.

The dadibaajim oral practice was often informal but always respectful. In my own work, the elders' proficiency with customary protocols governing traditional mawadishiwem established the tone of the dadibaajim sessions. Their knowledge about historical events and contexts and what they deemed to be most significant in the affairs of the community guided our conversations. Whenever the speaker's original subject seemed to morph into what I thought was something entirely different, the discussion proceeded along various paths, directions, and digressions that in fact proved to be of relevance. Some participants spoke at great length while others used words sparingly.

Depending upon the setting, dadibaajim does not entirely preclude questions or comments. However, their use requires skill on the part of the learner to know how, when, and even whether to inject them into a conversation. Minimal engagement by the listener in a discussion of two or more participants avoids potential distortions and disruptions in the dadibaajim flow. In the case with my own work, one elder continued to speak over my question. It became evident later, after replaying the recording several times, that the answers to my query emerged as the elder had intended, over the course of the entire dadibaajim. Misplaced comments became lessons about trust in dadibaajim protocols that allow us the freedom to follow the elders' lead for how to proceed. As scholars Marie Françoise Guédon, Margaret Kovach, and others have observed, to respect the elders' understandings is to learn the lesson that what is important for them is important for the research.[2] Listening with respect may not require any questions.

Dadibaajim's customary codes preclude a sense of entitlement to answers or clarification. By obliging listener-learners and researchers to earn the elders' trust and right to their knowledge, dadibaajim teaches respect for the elder-speakers' prerogative to decide whether and to what extent they will grant permission to share the information with others. The call for such a principled approach is particularly evident when elders speak in their heritage language.

Anishinaabe principles of ethical treatment of fellow humans govern the social and linguistic dynamics of an Anishinaabemowin exchange. For example, there are particular methods of interaction in the epistemological context of seeking, exchanging, sharing, confirming, and adopting knowledge. Referring to a drum in one of the photographs he brought with him, Oo'oons (O) describes it to Dedibaayaanimanook (D), who is the more senior of the two elders in the following:

O: First powwow gaa-gii' ayaawaad, aantagiin [laughter],
majote'-ojiigizôn.
D: Oziinjiigizôn [laughter]!
O: Oziinjiigizôn.[3]

O: First powwow they had, now what is it called [laughter],
when someone throws [it] into the fire, burns its edges.
D: Tightens it by heating it [laughter]!
O: Tightens it by heating it.

Oo'oons acknowledges the inaccuracy of ojiigizôn, which suggests that
the drum hide is actually on fire, with subdued laughter. Considered in
several ways, it is specifically his use of the suffix "-tagiin" that is helpful in
alleviating this incorrectness in an appropriate manner. For example, he
expresses his desire for a more accurate term without posing a question
to Dedibaayaanimanook directly. He thus conveys awareness that the
decision of whether and how to provide him with the correct wording is
Dedibaayaanimanook's alone, demonstrating his respect for the protocol
that discourages use of direct questions. Recognizing that he is appealing
to her generosity by seeking to access her linguistic expertise, Oo'oons's
"aantagiin" is also a gesture of deference to Dedibaayaanimanook herself
as the senior elder and to her linguistic authority. Dedibaayaanimanook
then acknowledges his usage, provides him with the correct term, and,
noting the humour in "ojiigizôn," shares in his laughter.[4] By using such
devices as morphemes, Anishinaabe people are able to combine humour
and laughter with humility and respect when conducting their relationships and interactions.

At this point, I will illustrate my own understanding of what respect
means for Namegosibii Anishinaabe people. Although I am not aware
of any specific Anishinaabemowin term that corresponds to the English
"respect," Oo'oons's dadibaajim narrative illustrates the concept as I see
it practised. He explains that his grandfather Jiiyaan demonstrated belief
in the soundness of respectfulness by how he prepared for Treaty Time:

Nimishoomisiban Jiiyaan, mii'iwe e'-diba'amaading gaa' izhi
wawezhiid. Minziweshkigan ogii'ako bizikaan suit, tie. Mii
e' wawezhiid ewii' diba'amaading.[5]

My late grandfather, Jiiyaan, when it was Treaty Time, he
began to prepare. He would put on a suit, tie. That was how he
prepared for Treaty Time.

Oo'oons points out that his grandfather wore a suit and tie for diba'amaadim
Treaty Time. Although community members long understood the lack of
honour in the wemitigoozhi's administration of treaties, they gathered for
Treaty Time to accept payments and observe the signing of the treaty. The
event never represented the principled reasons for which Anishinaabe
people historically entered into treaty; therefore what they celebrated by
expending their time and energy to put on their best attire and gather
together was the spirit in which the forefathers and foremothers agreed
to the treaty. Wearing a suit and tie was Jiiyaan's way of remembering and
honouring the intent of the aanikoobidaaganag ancestors, who understood that the Anishinaabe principles of treaty were important for the
community. Commanding ceremony and dignity, historical events such
as the signing of a treaty embody Anishinaabe ideals of respectful collaboration. How Anishinaabe people commemorate treaties is not a matter
of either naïveté or gullible thinking. They are maintaining the forebears'
concepts of how to live an honourable relationship.

Attention to what is voiced and what is silenced is a part of respecting the
dadibaajim narrative process. In the next conversation, Dedibaayaanimanook's
description of a journey she once took to Ikwewi-zaa'igan Woman Lake with
her siblings helps to illustrate how silences function:

> **Insayenziban, madaabiibatoopan, "Wemitigoozhiwag
> i'imaa ayaawag," indigonaan. Ezhi gichi zegiziyaang,
> Gweyesh. Anishaa e'ikidoj.**[6]
>
> My late elder brother came running down from the forest,
> telling us, "There are European settler men over there!"
> Gweyesh and I were overcome with fear. But he was
> only joking.

The immediate fear experienced by the two sisters may seem curious.
At this juncture in the narrative, a Western imperative would compel

the speaker to explain why two young Anishinaabe women would react
as they did at the thought of encountering wemitigoozhiwag European
(-descended) men in the homeland forests. Anishinaabe protocol,
however, considers the historical context of an event that took place
during the 1930s. It was a time when racism and sexism were overtly
the norm, particularly in the noopimakamig hinterland regions of northwest Ontario where a "wild west" frontier mentality typified the wemitigoozhi European settler, as indicated by Richthammer.[7] Awareness of
Anishinaabe sensibilities is an important feature of Anishinaabe dadibaajim protocol that exhorts us to refrain from probing for further information when none is offered. Anticipating situations of potential angst
or painful memories and being cognizant of historical impacts upon the
lives of Indigenous people individually and collectively are in keeping
with Anishinaabe ethical principles of a respectful engagement with the
dadibaajim narrative custom.

Ethicalness thus includes paying attention to Anishinaabe realities,
narrative contexts, and the spirit in which narrators speak in order to avoid
distortions, misrepresentations, and even the temptation to fit dadibaajim
into the listener's purpose at the expense of accuracy. An example of being
mindful of social, cultural, historical, and political realities is recognition
of the impacts of wemitigoozhiiwaadiziwin at the individual level with
the diminution of ancestral language use. It is important to remember the
reasons for such effects. Narrators do not always critique wemitigoozhi's
ways directly, but it becomes evident that witnessing or experiencing the
damage to language and other intergenerational after-effects of attempted
genocide, suppression, and domination is often the subtext of their dadibaajim. These historical realities are the backdrop that becomes evident
as the speaker progresses through each dadibaajim discussion.

Circumspection extends to matters of confidentiality. When individuals or families deem certain subjects to be the exclusive domain of
their babaamiziwin internal affairs, they are not for outsiders. Such topics
include those that relate to the historical forces of wemitigoozhiiwaadiziwin, minikwewin alcohol addiction, details about boarding school, the
traumas of having to disguise spirituality, and so on. In a similar manner,
use of the term "onjinem," relating somewhat to the notion of getting
what one deserves, can signify a desire to thwart, deflect, or otherwise
discourage discussion because the topic is of a sensitive or confidential

nature, particularly with Namegosibii Anishinaabe senior elders. Beyond simply omitting strategic pieces of information, in such cases, narrators may choose to remain silent, literally refraining from any further speech.

Anishinaabe protocol presumes that experiential evidence is the debwewin truth basis for an individual's dadibaajim narration. One participant in this work, elder Oo'oons Kejick, spoke of the fear he and others of his community experienced in the face of law enforcement:

Amiish geyaabi o'owe apii jigii' izhichigewaapan iwe aaniin gaa-gii' izhi gikinô'amawindô Anishinaabewichigewin, jigii' doodamowaapan. Gaawiin idash. Mii'iwe gotaajiwin. Zegiziwin. Ji-onji dibaakonigooyan.[8]

To this very day, they [the youth] should have been practising the Anishinaabe way of life as they were taught. But that is not the case. It is fear. Being afraid. That you will be charged, arrested, jailed.

By subjectively speaking about the personal terror he and his family lived through, Oo'oons explicates the prevailing fear that prevented him from living on the land as his aanikoobidaaganag forebears had taught. Evidence is not necessary to accept the dadibaajim of elders such as Oo'oons and Dedibaayaanimanook as truth. Commanding wide respect, their narratives are a valued contribution to the community's body of knowledge because members recognize them as rooted in the debwewin truth of their experiences.

An ethical approach extends to the foundational concepts, theories, and values from which the mentor-participant elders of this work speak to dadibaajim's contexts of historical experiences and practicalities. Having always striven to the best of their ability to abide by the customary codes of conduct such as behaviour rooted in humility and speech embedded in debwewin truth, the elders possess a special understanding of what is significant within the community's circumstances. Certain principles of ethics, to illustrate, make it possible for people to appreciate and understand that the narrator in the following dadibaajim speaks in non-racist, non-racialized terms that indicate the fundamentals of Anishinaabe thought:

Wegonen gewonji izhiwebak? "Wemitigoozhi osha
gaa izhichigej," osha gii'ikidowag, mitigoo' maawaj
gii'nisaawaaj[9]

Why is the weather like this? "It is clearly the European settler
who does this," is what they would say, especially as they
destroyed the trees.

The focus of this discussion is conduct. Elder Dedibaayaanimanook
alludes to the detrimental effects of wemitigoozhiwag's behaviours on
the natural environment and, by extension, on Anishinaabe people
and the wemitigoozhiwag themselves, something the aanikoobidaaganag grandparents often warned of. There is no doubt that Anishinaabe
people observed and experienced most of wemitigoozhi's ways of doing
and being as characteristically destructive. Critiquing an attitude and its
consequences rather than an ethnicity per se, Anishinaabe condemnation centres primarily on behaviour-related phenomena.

When working with dadibaajim narration in a cross-cultural setting,
use of the heritage language is a critical factor for retaining and facilitating the communication of its cultural meaning. Anishinaabe linguist
Roger Roulette of the Sandy Bay First Nation refers to the language
I learned from Dedibaayaanimanook as "old" Anishinaabemowin. As
with all languages, it has evolved over time to accommodate changing
conditions. Younger speakers in urban settings are unfamiliar with some
of the elders' land-based terminologies. The elders, at the same time,
will devise terms for what are to them urban-based contrivances such as
computers (gaa-jachakinaman) and remote controls (gaa-onji-zhenaman
and gaa-onji-gibitinaman), or they will resort to indigenizing words or
names (e.g., Menii for Mary, Aanjinoo for Andrew, Aanibat for Albert,
and Waadan for Walter).

Assisting with the work of conveying cultural meaning is a brief
morphological analysis that examines three terms to help clarify how
Anishinaabemowin functions: "dawisijigem" (clearing spaces), "dadibaajim" (the narrative or the narrative practice), and "mawadishiwem" (the
visit as an act or practice). A verb often transforms into an idea or concept.
"Dawisijige," she/he is clearing away space, to illustrate, becomes "dawisijigem," the act or practice of clearing spaces. Similarly, "dadibaajimo," she/

he is telling a narrative, becomes "dadibaajim," the practice, act, or content of narration. The verb "mawadishiwe," she/he is visiting, converts to the noun "mawadishiwem," the practice or act of going for a visit. In theory, every Anishinaabemowin verb has the capacity to become an abstraction.

A better understanding of Anishinaabemowin functioning is also possible by studying its structural characteristics. Many scholars have gained expertise about Indigenous languages from the Western perspective of linguistics. Anishinaabe writer Louise Erdrich observes that "two-thirds of the words are verbs, and for each verb, there can be as many as six thousand forms," making it possible to combine a multiplicity of concepts in a single word.[10] Anthropologist Maureen Matthews's discussion notes that singular pronouns are animate or inanimate, rather than gender-based.[11] This feature enables a better insight into how concepts and concrete realities about personhood, the self, and gender appear in distinctive ways to those who speak and think in Anishinaabemowin. For such reasons, use of Anishinaabemowin suggests the possibility of having a direct engagement with Anishinaabe ontological thought.

It is also helpful to note that certain nouns cannot stand alone in the same way they do in English. The word "oninj," for example, translates to English as her/his/its hand; "nininj" is my hand, and "gininj" is your (singular) hand. However, no discrete word exists simply for "hand" because Anishinaabemowin conceptualizes certain words by embedding them within a relationship rather than in isolation. The English word "hand" becomes "oninjiimaa," the state of having or being a hand, or hand-ness. It is more of a conceptualization than a physical object.[12] These examples help to explain why use of Anishinaabemowin is itself the most effective way of understanding the world view in which it is embedded and becoming familiar with its layers of nuanced and often overlooked meanings.

Importantly, Anishinaabemowin usage conforms to Anishinaabe ethical principles by preserving the dadibaajim frame of reference so easily distorted in translation. Although, for example, a literal English version of "Ojoozhimimaa" as "Parallel Nephewhood" is awkward and sounds odd for a person's name, no such problem exists within an Anishinaabemowin frame where various concepts blend seamlessly and logically. Personal names are especially best when left in their original Anishinaabemowin form, particularly when an English rendition counters the ethical principle of respect by sounding absurd or undignified.

A more respectful and ethical approach applies to Anishinaabemowin translation in other ways. To illustrate, avoidance of "bush" for "noopimakamig aki" eludes the historically negative connotations (backwards, rough, uncultivated, wild, etc.) that often occur within settler Canadian narratives. Words such as "boreal," on the other hand, draw forests and trees into the discussion, reflecting the Anishinaabemowin association of noopimakamig aki with positive characteristics. By merging dignity and beauty with generosity and strength, such terms more accurately communicate the Anishinaabe conceptualization of the natural environment. However, this does not preclude acknowledgement of assertions that "bush" can also hold many of the affirmative meanings of noopimakamig aki.[13] Here, my objective as a disciple of Anishinaabe intellectuality is to uphold and encourage the use of Anishinaabemowin rather than attempt to rehabilitate English words whose meanings are often awry.

While context imbues all forms of communication with meaning, the presence of Anishinaabemowin within the text increases the likelihood of achieving a completer and more accurate rendition. To illustrate, the noopimakamig aki phrase includes all of the aquatic, terrestrial, and celestial features of the boreal world. Water, land, and the day and night skies all have significance for Anishinaabe people, who observe and experience these elements from the unique vantage point of their noopimakamig aki places of home. The fullest meaning of the phrase "noopimakamig aki" embraces all of these concepts. As a way of respecting Anishinaabe sensibilities, meanings, and understandings, the use of Anishinaabemowin terms can present a wide range of ideas that an English counterpart may omit due to the nature of the English language. Hence, I particularly prefer Anishinaabemowin terms where translations into English cannot respectfully, accurately, or completely convey the concepts embedded within them.

Similarly, use of Anishinaabemowin place names is generally best, especially for geographical and map-based discussions. While maps supplement dadibaajim's information about places that have either disappeared from our conversations or literally ceased to exist, original names reflect the ontological viewpoint of the aanikoobidaaganag ancestors, helping us to understand their relationship with the aki homelands. Unlike the name

"Trout Lake," for example, "Namegosibiing" is a continual reminder of the unique attributes that people so greatly appreciated about the lake and the value system that regards the natural environment so highly.

The old Anishinaabemowin language of the senior elders' aanikoo-bidaaganag reveals how they thought about their identity. The expression for "lineal descent," for example, reflects an intimate sense of affiliation with the noopimakamig aki boreal land, as Dedibaayaanimanook relates in the following dadibaajim:

> **Mii' iwe gaa inaakwadabiigishing mitigoog gii maajiiyaakwadabiigishinowaaj anaamakamiing. "Bezhigwan ezhiseyaang," ako gii' ikidooban my mom.**[14]
>
> That was her lineal patterning, similar to how tree roots extend themselves beneath the ground. "It is the same with us," my mom would say.

Using the word "inaakwadabiigishing," by which wadabiig refers to the roots of a spruce tree, Namegosibii Anishinaabeg articulate the concept of descendant lines. They concretize the abstraction of the linkages existing among their selves, descendants, and ancestors by using the same term they use for describing how tree roots literally configure themselves as they propagate. In the Namegosibii Anishinaabe way of thought, both they themselves as human people and the spruce tree roots are encompassed in the concept of inaakwadabiigishing. Through this land-language aggregate, they indicate how strongly their identities are grounded in the boreal lands. This characteristic of old Anishinaabemowin suggests one among many reasons why its use was threatening to the European(-descended) settlers who desired Indigenous lands for themselves: it confirms the people's connection to noopimakamig aki.

In another dadibaajim conversation, Dedibaayaanimanook used the slight variation "gichiwaakwadabiigishin," in which "gichiwaak-" imparts the idea of holding onto something firmly. So long as the boreal trees and roots of noopimakamig aki thrive, so too do Anishinaabe populations, and when people persist in using the language, they safeguard their noopimakamig land-anchored selves. Indicating the land-human relationship, these types of expressions present a compelling argument for using the Anishinaabemowin heritage language.

Interestingly, the Anishinaabemowin of the senior elders enables a critical investigation into the origins of certain popular expressions used in English. Two elders discussed the terms "Turtle Island" (in reference to the North American continent) and "Mother Earth." Both elders concluded that neither was a part of the Namegosibii Anishinaabemowin vocabulary and did not reflect the ancestral world views or ideas about relationships with the noopimakamig aki natural environment of Namegosibiing. Particularly when the elders retain Anishinaabemowin (or other Indigenous language) as a first language, their linguistic expertise becomes a valuable resource for research into origins and derivations.

Use of English or other colonial languages perpetuates the domination of the wemitigoozhiiwaadiziwin way of thinking. Illustrating how the use of an Indigenous language can act as a counterforce to that dominance, my daughter told me of a meeting she attended where English legalese was the domineering language. At one point in the proceedings, a group of elders decided to switch to Cree in order to converse more readily amongst themselves. Lawyers were suddenly nonplussed by their unexpected inability to participate and, probably sensing a loss of control, fell uncharacteristically silent. Although it was not likely that their intent was to cause befuddlement, the elders' shift had the powereful effect of disrupting the long-standing presumption of English language authority. My daughter's dadibaajim shows how strategic use of language becomes a form of power, indicating the ability of Nēhiyawēwin Cree, Anishinaabemowin, or other Indigenous languages to draw negotiators into spaces where the possibility of alternative solutions lies.

The dadibaajim narratives of senior elders who speak with Anishinaabemowin fluency and experiential knowledge are of particular significance. The value of their narratives is found in their content and, as an institution of teaching and learning, in their ability to embody the relational and context-related principles of an Anishinaabe epistemological framework. Particularly when one has assistance from language specialists such as instructor-elder Roger Roulette, whose expertise covers a wide range of contexts, it becomes evident that Anishinaabemowin dadibaajim narratives create permanent dawisijigem spaces where the cultural journeys of both exploration and continuity can take place across time and the generations.

Most easily when it takes place within a traditional mawadishiwem setting, Anishinaabemowin is critical in the intercultural work of seeking the meanings embedded within Anishinaabe dadibaajim oral narration. The quality of cross-cultural work, moreover, is enhanced and enriched with recognition of self as the ego. Similar to the necessity of correctly identifying ego's position on a kinship diagram, acknowledgement of the self's location-positionality as a listener-learner of dadibaajim's subject matter helps us to study, comprehend, discuss, and make comment on its intended meanings.

Wenji Inendamang

Subjectivity

Awareness of positionality is integral to the work of listening to, exploring, and documenting identity dadibaajim narration. To explain, when the narrator speaks, my location as the listener influences my understanding and shapes the end product of what I produce. Educator Susan Hopkins affirms that doing what we do is never "a disembodied process"[1] because the signatures of our subjective selves and our frame of reference are woven into whatever we do. Even quantitative projects of the pure sciences are imbued with positionality and world views, as cultural anthropologist Julie Cruikshank suggests in her research work with colonialism in the Yukon.[2] Yet, they are not always acknowledged. Statements of self-acknowledgement are essential for the honesty of transparency[3] and the contextual integrity that staves off unnecessarily pan-Indian inclinations.[4] By making a special point of declaring their positionality in some manner, those who include the self are not so different from those who don't because they are less objective but because they are more transparent about their identity. Moreover, intentional expressions of subjectivity become a form of power by allowing us to control the identity discourse.[5]

While reading about Indigenous use of plants recently, I came across the observation that recognition of self encompasses the responsibility of acknowledging the many relationships we have with our sources of knowledge.[6] This is of special concern when working directly with individuals and communities. Referring to her own work, Anishinaabe scholar and educator Minogiizhigokwe Kathleen Absolon states that including herself serves to underscore her loyalties, making her accountable for her work and demonstrating that who she is is as important as what she produces.[7]

Today's cultural anthropologists increasingly agree with Absolon that "once you have identified your own social location, you will be better able to understand your unique perspective—your situated subjectivity—that informs your research choices."[8] With outsiders who work among Indigenous communities and take their situated subjectivity into consideration, in fact, inclusion of positionality becomes practically standard practice.[9] Every project is ultimately also a dadibaajim narrative about positionality and, as a reflexive product of its creator, it is a reflection and extension of individual and even community identity. Narratives thus inform and are informed by the spaces in which a person self-situates, comprising her or his frame of reference.

Using myself as an example of a Namegosibii Anishinaabe community member, I am able to articulate, move between, and draw from divergent world views due to certain factors. Being a great-grandchild of Giizhig through my mother and the daughter of a Norwegian immigrant are core ingredients in my positionality, although I largely secure my sense of self within the community of my mother's people, the descendants of Giizhig. Many of my concerns, interests, and preoccupations manifest themselves in ways that reflect my tendency to self-locate among the Namegosibii Anishinaabe people rather than Scandinavian spaces because I was raised in the Namegosibii Anishinaabe traditional homelands and learned Anishinaabemowin at an early age.

Figure 11.
Makakoshkwemagoon as identity expression. These are examples of
how I used birchbark, available in abundance in boreal noopimakamig,
and braided sweetgrass (not a traditional component of Namegosibii
Anishinaabe cultural practice) for my version of what Gaa-madweyaashiik
Emma, my maternal grandmother, made for storing food (Agger, 2008).

Figure 12.
Gathering wiikenzh sweet flag, Namegosibiing (2009). Canoeing to a nearby location for wiikenzh depicts our identity as members of the Namegosibii Anishinaabe community.

In her dadibaajim narratives, my mother mentions that her mother made makakoshkwemagoon birchbark containers for food storage. I gathered birchbark and attempted versions of my own, which, predictably, proved to be more symbolic than functional (see Figure 11). Wiikenzh sweet flag outings each time my family and I return to Namegosibiing are similarly indicative of identity-related interests (Figure 12). These and other enactments of ancestral customs are small but meaningful experiences of how our aanikoobidaaganag ancestors lived their lives, confirming our ideas about ourselves as Anishinaabe individuals. Situated within the context of such expressions, wiikenzh and makakoshkwema-goon are material manifestations of my own Anishinaabe subjectivity and frame of reference.

Literary theorist Renate Eigenbrod suggests that the situational and relative nature of subjectivity and positionality interconnects with both perception and context.[10] For example, how I perceive a mentor-partic-ipant's ideas about who I am throughout our interactions; whether I am an insider, outsider, or a little of both; and meanings I draw from scholarly writings in English and from the dadibaajim of the Anishinaabemowin speakers are relevant to my perceptions. I may imagine myself an outsider to the extent our conversations focus on academic work, an insider when we discuss our ancestors, and then again, an outsider when the elders talk about Anishinaabe philosophy.

Some self-identify by their sense of spirituality, a force that guided the lives of their ancestors. Also, there are people who blend aspects of the old Anishinaabe system of spirituality with Western organized reli-gion as a combination that plays a significant role in ideas about their personal selves. In addition, there has been a merging with the practices and beliefs of various other Indigenous cultures that helps to fashion a unified and meaningful self-concept. Creating these syntheses, however, can be complicated, confusing, and even contentious. In the process of searching for meaning in today's conditions, particularly with the youth, it becomes evident that many teachings of ancestral ceremony became lost or fragmented due to the historical forces of wemitigoozhiiwaadiziwin. In my own community, few material objects or openly observable practices that predate the establishment of colonial authority have survived. Overt components of ceremonial life were intentionally obscured in response to the foreigners' religions, genocidal policies, and forced schooling.

Figure 13.
Her real self. Baswewe wore a black silk headscarf that she folded
into a triangle and secured with a knot at the top. Courtesy of
Dedibaayaanimanook Sarah Keesick Olsen.

Figure 14.
Giizhig's dress, c. 1928. The fabric for Giizhig's choice of clothing and the birchbark and spruce poles of his residence all express his identity as an Anishinaabe of that time period and place. Courtesy of Dedibaayaanimanook Sarah Keesick Olsen and John Richthammer.

There are alternative terms and concepts that have the potential to be less problematic. Basil Johnston speaks of "reverential," an arguably more accommodating and accurate term than either "spiritual" or "religious," as it focuses on attitudes applicable across all areas of life.[11] As well, there are multiple other ways of conveying identity and positionality, including community affiliation, heritage language use, cultural activities, parentage, and odoodemiwin.

The quest for autonomy often begins by reformulating and elaborating on ideas about the identity of the self. In fact, it is the sense of ancestral self-determination that nuances participants' dadibaajim narratives with added layers of meaning. Considering that the multidimensional nature of Indigenous self-representation includes effects of historical and continuing domination, Indigenous people challenge the accuracy of how dominant society portrays them.

The concept of authenticity—what is "real"—is highly contextual and dependent on positionality as it relates to Anishinaabe identity. When women of the Namegosibii Anishinaabe community such as Baswewe wore folded black head kerchiefs throughout the early to mid-twentieth century, it was possible to view them as "real" because they adhered to the prevailing Anishinaabe custom (Figure 13). But a woman with a tam in the 1940s may have compromised the genuineness of her Anishinaabe identity as perceived by her peers while seeming fashionable and modern in the eyes of Red Lake's dominant society. Wearing the same style today could appear to be the political statement of an activist or a descendant's tribute to the ancestral grandmothers.

The same logic applies to my great-grandfather, Giizhig, who wore factory-made clothing in the early twentieth century (Figure 14). An externally constructed identity might focus on the material and style of Giizhig's clothing and form the conclusion that his attire made him less Anishinaabe. On the other hand, his residence, made from spruce poles and birchbark in the customary madogaan tipi design, could present him as an authentic, traditional Anishinaabewinini man. His combination of pieces from divergent cultural practices is an example of hybridity, reflecting contexts in constant flux and necessary adaptations and adjustments in the lives of Anishinaabe people. As it relates to Anishinaabe identity, an expression of Anishinaabe "authenticity" lies along a continuum from the pre-wemitigoozhiiwaadiziwin era on the homelands to colonialism

that came with removal from the traditional noopimakamig territories
and forced assimilation. Hence, it is a relative term, the meaning of which
depends on where on the spectrum of temporal, political, historical-co-
lonial, social, economic, and land-related conditions and circumstances
the subject and observer are situated.

Anishinaabe people identify with the spaces of home in particular
ways. As a female Anishinaabe scholar, Absolon describes a set of ontological points around which personal realities and experiences of the world
revolve.[12] These sites emerge from how we think about and speak of the
ancestors and their histories, stories, customs, and philosophies about the
land. In my own experience, facing the direction of waabanong east where
tomorrow begins to dawn is a reminder of Ikwewi-zaa'igan Woman Lake
and Bizhiwi-zaa'igan Cat Lake, the places where kinfolk were historically
located. I perceive our Biigaanjigamiing Pikangikum relations' homelands
to be on namanjiniking my left, toward the giiwedinong north, as I remain
facing the waabanong east. Our Obizhigokaang Lac Seul brethren, on
the other hand, are on ingichiniking my right, past Gojijiwaawangaang
where the ancestors are resting, in the zhaawanong south. Even if I close
my eyes and only picture myself standing on the neyaabikaang rocky
point of land, that land compels me to imagine myself facing the east.
This is one way I experience the literal specificities of place that provide
me with land-derived subjectivity. Moreover, the act of thinking about
and describing the ancestral lands by using Anishinaabemowin terms
elicits additional layers of cultural subjectivity that heritage language users
understand and share in common.

While Anishinaabe people have always conceptualized their selves
in relation to the land, evolving conditions affect land-based subjectivities and relational identities. The noopimakamig territories of today
appear markedly different from how the ancestors and even the senior
elders of today once encountered and related to these spaces. For the
aanikoobidaaganag forebears, for example, the autumnal travel between
Namegosibiing Trout Lake and Obizhigokaang Lac Seul consisted of four
or five days of canoeing, gathering food products and medicinal plants,
trapping and snaring, and fishing (see Figure 8). People invariably thought
of themselves in terms of their physical mobility, strength and endurance,
and ability and willingness to transport themselves across the home territories, up the river against the current, when they returned home for the

Figure 15.
Elder Dedibaayaanimanook Sarah Keesick Olsen. Dedibaayaanimanook
lived at her Red Lake residence for nearly forty years. Although she
now lives in Winnipeg, Dedibaayaanimanook still thinks and speaks of
Namegosib, the place of her birth, childhood, and much of her adulthood.

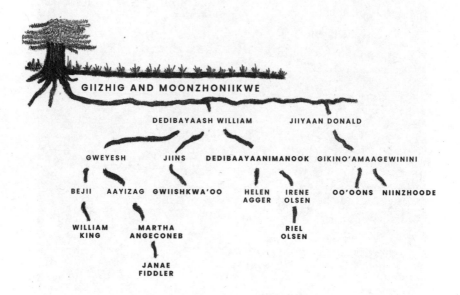

Figure 16.
Relationships among participants of this work. Dedibaayaanimanook's
dadibaajim explains how the eight participants are related as descendants of
Giizhig and Moonz(h)oniikwe.

winter. In contrast, today's descendants may think of themselves in terms of their being able to take a five- or six-hour drive up the highway and their perceived dependence on motorized travel. Contexts of continually changing circumstances, situations, conditions, timescapes, and landscapes are critical considerations as we listen to dadibaajim's presentation of Anishinaabe subjectivity and positionality.

As the basis of this work, the dadibaajim narratives of eight community members describe the Namegosibii Anishinaabe community's positionality. Figure 16 illustrates the location of these individuals in terms of how they are related to each other. The participants represent three generational groups whose dadibaajim narratives present personal experiences and observations as wemitigoozhiiwaadiziwin's domination increasingly impacted their lives. The first group consists of elders who are recognized and honoured throughout the community. They share their insights, observations, and knowledge from having lived on the land, and they still remember the dadibaajim narratives of their own aanikoobidaaganag senior elders. Importantly, they retain the ability to speak from the culturally rich perspective of the Anishinaabemowin language.

Dedibaayaanimanook Sarah Keesick Olsen is the eldest participant (Figure 15). Through the insightfulness of her parents, she evaded boarding school, achieving her education from within the dadibaajim learning system of the Anishinaabe epistemologies. Born in Gaa-minitigwashkiigaag Namegosibiing around 1922, Dedibaayaanimanook took the annual canoe journeys with her parents and sibling-cousins to the Lac Seul region where she became exposed to wemitigoozhi's ideas of treaty when her parents and family members attended diba'amaadim Treaty Time. Over the years, Dedibaayaanimanook has shared certain of her knowledges with various individuals, including representatives of the Ministry of Natural Resources and Forestry (MNRF), academic institutions, and the Lac Seul First Nation, as well as not-for-profit organizations, corporate representatives, and private individuals who pursue research for personal reasons.

Dedibaayaanimanook remains firm in her belief in the validity, applicability, and veracity of the ancestral teachings she received, noting that with each passing year, the progressively negative effects of Western global capitalism corroborate the soundness of those teachings. She retains Anishinaabemowin as her first language and maintains proficiency in the use of Anishinaabe syllabic writing and reading. Despite approaching her tenth decade, she continues to share vivid and powerful memories of the life she once lived. Dedibaayaanimanook remains my last direct link to the ontologies of the Namegosibii Anishinaabe aanikoobidaaganag ancestors. She speaks from a truly unique perspective.

Oo'oons John Paul Kejick, now deceased, was loved by his people and honoured for his many contributions to the community (Figure 17).[13] Although he attended boarding school and lived much of his life in the municipality of Red Lake rather than the homelands of Namegosibiing proper, he spoke Anishinaabemowin and retained segments of the ancestors' dadibaajim narratives. He led an active life and took every opportunity to visit Namegosibiing. As a grandson of Jiiyaan Donald Keesick, great-grandson of Giizhig, and great-great-grandson of Jiiyaan Cheean, he was Dedibaayaanimanook's first cousin once removed.

The third participant of the first group is Gwiishkwa'oo Eliza Angeconeb (Figure 18). She is one of Giizhig's great-granddaughters and a community elder who speaks Anishinaabemowin fluently. As with Oo'oons, however, boarding school interrupted her Anishinaabe learning. Her knowledge about the noopimakamig homelands derives from the dadibaajim of her elders, observations of others' activities, and her own first-hand experiences. During her early childhood, she and her family and various community members who still followed the customary ways embarked on lengthy journeys throughout the regions of Namegosibiing Trout Lake and Red Lake during the late autumn and winter months. Gwiishkwa'oo and Dedibaayaanimanook each maintains a residence in Namegosibiing where they return as frequently as every year to visit. A strong sense of connection to the lands of Namegosibiing clearly emerges from the dadibaajim narratives of all three elders.

The second group of mentor-participants also consists of three individuals. When I approached Niinzhoode Wilfred Kejick (who is now also deceased) and William King about my project, they agreed to speak but indicated a preference to do so together (Figures 19 and 20, respectively). Niinzhoode, as William currently does, resided within the Red Lake region. Both worked in Namegosibiing as tourist guides for many years, attended boarding school, and heard ancestral dadibaajim narratives in Anishinaabemowin. For each, silence speaks volumes. Niinzhoode Wilfred was Oo'oons Kejick's younger sibling. William is Giizhig's great-great-grandson through his maternal grandmother, Gweyesh Angeconeb.

Figure 17.
Oo'oons John Paul Kejick. Namegosibii Anishinaabe elder Oo'oons John Paul Kejick of Red Lake, Ontario. He was Dedibaayaanimanook's first cousin once removed.

Figure 18.
Gwiishkwa'oo Eliza Angeconeb. Gwiishkwa'oo, Dedibaayaanimanook's niece, has lived most of her adult life in Winnipeg, where she remains close to her progeny.

Figure 19.
Niinzhoode Wilfred Kejick. Niinzhoode Kejick was Oo'oons Kejick's younger sibling. After retiring from guiding in Namegosibiing, he took up residence in Red Lake to remain close to his relatives.

Figure 20.
William King. William "Spider" King grew up in Namegosibiing, where his parents and relatives trapped, hunted, and worked for wages.

Although a desire to live in Namegosibiing clearly emerges from their dadibaajim, various logistical, financial, and health-related reasons have stood as barriers to fulfilling their wish.

The youngest of this group is Martha Angeconeb Fiddler, who was born in Namegosibiing (Figure 21). Spending time with her paternal grandmother, Gweyesh Annie Angeconeb, she learned Anishinaabemowin and its embedded ontologies while her parents worked at a nearby tourist camp. She too attended residential school as a young child and as a result speaks both Anishinaabemowin and English. Although she lives in the Nengawi-zaa'igan Sandy Lake homeland territory of her mother's people and her children's father, Martha continues to ground her identity in terms of Namegosibiing. She is Giizhig's great-great-granddaughter, Dedibaayaanimanook's great-niece, and my first cousin once removed.

The two individuals who comprise the third group of participants are generationally furthest removed from the Namegosibii Anishinaabe aanikoobidaaganag ancestors. They are not fluent Anishinaabemowin speakers but, having a basic understanding of the language, are able to speak in short sentences. The younger is Martha's daughter, Janae Fiddler (Figure 22). With few opportunities to visit Namegosibiing, she has spent a great deal of time in the Sandy Lake First Nation home community of her father and maternal grandmother. She therefore sees her Namegosibiing identity from a more distant relational location than does her mother. Although Janae traces her lineage to the aanikoobidaaganag forebears of the Namegosibii Anishinaabeg, her sense of attachment to these ancestors is comparatively remote.

Riel Olsen, second participant in the third category, is a grandson of Dadibaayaanimanook and great-great-grandson of Giizhig (Figure 23). During his childhood years, Riel encountered few ancestral narratives of his maternal foreparents, either in Anishinaabemowin or English, due to factors such as public schooling and urban ways of life. Despite circumstances that tended to remove him from exposure to his grandmother's community, however, Riel has spent considerable time in Namegosibiing as a tourist guide and continues to express a desire for life in the places of home on a more permanent basis.

By mentioning their special names, participants confirm that the Namegosibii Anishinaabe ogwiimenzim practice of name giving still existed at the time of their birth. The following brief explanation will help

Figure 21.
Martha Angeconeb Fiddler. Martha, who now makes her home in
Sandy Lake, Ontario, enjoys sharing memories of life as a small child in
Namegosibiing, particularly of those she formed while staying with her
paternal grandmother, Gweyesh Annie Angeconeb.

Figure 22.
Janae Fiddler. Janae is the youngest of the eight participants in this study.
Her perspectives of what is her homeland reflect the lineage of her father's
Sandy Lake community.

Figure 23.
Riel Olsen. Having spent sufficient time in Namegosibiing Trout Lake in his youth, Riel articulates a strongly felt attachment to the homelands of his Giizhig ancestry.

to gain a better understanding of and deeper appreciation for the custom and why it served the community so well. Similar to how the odapi-naawasowin midwifery role establishes a special connection between the child and his or her birth deliverer, ogwiimenzim was intended to create and maintain lifelong relationships. Dedibaayaanimanook's ongoing dadibaajim narratives explain that name givers were elders closely linked to the recipients, perhaps as grandparents, great-aunts, or great-uncles. The child's naming ceremony usually occurred soon after his or her birth and the giver(s) had spent time in deep meditation. To illustrate, Dedibaayaanimanook's name (a feminized form of her father's, Dedibayaash) was a gift from her paternal grandfather, Giizhig. Because she chose to use the name her grandfather gave her, Dedibaayaanimanook is able to draw upon the energizing forces of his compassion in times of duress, thus exemplifying the dynamic of their ogwiimenzim relationship long after Giizhig's physical passing. She also received ceremonial names from her father and her paternal uncle Jiiyaan Donald, two brothers who enjoyed a particularly close relationship. In other cases, including those of Dedibaayaanimanook's aunts-in-law, the giver bestowed a special name when the recipient became a member of the family through marriage. The ogwiimenzim custom cultivated bonds of mutual affection among community members that served to reinforce their sense of belonging at the same time it conferred respect and honour to the name giver. As a gift from a senior family member, the name became an *aide-mémoire* that kept communal and lineal origins alive and guided the recipient through life's many challenges and responsibilities.

When Dedibaayaanimanook was a child, the community as a social unit, use of the heritage language, and the people's beliefs and principles were still largely intact. Today, however, the ogwiimenzim tradition that she and other senior elders of her era cite is commonly copied but rarely duplicated because its essential components have become frayed, frag-mented, or lost. Without the close-knit community that nurtures character traits such as zhawenjigem compassion, few people, if any, hold the qual-ifications that the Namegosibiing forebears needed in order to conduct a naming ceremony. Instead, practitioners today reconstruct the remnants as processes of recovery from wemitigoozhi's imperatives.

Although I have included participants' Anishinaabe names when they shared them, I did not ask for their meaning. Anishinaabe protocol respects the specialness of an individual's personal information. Today, the social structures and values of dominant society have destroyed and replaced many Anishinaabe customs, altering, for example, the sense of sanctity with which people once negotiated their relationships and engaged with the ceremonies, symbolisms, and teachings of ogwiimenzim. Despite these setbacks, participants shared their special names and confirmed their regard for ancestral customs, ontological systems, and their own Anishinaaabe identity. Figure 24 illustrates the ancestry of the Namegosibii Anishinaabe people as the spoken narratives of senior elder Dedibaayaanimanook and information from the written text indicate. Inevitably, however, this diagram does not include all of those who descended from Jiiyaan, and dadibaajim does not provide any details about Jiiyaan's six wives. We do not know which was the mother of each child, and the children's correct chronological ordering is not clearly evident from Dedibaayaanimanook's dadibaajim. Judging from the fact that her father, Dedibayaash (Giizhig and Nookomiban's fourth son), spoke of having many elderly relatives (i.e., cousins), it is likely that Giizhig was among the younger of Jiiyaan's children. Dedibaayaanimanook herself remembers observing a person she referred to as Jakaabesh when she was a small child, but most of the other paternal relatives of Dedibayaash's generation may have been deceased by then (see Figure 25). Jiiyaan, the Che(e)an in both the Hudson's Bay Company and Indian Affairs records, left a widow whom the 1883 treaty pay list mentioned as "M deceased." Despite the ambiguities associated with Figure 24, merely having knowledge of these names and simply being able to articulate them is inexplicably gratifying for us, their descendants. The possession of the knowledge of their names contributes to a sense of belonging to the ongoingness of the Namegosibii Anishinaabe community's genealogy. I will discuss these and other individuals in greater detail in Chapter 9.

This project, working with only a tiny fraction of those who express their identity in terms of Namegosibiing, recognizes other relatives who communicate their attachment to and concern for ancestral homelands in varying ways. For example, a local working group in Red Lake is dedicated to Anishinaabe advocacy. One project sought ways to protect Gichibaawitig Big Falls on Namegosi-ziibi Trout Lake River from the proposed construction of a hydro facility. The significance of these efforts lies in the attention they draw to the fact that the home territories consist not only of

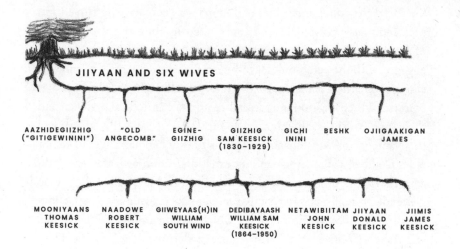

Figure 24.

Descendants of Jiiyaan and his six wives. Dedibaayaanimanook has stated
that she was seven years old when her paternal grandfather, Giizhig, passed.
According to the written record, Dedibayaash was born in 1864.

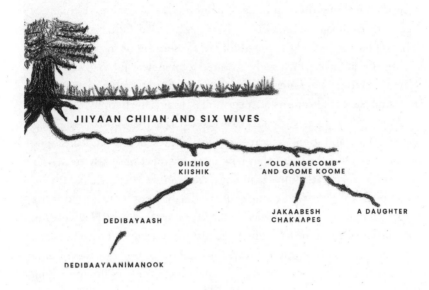

Figure 25.
Probable relationship of Dedibayaash and Jakaabesh. Both
Dedibaayaanimanook's dadibaajim and Gary Butikofer's notes mention the
person whom Namegosibii Anishinaabeg referred to as Jakaabesh.

Namegosibiing itself but all of the areas in which the aanikoobidaaganag ancestors and their descendants—including at least one participant of this work, Dedibaayaanimanook—lived and travelled. Other Anishinaabe relatives have explored the possibility of a reserve in or near the municipality of Red Lake. One family acquired a cabin near Jiibayi-zaagiing in Namegosibiing where members are able to revitalize relationships with ancestral places of home as Namegosibii Anishinaabe people.

Most of the eight participants have taken part in these and other efforts to re-establish and strengthen the Anishinaabe presence in Namegosibiing Trout Lake. Over the years, they have attended meetings with the MNRF to advocate for greater input in policy development. All participants who wish to advance the well-being of Anishinaabe people throughout the region recognize and acknowledge these examples of how Namegosibii Anishinaabeg continue to reaffirm the historical origins of who they are.

Subjectivity and positionality are thus components of a person's frame of reference, with particular circumstances and events of life informing their views and beliefs about the world. My own case, for example, consists of a childhood in Namegosibiing among Anishinaabe relatives, hearing Anishinaabemowin language from birth, and learning about dadibaajim customs that commingled with a Norwegian immigrant father's Western perspectives and parental philosophies. From these diverse ontological systems of thought emerged and evolve my own understandings and world views.

As the historical forces of the wemitigoozhi spread over the land, dominant discourses affected Anishinaabe people in particular ways. It is important to look briefly at the means by which Europeans subjugated and continue to subjugate Anishinaabeg as Indigenous people and make every effort to destroy their value systems and alter their ideas about themselves and their place in the world and the aki earth. The documentation of these actions is nothing less than a record of attempted genocide.

Ezhibii'igaazoyang
How We
Are Written

The historical processes of dominant discourse—a concoction of wemitigoozhi's imaginaries and realities—have excluded Namegosibii Anishinaabe dadibaajim while empowering wemitigoozhi's texts, maps, and ethnographies. In this chapter, I examine written texts for how historical figures, academic researchers, and Anishinaabe writers themselves have characterized Anishinaabe people. From there it is possible to fully appreciate how Anishinaabe people conceptualize and articulate—and write about—who they are. Then it is also possible to present the Anishinaabemowin dadibaajim narratives, thus making visible and validating the Anishinaabe people's presence in the physical spaces of their homelands, and to establish broader historical contexts for a more balanced, ethical discourse.

By way of critically assessing the historical use of text, there are certain writers who document its function as a coercive implement of control and the attempted extermination of First Nations peoples culturally and literally. For example, Walter Mignolo, whose speciality lies in ideas about Eurocentrism, geopolitics and colonialism, and the use of language as a weapon of subjugation, explains that a certain "philosophy of language based on the celebration of the [written] letter and of vernacular languages began to emerge in Europe" around the close of the fifteenth century.[1] The text, according to Mignolo, was a manifestation of coloniality, which he describes as the "invisible and constitutive hand of 'modernity.'"[2] Noted for his analysis of colonial legacies in the Americas, Damián Baca is an academic who clarifies what was at the core of that modernity. He asserts that the arrival of the Europeans to this continent was accompanied by a "universal hegemony over political ideology, cultural meanings, and historical narrative" driven by a belief in their linguistic, intellectual, and moral superiority.[3] Armed with an inordinate desire for Indigenous resources, Europeans granted themselves permission to treat Indigenous peoples as though they were not quite human.[4] The latecomers' use of the text was an essential feature that seemingly confirmed such attitudes about themselves and Indigenous peoples.

Expanding and maintaining domination over Indigenous places and populations, European inscription was the voice of authority. Basil Johnston (1929–2015), an Anishinaabe scholar, lecturer, and advocate of Anishinaabemowin use, stated that this was possible because "the blade, the bludgeon, and the bullet" enforced the new order.[5] To more effectively destabilize Indigenous spirituality and culture for purposes of exploitation and genocide, colonizers used roman orthography and syllabic text in many Indigenous languages including Anishinaabemowin.

Dissemination of and access to texts were implicated in the political economy of control and domination. Margaret Bender is a cultural and linguistic anthropologist who asserts that language in the form of text "connects to . . . power structures . . . such as those involved in colonial administration [that] necessitate[s] graphic representation."[6] The power of the text, she explains, has fundamentally resided in its exclusive accessibility to those with the advanced education to find the key to its workings and unlock its meanings. Concomitantly, the globalizing colonizer settlers attempted to destroy the Anishinaabe people's oral systems, pressuring them to become literate. With Indigenous peoples now, to a great extent, subsumed in a Western capitalist way of thinking and being, Cherokee scholar-educator Ellen Cushman reminds us about the "dominance of the letter, writing, and the book."[7] It is important to keep in mind that effective forms of knowledge transmission existed long before the Europeans imposed literatism. The text is a human construction, neither natural nor neutral.

Although the canonic text may appear disinterested, it is not so benign for Anishinaabe people. The ethnographers' method of using geographical regions to facilitate their research, for example, detailed several identifying characteristics of Anishinaabe communities. Among these were birch-bark canoes and storage containers, distinctive snowshoe patterns, use of spruce roots, beadwork designs, unique ceremonial pipes, the vision quest, and forms of bloodletting.[8] Others drew attention to what appeared to be shared practices, mentioning neighbouring communities such as Pikangikum and Lac Seul. Discussions about the Lac Seul Anishinaabeg of the nineteenth century, to illustrate, according to anthropologist Charles A. Bishop, noted that populations were "evenly dispersed throughout the area in family units" as a strategic response to prevailing scarcities.[9] Although these attributes are essentially similar to how dadibaajim presents Namegosibii Anishinaabe traditional customs, the ethnographic findings failed to recognize the Namegosibiing Trout Lake Anishinaabeg as a distinct—albeit relatively small—community of people in their own right. The analysis of these findings thus homogenized both the people of Namegosibiing and those they did recognize and mention. The ethnographers had in effect made the Namegosibii Anishinaabeg and all of their unique qualities invisible.

Another example of a seemingly innocuous ethnographic text used maps that depict northwest Ontario, the so-called Northern Ojibwa country of North America's Subarctic Shield.[10] Although one map portrays and identifies Namegosib as Trout Lake, the area of research actually lies just to the east, thus technically excluding Namegosib.[11] The lake is on a map, but because the text fails to describe or even mention its Anishinaabe occupants, it risks portraying the region as uninhabited, empty of and unused by humans.

Charles Bishop, on the other hand, noted that the Hudson's Bay Company distinguished Namegosibiing Trout Lake from Big Trout Lake of the Hudson Bay drainage basin by how records described the location of Namegosibiing relative to Lac Seul and Big Trout Lake to Osnaburgh House.[12] However, the two maps he used—both showing Big Trout Lake, with one referring to it as Big Trout Lake and the other as simply Trout Lake[13]—do not show or name Namegosibiing. While Bishop seemed to have been aware of Namegosibiing's existence as a lake, his text and accompanying maps overlooked the community of people who made it their home. As a result, he produced an account that is not particularly useful for the needs of Anishinaabe communities and individuals who seek to corroborate their identity in Western terms. These research approaches have reinforced the invisibility and marginalization of the Namegosibii Anishinaabe people and the notion of *terra nullius*.

Important to bear in mind, use of ethnographic records that cite Trout Lake by name must also contain information that identifies whether it is Namegosibiing or Big Trout Lake located within the northern region of what is now Ontario. When, for example, anthropologists Edward Rogers and J. Garth Taylor stated that treaties were negotiated and signed "in 1929 and 1930 . . . with the people of Trout Lake and Caribou Lake," they were referring to Big Trout Lake.[14] Big Trout Lake is a community that self-identifies as the First Nation of Kitchenuhmaykoosib Inninuwug, literally translated as the People of the Great Trout Water. Although Namegosibiing Trout Lake community members retained a close association with Lac Seul throughout the fur trade and treaty-making periods and are still off-reserve members of Lac Seul First Nation, they historically expressed an interest in acquiring their own band status, as some members continue to do today.

I would argue that no work focusing on the identity of Anishinaabe people is complete without a comment on the ethnographic texts of renowned American anthropologist Alfred Irving Hallowell. Highly regarded and often quoted as an authoritative researcher in academia, Hallowell began his work by surveying ethnographic material on Anishinaabe peoples' special relationship with the makwa bear.[15] Subsuming Lac Seul in the northern Saulteaux of the eastern North American woodlands, Hallowell included a description of a Lac Seul man who refused to relinquish his sacred bear poles along a journey from Lac

Seul to Lac St. Joseph.[16] He then reviewed the religion of Anishinaabeg in the Pigeon River areas east of Lake Winnipeg, focusing on settlements of the Pikangikum band.[17] Given the relational ties among the communities, it is not surprising for Hallowell to have noticed a number of features that are strikingly similar to Dedibaayaanimanook's descriptions. Fisher pelts, for example, were highly valued, and individuals could assume the role of spiritual leader only if they had undergone a dream journey before puberty. Hallowell also reported that an unidentifiable wemitigoozhi sometimes participated in spiritual events and described the loud sounds and violent movement accompanying a gozaabanjigan "conjuring" tent ceremony.[18]

Hallowell later mentioned signs of Christianity, including its condemnation of polygyny.[19] In regard to the missionaries' drive to disrupt Anishinaabe cultural practices relating to familial stability, he asserted that "the decline observable in our sample thus represents a continuation of this process of [polygyny] extinction, under conditions of acculturation that were spreading to the bands previously unaffected."[20] Continuing his anthropological scrutiny, Hallowell looked at practices related to death, the deceased, and the afterlife, aspects of which constitute the subject matter of Namegosibii dadibaajim.[21] Among these were the sharing of food and tobacco when visiting the deceased ancestors at their places of rest, crossing a river to achieve afterlife, safeguarding the spiritual signification of the shoulder blade, and protecting the means by which people returned after death. Hallowell identified them as customs of Berens River and Lac Seul, both communities that were relationally connected to the Namegosibiing Trout Lake people.

Of significance is Hallowell's observation that putting food into an open fire as an offering was still practised "up the River."[22] This remark suggests that the further east he travelled along Berens River toward Pikangikum and beyond, the more likely communities were free from proselytism. Ironically, it is this remark that acts as an oblique reference to the Namegosibii Anishinaabeg by confirming that traditional spirituality was still relatively unscathed among communities located in the vicinity of Namegosibiing. Notwithstanding all these observations, the specific identity of the Namegosibii Anishinaabe community would appear to have escaped Hallowell's anthropological gaze.

After Hallowell, research adjoining his work by focusing on communities east of Lake Winnipeg began to proliferate. Ethnohistorian Jennifer

Brown and cultural anthropologist Maureen Matthews, to illustrate, allude
to Christianizing efforts among Anishinaabe people—among whom
would certainly have been acquaintances, friends, and relatives of the
Namegosibii Anishinaabeg—west and north of the Red Lake district.[23]
Interestingly, these evangelizing activities included the occasional Sunday
visit to Namegosibiing during the late 1950s, when Mennonites based
in Red Lake provided my siblings and me with religious enlightenment.

Other studies looked at the southwest regions of northwest Ontario.
American cultural anthropologist Ruth Landes investigated traditional
Anishinaabe lifeways from a female perspective, basing her study on
seven months of fieldwork with a mentor from Emo, south of Kenora.[24]
Her depiction of marriage and divorce among the Anishinaabe people
whom she researched aligns with certain customs of the Namegosibii
Anishinaabeg. From the perspective of colonial disruptions to land access
and the coping strategies of Anishinaabe families in the Rainy River
regions, anthropologist Laura Peers and ethnohistorian Jennifer Brown
corroborate and make several references to Landes's findings.[25] These texts
contain information about and names the communities of Lac Seul, Rainy
River, Pikangikum, and Berens River, but the Namegosibii Anishinaabe
people and their Namegosibiing homelands receive no specific mention.

Whereas these writings are an outsider's etic construction of
Anishinaabe identity, dadibaajim narration is an insider's view that
describes variations in how Anishinaabe people themselves conceptualize and portray who they are. For example, Dedibaayaanimanook's
dadibaajim notes that Namegosibii Anishinaabe women purposely distinguished themselves from those of Lac Seul by adorning their clothing with
ribbons.[26] Although anthropologist Jack Steinbring's description of the
vision quest suggests that only boys participated in the spiritual practice,[27]
the ando-bawaajigem dream quest of the Namegosibii Anishinaabeg was
inclusive of both boys and girls.[28] This detail demonstrates the egalitarian
nature of Namegosibii Anishinaabe thought.

The wiindigoo concept is a popular subject with certain writers,[29] but
by way of avoiding such topics, the Namegosibii Anishinaabe elders of my
work chose to remain silent. Their silences are examples of the waawiimbaajimowin custom, indicating that the subject is appropriate for discussion only within the community. Of note, even though "waawiimbaajimowin" is not a term in common use among Namegosibii Anishinaabeg,

I use it here in reference to obfuscation in speech, or the discreet form of communication that works to protect and respect community protocols and sensibilities.

Without careful consideration, work that is organized around geographically demarcated spaces can give the false impression that communities falling within these researcher-defined boundaries must all be alike. These texts identify what they regard as commonalities and tend to overlook a wealth of diversity by excluding variations among individual Anishinaabe communities that actually self-identify in very particular ways.

It is necessary to keep in mind the role of power in the creation of texts about Indigenous peoples in order to understand the historical lack of Namegosibii Anishinaabe voice in dominant discourse. When, for example, we examine the long-standing connections of research, the academy, and the state, structural linkages become evident.[30] Coercive uses of power enabled outsider researchers who subscribed to unilineal cultural evolutionism and other similar notions to gather data for ethnographic texts that served as "evidence" to support state assimilationist arguments against Indigenous populations.

Diamond Jenness's ethnological approach serves as a good example of research projects that the Canadian state directly funded for evidence to justify the treatment of Indigenous people. Helping to perpetuate the dominant society's pejorative ideas that included the people's objectness, Jenness described his own active participation in physical examinations and anthropometric measurements of over 100 men and women living in the Far North over the course of two years.[31] The statistics he compiled contributed to the creation of a body of information about eyes, hair, skull and face shapes, proportions, heights, and other physical features. Jenness then went on to criticize the government, asserting that policies such as those that denied Indigenous people their right to vote, outlawed crucial ceremonial practices, and foisted a fallacious governance system upon them were not sufficiently assimilationist!

At various times an employee of the Department of Human Anatomy at Oxford University, Britain's physical anthropologist Beatrice Blackwood travelled to First Nations communities throughout this continent using similar methods. She collected hair samples as biological specimens and conducted the same type of invasive measurements as those of Jenness with the support of the Canadian state.[32] Importantly, state actors used ethnographies to evince notions of racial hierarchies in order to advance the erasure of Indigenous peoples, whether the authors themselves opposed or agreed with these underlying motives and ideologies. Jenness and Blackwood are both prime examples of how the work of anthropologists was the handmaid of a racist state. This begs the question of why anyone could possibly imagine that people willingly agreed to undergo such soul-destroying treatment.

Contexts of subjugation from which most outsider texts, whether academic or otherwise, about Indigenous peoples were—and often still are—generated can be characterized as pernicious forms of power inequity. These are evident in one of Western research's central preoccupations: the investigation of traditional spiritual ("pagan") customs and practices. When Hallowell arrived in the relatively remote communities of the Berens River during the middle years of the twentieth century, he indicated that the Berens River Anishinaabeg were losing their self-determination and traditional lifeways as access to their land and natural resources was rapidly diminishing.[33] He formed a close relationship with Chief William Berens, who agreed to be his principal participant (informant). With economic, cultural, and spiritual duress in plain view everywhere, evidence of diminution and vulnerability could not conceivably have eluded the attention of an exceptionally observant anthropologist any more than the status, influence, and power permeating him as the wemitigoozhi from the dominant world would have gone unnoticed by community members.

From the perspective of an Anishinaabe understanding, it is also inconceivable that the people anthropologists studied would not have felt compelled to appear, at the very least, cooperative. They may have even had hopes of deriving some form of benefit—the ability to regain a measure of self-sufficiency, perhaps—in exchange for their (real or apparent) collaboration. Generally, however, people knew that wemitigoozhiwag would never return the land and its resources or abandon the all-encompassing pursuits they had begun.

Benefitting so enormously as they had from the Anishinaabe people's disadvantaged circumstances through advancements in professional careers and reputations, researchers largely failed to consider the moral and ethical repercussions of their activities upon their subjects. They often began by enlisting individuals they presumed to be leaders to act as intermediaries because it was likelier that the rest of the community would then participate. Accepting it to be true that leaders as converts would set an example for others of the community to follow, missionaries often used a similar strategy.

Chief William Berens had become a Christian believer; nonetheless, he expressed angst in having compromised customary taboos by disclosing aadasookaanan narratives during the summer.[34] Specifying that these special narratives can be spoken only during the winter, the Anishinaabe people's belief system warns of consequences if this proscription is ignored. However, the demands of Hallowell's academic schedule took precedence, and the anthropologist continued to return each summer for several years in order to finish his fieldwork, despite being aware of his mentor's moral dilemma.

Aside from the timing of Hallowell's visits, some of the subject matter the anthropologist investigated was the exclusive concern of the community. It is inappropriate and unethical to expose babaamiziwin internal information to outside scrutiny. Even today when Indigenous people have largely adjusted to dominant culture, there are senior Anishinaabe elders who are uncomfortable discussing certain topics with those who do not have experiential and contextual understanding or grasp their spiritual signification. The elders' hesitancy is a matter of trust and how well the researcher understands the sanction. Situated within the community's intellectual and sacred domain, these aspects of Anishinaabe knowledge were an inalienable extension of the community members' spiritual selves that Hallowell's research compromised. For him to persist with his research without first resolving the babaamiziwin issue with his participants and their community by either refraining from discussing the aadisookaanan narratives or visiting the community during the winter was unethical and disrespectful, no matter how close his friendship with Chief Berens may have been.

Hallowell's quest to document the babaamiziwin philosophies and spiritual practices of his hosts disregarded the most fundamental Anishinaabe ethical concerns relating to those belief systems. In so doing he not only dishonoured the people as well as his work and himself, he trampled on their sensibilities and exposed them to the risks associated with breaking taboos. Seeming to escape the consideration of many outside researchers is the notion that Anishinaabe people may have preferred to exercise their autonomy, follow their criteria and guidelines, and use their discretion about what information to release and what to protect in the same way that researchers seek to make choices about their work, free of duress and without pressure. Anthropologists failed to examine the question of why any Anishinaabe people would abandon the spiritual beliefs, teachings, principles, practices, and values of their elders and ancestors had they had the choice to do so without coercion in any way, shape, or form, directly or indirectly.

The process of acquiring the knowledge of babaamiziwin requires what Anishinaabe people refer to as "gikendamaawiziwin," a kind of inner discernment or ability to intuitively perceive effects and conditions existing within the immediate or ongoing environment. In all settings, it is an essential form of intelligence. Anishinaabe people whom researchers studied did not lack gikendamaawiziwin, that positional frame that includes awareness and experiences of the realities, circumstances, and exploitative conditions during the time of Hallowell's visits. The comparative power and privilege of wemitigoozhi researchers—outsiders—such as Hallowell contrasted with the lack of autonomy of their subjects, undoubtedly affecting their thoughts and decisions about whether they might divulge details about their practices or stage performances.

An important aspect of gikendamaawiziwin is awareness of the contextual location from which outside investigators seemingly have free access to matters of babaamiziwin such as the sacred dadibaajim narratives, aadasookaanan. Not only do Anishinaabe researchers usually know the importance of looking to community principles for ethical guidance, they examine professional and personal motives and, importantly, funding arrangements. The concern for the identity of funders is a critical component of gikendamaawiziwin because those who provide financial support have the power to influence agendas, ethical guidelines, objectives, goals, expected findings, and what is in everyone's best interest from their particular perspective. Close attention to these issues is an example of how gikendamaawiziwin helps to better understand and evaluate the processes of research and keep them on an ethical path. Fairly recently, an unfortunate example of how a project can derail due to lack of proper consideration for Anishinaabe ethical sensibilities occurred in Namegosibiing.

Fieldwork and its analysis that lack respect for the belief systems, spirituality, and sensibilities of a community and its elders often result from valuing expediency over principle. Without that foundation, comprehension and interpretation are necessarily limited. At best, the work is shrouded in ethical ambiguity, with the *how* as important as the *what*. The integrity of both the process and conclusions of texts that arise from taking advantage of the disempowering effects of wemitigoozhiiwaadiziwin on Indigenous communities or the nation-state's racist ideologies needs rigorous investigation. At the same time, however, the process and the conclusions are useful for making comparisons with texts that derive from more ethical methodologies, thereby allowing for the examination of power imbalances and their impact on anthropological work.

There are few exceptions to the norm of making only indirect references to the Namegosibii Anishinaabe people of northwest Ontario. One such exception is anthropologist Robert Dunning's study that included the Red Lake Anishinaabeg, some of whom would have been the Namegosibii Anishinaabeg who frequently visited Red Lake or had relocated there.[35] The work of archivist-historian John Richthammer is another departure from the norm of the Namegosibii Anishinaabe community's ambiguous treatment. Framing his work from a settler pioneer's perspective, Richthammer speaks from his own first-hand experience of the region's social-historical contexts and is clearly mindful of the presence of the local Anishinaabe people. He discusses, for example, the importance of land to their identity, lives, and well-being by noting that "the Anishinaape, with their great reverence for the land and its animals, were distraught at the denuding of both the land and its wild game" throughout the twentieth century.[36] Although his observation may seem understated to the Namegosibii Anishinaabeg themselves, Richthammer, unlike Dunning, grew up in Red Lake. As a result of personal interactions, encounters, and friendships with Namegosibii Anishinaabeg, he helps to make the community visible by drawing from his personal observations of the effects of settler activities on how they sought to live and self-identify.

Importantly, Indigenous writers and researchers have striven to redirect the creation of text to a more respectful, emancipatory, and reciprocal discourse. Nonetheless, distinctive power structures, hierarchies, and processes of Western organizational thinking become apparent in how Christian conversion or a Western education historically afforded certain advantages to some people. These comparative privileges are evident, for example, in the undivided attention Christian convert William Berens received from the highly prolific anthropologist Hallowell, and the ability of Western-trained Dakóta physician Charles Eastman to publish his ethnographical work.[37] Conversely, the comparative absence of non-Christianized, non-schooled voices also becomes evident.

With regard to fieldwork itself, Charles Eastman recognized the adherence of southwestern Anishinaabe communities to strict protocols that prohibited wemitigoozhiwag from even looking at certain ceremonial objects. Eastman grew up learning about the spiritual and philosophical systems for living on the land as an Indigenous person and became familiar with the belief that to countervail these teachings is to defile, desecrate, and endanger the integrity of their sacredness. Given that he was living in the juxtaposition of two convergent world views and its asymmetrical power relations, Eastman and his work personify the difficult decisions facing Indigenous people, including those who were not converted or schooled in the Western sense, about how to balance resistance and cooperation with what information—and material objects—to disguise, conceal, or relinquish completely.

Appropriate standards for any research arise from a genuine appreciation and respect for the customs and values of the mentor-participants and their communities. George Copway, for example, was a member of the Mississauga Anishinaabe band who spent his childhood learning the hunting and trapping lifeways of his ancestors.[38] Combining conversations with male community elders and his personal experiences, he expressly avoided the common disparaging terms used by Christians despite his Christian conversion. Instead, Copway showed his regard for his mentor-participants by referring to them as "wise men."[39] In his discussion about ancestral belief systems, he applied such descriptors as "ridiculous" only to how Europeans judged practices such as ceremonials. The value of how Copway conducted his work lies in the non-threatening, respectful treatment of participants, allowing them the dignity to decide how and to what degree they would engage in his research. This line of logic leads to the conclusion that his was an ethically derived work that reflected not only the soundness of his methodologies but also the spirit of integrity in which he worked. So long as he proved himself trustworthy and respectful toward his participants, they were willing to share the information he recorded and we are assured that his work is solidly ethical and accurate.

Similar in his methodology to that of Copway, William W. Warren based his work on the information he gathered from visits among Anishinaabe communities throughout Michigan and Minnesota. Warren, born in Minnesota of Anishinaabe-European heritage, used the words "true and perfectly reliable" to describe the individuals under whose guidance he carried out his fieldwork.[40] The ability to build on their Indigenous experiences and kinship relationships combined with a deferential attitude toward community customs enabled both Copway and Warren to engage in ethical methodologies. With the influences of an Anishinaabe heritage, combined with Western learning, religion, and dominant forces and structures of power at play, Indigenous writings generally call for a different kind of critical reading from what the work of non-Indigenous researchers requires.

It is unlikely that researchers and academics would have wished to submit themselves as subjects for the dehumanizing, spirit-shattering methodologies of the Beatrice Blackwoods, Diamond Jennesses, and others of the era. The Indigenous populations in Canada, however, had very little space for decisions about collaboration, contestation, or resistance.

Various ideas exist about why disreputable methods were so common during the late nineteenth and early to mid-twentieth centuries. According to one popular theory, anthropologists believed that the disappearance of Indigenous peoples was imminent. Hopes of seeing their ethnographies become the final authority about a vanished people may have incentivized them to set aside concerns for ethics. But increasing numbers of Indigenous people themselves began to write about who they were and record their dadibaajim narratives, thus becoming autoethnographers. As anthropologist Laura Peers and historian Carolyn Podruchny note, the "postcolonial turn in the social sciences . . . focus[es] on issues of power, both in the past and in the present, including the cultural and racial politics of scholarship and the production of knowledge."[41]

When George Copway wrote *The Traditional History and Characteristic Sketches of the Ojibway Nation* and William Warren published *History of the Ojibway People* in the nineteenth century, Indigenous scholarship and publications were barely in their infancy. Today, there is an expanding body of text that focuses on the use of Indigenous languages and expounds Indigenous knowledges using an Indigenous voice and reflecting Indigenous subjectivity and thought. Conveying an experiential understanding of the connections that exist with heritage languages, places of origin, and historical contexts, that literature inevitably enunciates notions of decolonization, the self-determination enterprise.

One self-determination-related reason why Indigenous writers strive to use heritage languages in text is to more effectively articulate the connections that exist with language and land-centred identity. Indigenous educator Belinda Daniels-Fiss explains that the nêhiyawêwin Cree language confirms her identity as nêhiyaw because it is inherently rooted in the land.[42] Similarly, Myrle Ballard underscores the land-based intelligence of her heritage language, warning that when a community loses its language, it loses a vast body of knowledge about the land, the ecosystem, and our responsibilities and obligations to the natural environment.[43] Ultimately, then, it is the aki land-natural environment itself that evokes the desire to rethink what is truly relevant and of importance because, as my own mentor, senior elder Dedibaayaanimanook, teaches, it is where truth lies.

Anishinaabe writers who were not raised as fluent language speakers argue for the applicability and value of dadibaajim's teachings in today's contexts. Versed in Western logic, John Borrows demonstrates the relevance of the Anishinaabe oral tradition in Western society's legal system, suggesting that its purported shortcomings often indicate a flawed assessment.[44] As he points out, the oral custom urges us to think beyond the constraints of dominant conceptions and see the dadibaajim narrative as a source of inspiration in times of duress. Borrows's father's story about his disappointment in forgetting the location of an important archaeological discovery reminds us that "a range of choice in structuring thoughts, behaviour, and relationships" is available for us.[45] Of necessity using the English language in discussions about principles, character traits, and the dynamic of relationships, Borrows presents the narrative as an instructive form of communication that is similar to how beading or creating birchbark containers and gathering blueberries are forms of language that express and convey meaning.

People originally conveyed the old Anishinaabe dadibaajim narratives in Anishinaabemowin, but scholars and academics who do not speak fluent Anishinaabemowin often mimic the language by how they tell a dadibaajim narrative in English. Borrows, to continue with his technique as an example, uses an uncomplicated English as though he had translated word for word from Anishinaabemowin.[46] Literal Anishinaabemowin-to-English translations, however, can present Anishinaabe ontological expression and thought as almost childlike in their seeming simplicity because English terms rarely carry the deeper, more encompassing meanings that lie within Anishinaabemowin. This is one reason why Anishinaabe narratives written in English are often mistaken for children's stories when, in fact, they are legal, historical, political, cultural, and spiritual records of prime significance for Indigenous self-identity.

In Borrows's narratives, Mishoomis's grandmother "laughed when she saw people trying to escape life's cycles and eliminate their conflicts."[47] The English word "laugh," however, fails to express a gookom's underlying compassion implicit in the Anishinaabe phrase "gii' baapi" (s/he laughed) that is embedded in the context of a grandmother speaking to her grandson. When we appreciate the relationship of a grandmother and the grandchild she is teaching, "she laughed" for "gii' baapi" communicates the correct idea that a gookom is caring and gentle. Cree language specialist Freda Ahenakew suggests that when a dadibaajim narrative stays within the framework of its own language and ontology, it remains intact and its complete meaning becomes self-explanatory.[48] Hence, the inner complexities of Borrows's narratives re-emerge when they return to their Anishinaabemowin places of origin. These are critical reasons why Anishinaabe thinkers advocate for the use of Anishinaabemowin.

One method for highlighting the primacy of Anishinaabemowin is to choose a specific Anishinaabemowin word as a centring concept or theme. By using the term "mino-bimaadiziwin" (life lived well), for example, Anishinaabe educator Brent Debassige illustrates the many functions of language and culture in Anishinaabe research.[49] He hyphenates the term "oshkabaywis" (ceremonial assistant) with the English word "academic," oshkabaywis-academic, to symbolize the role of Anishinaabe scholars who concomitantly respect community protocols and fulfill the academy's requirements.[50] With her use of Anishinaabemowin, educator and scholar Mary Young concurs that heritage language use is the most effective means for capturing its spirit and for understanding the world views it carries.[51] While all languages may be similarly characterized, it is the contrasts between Indigenous and European ontologies, the active erasure of Indigenous languages, and the privileging of those that are dominant that demand attention to the distinct meanings and nuances of Anishinaabemowin expression. Hence, Young convincingly argues that her use of Anishinaabemowin invigorates and substantiates her Anishinaabe identity. At the same time, she suggests that the use of Indigenous languages becomes a form of power that overcomes the hegemony of the English language.[52]

For those who seek greater use of Anishinaabemowin—or other Indigenous languages—Anishinaabe scholar Basil Johnston's statement takes Young's assertions in the following critical direction: "Without knowledge of the language scholars can never take for granted the accuracy of an interpretation or translation of a passage, let alone a single word to validate their studies, their theories, their theses about the values, ideals or institutions or any other aspect of tribal life."[53] Johnston notes that those who are without their heritage language must rely on others to provide them with meaning. Issuing an instructive message, he says that when Indigenous people lose their language, they lose their ability to "understand the ideas, concepts, insights, attitudes, rituals, ceremonies, institutions brought into being by their ancestors; and having lost the power to understand, cannot sustain, enrich, or pass on their heritage."[54] Perhaps most sobering is his forewarning that "they will have lost their identity which no amount of reading can ever restore."[55]

Johnston further explicates Anishinaabe thought by detailing the meaning of key concepts such as truthfulness, which he terms "w'daeb-awae."[56] He chooses that word to illustrate how we must rely on, trust, and believe his way of understanding w'daeb-awae if we are non-speakers. Again, these essential meanings will disappear along with Anishinaabe ontological contexts when Anishinaabemowin falls into disuse.

Considering that this book is a textualizing project, it is necessary to look briefly at the spokenness of Anishinaabemowin. Anishinaabe scholar Leanne Betasamosake Simpson, for example, looks at the value of orality in preserving and protecting Anishinaabe knowledge from loss of control, meaning, and contexts that comes with textualization.[57] Not holding ownership of dadibaajim oral narratives, she herself does not publish them because the ethical right to appropriate that responsibility is not hers. As with other non-speakers who present an Anishinaabe narrative using the English language in such a way as to mimic Anishinaabemowin, Simpson uses her heritage language within the text to a lesser extent than do speaker-scholars such as Johnston. She continues to spend considerable time on the land in order to learn from speakers who instruct her in the land-rooted language of the Anishinaabeg. As Johnston implies, people who learn the language are no longer dependent on others for meaning.

As an essential component of this book, the in-text use of Anishinaabemowin is a form of power that lies in the innate ability of the language to speak to history, spirituality, ceremony, and land-based identity. The philosophies that ground Anishinaabe people in Anishinaabe world views reside within the language and how it is structured. As Anishinaabe scholar and advocate of Indigenous language revitalization Brock Pitawanakwat indicates, we can still be confident and optimistic about maintaining and expanding upon our Anishinaabe identity as we strive toward becoming fluent speakers.[58]

There are many fluent Anishinaabemowin speakers who textualize dadi-baajim, as this book evinces. Anton Treuer edited an Anishinaabemowin-English anthology of more than fifty narratives of elders who describe how they live the language in discussions about the role and relationship of Anishinaabemowin with land, self-identity, and the colonial experience. Miskwaanakwad Melvin Eagle, to illustrate, explains why the spirit beings gave Anishinaabe people responsibility for—rather than ownership of—aki in his dadibaajim narrative.[59] Through his use of Anishinaabemowin, Naawi-giizis Jim Clark clarifies the importance of mawadishiwem, the customary practice of Anishinaabe people of maintaining community cohesion across the homeland distances.[60]

Treuer himself expresses grave concerns for the preservation of Anishinaabemowin. Calling for nothing less than language fluency, he explains his rationale by framing the value of language in terms of its ability to impart Anishinaabe identity and its proclivity to dialogically centre self-determination.[61] Treuer illustrates his reasoning by writing entirely in Anishinaabemowin as follows: "Anishinaabeg igaye wiinawaa odaa-ayaanaawaan odakiimiwaan miinawaa odinwewiniwaan giishpin waa-anishinaabewiwaad miinawaa waa-bimaadiziwaad daabish-koo go anishinaabeg ogimaataazowaa."[62] Here Treuer asserts that understanding self-identity (ezhi-nanda-gikenindizowaad) as Anishinaabe people (waa-izhi-gashkitooyang geget ji-anishinaabewiyang), self-determination

(ogimaataazowaa), Anishinaabe expertise and knowledge (anishi-
naabe-gikendaasowin), the homelands (odakiimiwaan), and the power
that inheres within Anishinaabemowin usage ([g]iishpin gii-anishinaabe-
widooban gaa-izhichigebang apii nawaj daa-mashkawiziimagad noongom)
are all at stake. Linking a sense of Anishinaabe identity to the ability to
maintain spiritual connections through language use, he states, "Giishpin
wanitooyang gemaa gaye aabajitoosiwang, manidoog gaawiin oga-nisi-
dotawasii-waawaan anishinaaben."[63] Treuer underscores the weight of
our responsibility to maintain our Anishinaabe identity and spirituality
through language with the root "nisidotaw-," which translates as recognizes
by sound or understand and comprehend someone when she or he is
speaking. He advises that the spirit beings will understand and recognize
us as Anishinaabeg optimally when we use our Anishinaabemowin speech,
even when less than fluent.

Treuer's work articulates a profound appreciation and respect for
Anishinaabemowin. He believes that the ability to conceptualize and put
forward various Anishinaabe philosophies in Anishinaabemowin within
the context of a conversation in English reflects the ability to understand,
value, and engage in the deeper subtleties and nuances of Anishinaabe
meaning. In a recorded interview in Minnesota in 1999, Treuer repeat-
edly uses the term "Anishinaabewisidoon" (literally, put it down in textual
Anishinaabemowin) in reference to translations of English terms into
Anishinaabemowin meanings.[64] The capacity to capture the essential
meaning of an English word and know whether or not it is translatable
into Anishinaabemowin that fits coherently into the ontological system
of Anishinaabe thought is the ultimate test of inter-ontological fluency.
Acquiring that skill is a reconciliatory endeavour.

The product and production processes of non-Indigenous research
throughout the early and mid-twentieth century were very often ethically and factually problematic. Experientially and literally marginal-
izing, the ambiguous treatment of Anishinaabe communities resulted
from how canonic researchers and scholars conceptualized, categorized,
and mapped Indigenous people from a myth-based, Eurocentric frame
of reference. That type of literature lacks the capacity and intent to

capture an Indigenous perspective or articulate Indigenous self-identity. Yet it has considerable value for those who wish to explore the notion of knowledge production within the context of its impacts on Indigenous people and in terms of its potential usefulness in reversing those historical processes and their effects. Hence, the utility of the historical canonic text includes its ability to generate theory, provide a basis for analysis, and highlight how a set of descriptions and data of Indigenous peoples were unethically generated.

Academe's presence, the ubiquity of dominant languages and Western epistemologies, and scholarly imperatives and ways of doing diminish the expression of ancestral, land-based identity by muting Anishinaabe voices and supressing original languages and knowledges. Indigenous researchers, academics, and writers, however, are reversing these processes and championing the value in building the capacity to engage with knowledge production by visiting the land and learning the language of the elders. The writings of Treuer, Johnston, Borrows, and Simpson[65] are examples of scholarship that privileges Anishinaabe aweneniwiyang self-identity, orality, the heritage languages of dadibaajim narratives, and land-centred perspectives. At the same time they enhance Western thought by contributing to a more comprehensive body of knowledge, they also manifest the increasing volume of work that is creating dawisijigem spaces where dadibaajim can once again thrive and teach.

Wenji-Anishinaabewiyang
Our Anishinaabe Selves

The knowledge in which the dadibaajim of today's gichi-Anishinaabe senior elders is anchored inevitably differs from what we now encounter. Even as they still remember and tell the narratives that all adult members of the community once understood, much of that corpus is no longer available for the younger generations of today to tap into. Nonetheless, as previously noted, careful attention to the context and historical frame of reference that each senior mentor-teacher speaks enables current listener-learners to rediscover some of the once prevalent understandings. Considering the contrastive forces of globalization that the wemitigoozhiwag instituted and the nurturing ontologies the Anishinaabe forebears lived for so many millennia, those—young and old—who seek to study ancestral narratives from a place of deference will find a worthwhile project in pursuing the dadibaajim expressions of our aanikoobidaaganag ancestors' life-supporting knowledges. By listening to the narratives of the mentor-participants, this chapter sets out to discover what those narratives and their knowledges were.

As a purveyor of culture and an institution of learning, dadibaajim was a means for intergenerational conveyance of Anishinaabe identity across the eons. Dadibaajim continues to carry out that function by describing the relationships and interactions, values and practices, beliefs and symbolisms, and activities and experiences of the speakers as Anishinaabe community members. The custom and its processes in themselves strengthen and preserve Anishinaabe cultural identity by instilling in each speaker the power to protect that Anishinaabe identity, and when Anishinaabemowin is being spoken, dadibaajim's role as cultural transmitter is immeasurably reinforced.

As each dadibaajim narrative unfolds, we can hear individual differences—some distinct, others subtle—stemming from the varying socio-political realities, contexts, and reference points in which speakers situate themselves and their narratives. Gichi-Anishinaabe senior elders such as Dedibaayaanimanook frequently cite conditions and events that are different from those in which the younger narrators live today. Narratives voiced in either Anishinaabemowin or zhaaganaashiimowin English—or both—can be specific and clear in their meaning or nuanced and even obscured. Lengthy accounts may abound with contextual information, while silences are replete with meaning for those that are brief. Whether spoken by an elder or a youth, whether extensive or terse, the narratives are the most accurate representation of the speaker's Namegosibii Anishinaabe identity. This work is about the history, identity, and origins of the Namegosibii Anishinaabe people; therefore, their dadibaajim narratives provide appropriate themes for organizing this chapter.

Enacting Dadibaajim

Engaging in the dadibaajim custom engenders speaker-listener-land relationships whenever narrators first tell a dadibaajim, then again when they and their audiences remember and relive its experience by re-recitation. Senior elder Dedibaayaanimanook's oral presentation of "E-gii' ishkô gimiwang" (when it finished raining), for example, describes how a mother expressed affection for her young child at the same time she strengthened their connection to the boreal land that surrounded them. The appealing nature of the narrative in itself makes it eminently agreeable for retelling, as is evident in the tone of delight—something that the written text cannot adequately capture—with which Dedibaayaanimanook presents it:

> E-gii'-ishkô-gimiwang, ebaashkineyaag idash, "Omagakiig osha igi gaa-baashkinawewewaaj," ako e-gii' izhipan my mom. "Gonige agwaawewag wiiyaas," ako e-gii' inenimagwaa. "Ambesh izhaayaan," ishako ingii' inendam ewii' awi bagoshi' agwô iya'iin, odagwaawaaniwaan [laughs]. Ewii' miijiwag ogaaskiiwagomiwaa, ako ingii' inendam.[1]

> When it stopped raining, and steam was wafting up, my mom would tell me, "Those are the frogs creating the smoke." "I wonder if they are smoking meat," I used to imagine. "I wish I could go over there," I would think, so I could beg for some of their smoked meat [laughs]. So I could eat some of their smoked dry meat is what I used to think to myself.

Dedibaayaanimanook's use of the word "ako" signifies that her mother repeated the omagakii frog narrative on more than one occasion, indicating its cultural reliability and usefulness. Note that when Dedibaayaanimanook wondered to herself about whether the frogs were smoking meat, she did not pose the question to her mother. When children are taught to listen, pay attention, and absorb what they hear, they are learning that the dadibaajim is complete as spoken. Young children need to learn how to engage with dadibaajim narratives, for they themselves will undoubtedly speak them one day.

Drawing from the natural components of the world around them and arising from the everyday experiences of life, each recital is a cultural mechanism for preserving the close mother-child-land relationship. Dedibaayaanimanook's own telling becomes a reperformance of her mother's narrative that renews and reinvigorates her own memories of those relationships. Reliving her sense of attachment to specific places located in the ancestral homelands, she mentions various natural phenomena as a confirmation of her sense of identity. Dedibaayaanimanook references rain, mists of rain, humidity, water, smoke, and the presence of omaga-kiig—we can almost hear them singing! All of these readily appeal to our sensory receptors. Although no longer able to physically experience these facets of her Anishinaabe childhood, Dedibaayaanimanook uses the dadibaajim as a mechanism for fortifying her remembrances of life in the noopimakamig aki boreal land at the same time she transmits them intergenerationally.

The next narrative focuses on other characteristics of dadi-baajim. Alluding to how it contrasts with textuality, for example, Dedibaayaanimanook ponders the oral tradition as a fundamental compo-nent of Anishinaabe thought, suggesting the reasons for its exceptionality within a milieu that places so high a value on the text as follows:

Gii'michi maamikawiwag. Gaawn wiikaa awiya ogii'ozhibii'anziin, aaniin ekidong. Nashke gaa-gii' dibaajimoyaan my story. Gaawn gegoon ingii' ozhibii'anziin. Miigo yetago ni maamikawiziwin gaa-gii' ozhitooyaan. Wiinge gichi inendaagwan gete dibaajimowin.[2]

They only remembered. No one ever wrote things down, what was said. Take, for example, my story that I told. I did not write anything down. It was only my memories that I created. The old narratives are held in absolutely the highest regard.

Dedibaayaanimanook expresses her understanding as a senior elder of the community, describing her role in a biographical work produced within the Western izhibii'igem system of text generation.[3] Comparing the oral system with that of the text, she indicates that the former requires that we work through the power of our intellectuality by engaging, cultivating, and stimulating our memory. The written method and its underlying structures and materiality, on the other hand, continuously produce and reproduce dependence on text for acquisition, retention, and transmission of information.

Dedibaayaanimanook intimates that dadibaajim depends upon active and direct speaker-listener linkages, and that its value lies not only in its content but also in its demand for physical proximity—that is, within hearing distance. She suggests that gete dadibaajim conveys the highest order and purest quality of knowledge of the Anishinaabe oral tradition, reinvigorating the cultural practice of gathering and celebrating the life-long remembrances of the community's senior elders. With Anishinaabe communities having their own unique sets of traditional narratives, dadi-baajim facilitates the expression of their sense of self-identity.

Speaking Dadibaajim

Similar to how the enactment of dadibaajim preserves and promotes Anishinaabe subjectivity, the content describes and illustrates the prac-tices that define and characterize that identity. A closer examination of "E-gii'-ishkô-gimiwang," for example, reveals that young children learned to pay attention to naturally occurring phenomena as everyday experi-ences in life and to become familiar with their associations and connec-tions. Playing a key role in the narrative, frogs were never only interest-ing subject matter for a children's tale. They were non-human persons whose affairs impinged upon and interacted with those of Anishinaabe people. Protecting Anishinaabe society's behavioural norms, omagakiig were an auspicious presence upon the landscape of Anishinaabe cultural identity. Their responsibility was to help safeguard aadasookewin, as Dedibaayaanimanook has often reiterated, by reminding people that the practice of telling that special type of dadibaajim includes telling it in very specific ways. Interestingly, what makes an aadasookaan narrative so special is that it can be told only during the winter. This means that it cannot be textualized because the written word is available for discus-sion at any time of the year.

The role of dadibaajim to preserve culture and cultural identity is also evident in Dedibaayaanimanook's "E, sii, dii, dii" narrative in which she describes how her mother taught her the English alphabet:

**A, B, C, D. Bizhishig ako ingii' gikinô'amaagonaan ji'
ikidoyaang, Gichi-jôj e' ani jibikang ako, e'gawishimoyaang**

oshako. Amiish i'i gaa' izhi noonde gawingwashiyaang.
Jackfish Bay goda i'imaa gii waaninaawangaang.[4]

A, B, C, D. She would always teach them to us so we could
recite them, Gichi-jôj and I, when it would get dark, when we
were going to bed. But then we would fall asleep too soon. Yes,
it was over there at Jackfish Bay where there is a sandy bay.

Using the historical building blocks of domination, this narrative
embodies the realities of contrasting ontologies by suggesting that the
ABCDS and the literate system they represent have little usefulness in
an oral society beyond putting children to sleep. Dedibaayaanimanook's
mother understood the letters in terms of their ability to represent any
number of meanings connected to wemitigoozhiiwaadiziwin because
she had learned the system at some point in her own childhood.

This dadibaajim relates to a time when an Anishinaabe mother
still exercised the freedom to rely on her own competencies, including the ability to provide for her children's safety, warmth, nutrition,
education, and cultural training even during the severest season of the
year. Dedibaayaanimanook upholds her own land-centred identity by
evoking constituent components of her Namegosibiing homeland. The
frozen bay, the sand beneath, and winter evenings at Jiibayi-zaagiing all
comprise an Anishinaabe lifeway that was essentially intact throughout
Dedibaayaanimanook's early childhood. A reminder of how children
so often poke fun at one another, she indicates that she teased her little
nephew for so completely mispronouncing the first four letters of the
English alphabet.

Also taking place at Jiibayi-zaagiing and originating from the same
time period, the narrative "E'michi nisiyaang" (with only the three of
us) illustrates how dadibaajim functions to preserve details of land-based
practices. It presents examples of the type of traditional ecological knowledge that helped to keep families supplied with fresh wild meat on a daily
basis. Dedibaayaanimanook's narrative is as follows:

Asiniin e'odakikowaaj. My mom e'inasookepan e-gii' nitaa
dadibaajimotawinangij ako Gichi-jôj e'ayagaashiinzhiyaang.
Indede e-gii' maajaawaaj noopimakamig e'izhaawaaj Jiins

**ningodôsogoniwaaj. Gaa'minowiisiniyaang. Waaboozoog
wiinge e-gii' wawiininowaaj. Gookooko'oogsh gaye
gimoodagwewaaj. Indede ako binamaa [giishka'ôj]
gaa'ogichi okik.**[5]

They had stone pails. My mom would tell us special narratives
when Gichi-jôj and I were small. My father would go away
into the forest (with) Jiins for six days. We ate very well. The
rabbits were very fat (and so) the owls would steal from the
snares. My father would first[cut down] a large jack pine.

Alluding to a specific kind of dadibaajim and signalling the time of year
that the event of the narrative took place, Dedibaayaanimanook begins
by using the term "inasookepan" in reference to aadasookewin. She
speaks to that aspect of a child's cultural training that conveys concepts
of other-than-human beings who coexist with Anishinaabe people. The
stone pails she mentions are associated with the non-humans whose
practices revolve around rocks, cliffs, water, and avoidance of direct
contact with Anishinaabeg—and an apparent ability to defy the natural
laws that govern humans.[6] With the terms "ako" (would) and "nitaa"
(used to), Dedibaayaanimanook stresses the early education children
received by emphasizing her mother's reiteration of the narratives.

This dadibaajim provides several examples of Anishinaabe traditional
ecological knowledge, which incorporates sustainable uses of resources,
and the location of animals on the food cycle, their eating preferences
and habits, and how that knowledge was best put to use. Thus assured of
the soundness of their knowledge and its ethical use, Anishinaabe people
exercised their ability to survive on the land, eat well, and speak of it
through dadibaajim for countless years, from one generation to the next.

Dedibaayaanimanook touches upon the spiritual dimension of
Anishinaabe thought in her recitation of the narrative "E-gii' nigamoj"
(that he sang). Recalling her father's explanation of his journey songs,
she suggests the nature of a hunter's interactions with the animal beings
in the following dadibaajim:

**Nigamoj. E-gii' inootawaaj ma'iingana'. Aya'aawisha'.
Minising gii nibaaj gaye. Nimishoomis onigamonan. Ogii'**

miinigoon ji nigamoj indaadii, gii maajaaj. Mii iniweniwan
nigamonan nimishoomis gaa-gii' ayaaj. "Bizaanigo nishike
ayaayan; ingoji ayizhidaayan, bizaanigo giga nigam
ingoding." Giizhiganinig-shgo gaye gii' nigamo.
[D]ewe'iganan, gaa-gii' ayaawaaj, gaa' aabaji'aaj e' nigamoj
e' giizhiganinig. Ingoding e' babimaakoshing [gii]' nigamo.
Aaniish wiin gaawn aadasookewin.[7]

He sang to honour the wolves. The animals. And when he was
sleeping on an island. My grandfather's songs. He gave them
to my father to sing when he [my grandfather] left [passed].
Those songs of my grandfather that he had. "Go ahead, when
you are alone anywhere on your journeys, and sing them
sometimes." He would also sing during the daytime. [T]he
drum he had was the one he used when he sang during the
day. Sometimes he sang while he was lying down [because] it
was not, to be sure, the type used for special narratives.

Dedibaayaanimanook indicates that her father received a repertoire of
nigamonan songs as a parting gift from his father, Giizhig. As a means
with which to honour and show respect for the animals, they had come
with instructions to use with care and discretion while he was journeying
alone. These songs fulfilled specific functions. Alone at night—perhaps
on an island—her father was assured of safety whenever he sang them.
Considering that the main purpose of his outings was to hunt, trap, and
kill animals, the power of their spirituality is evident by the fact that
they guided him through the animals' realm, mediating his relationships with them.

With this dadibaajim, Dedibaayaanimanook also contrasts sacred
songs with those her father used for relaxation by accompanying himself
with a hand-held drum (see Figure 26). Although the songs that were
recreational in nature came with fewer restrictions than sacred songs in
terms of who could hear them or when their owner could sing them,
Anishinaabe customary protocol and ethical considerations insisted that
they not be performed without the current proprietor's permission.

Figure 26.
Dedibayaash's dewe'igan. Dedibaayaanimanook's father's recreational drum
remains in her possession in her home in Winnipeg.

Remembering Through Dadibaajim

As the wemitigoozhiwag European(-descendant) peoples began to spread across the homelands in larger and larger numbers, prospecting, mining, trapping, hunting, fishing, logging, and damming, Namegosibii Anishinaabeg and other communities had to carefully re-examine issues of cultural and even physical self-preservation. "Jibwaa baatiinowaaj" (before there were many) demonstrates how people conceptualized and reacted to the arrival of the latecomers and their values, customs, priorities, and expectations of others. Alluding to details of life during the late 1920s and early 1930s when she was a child, Dedibaayaanimanook narrates as follows:

Jibwaa baatiinowaaj. Gii'wanii'igewag isago. Ya' [e' niibing gaye]. Gaawnshwiin niibiwa' gii'ondizisiiwag. Aanshinaa gaawiin wiin gegoon ogii'andawendanziinaawaaa'. Bakwezhiganan, waabishkibimide eta ogii' miijinaawaa'. I don't know about ziinzibaakwad. Dii sago. Maawaj asemaan. Miiwosha'i. Maawajigo gaa'izhi zaagichigewaagwen mewinzha Anishinaabeg. Gaa-gii' onji izhichigewaaj, ewii'onji ayaawaaj dii, asemaan. Gaawn gaye gegoon niibiwa' gii' inagindesinoon gaye gaa' onji wanii'igewaaj e'niibininig. Gaye more and more, biinish gii'ani-ayaawag gegoon ogii'ani ayaanaawaan. Aazha maawiin gakina apaneg Anishinaabewitoowaaj, o'omaa goda- wiin giinawindinake gaa'izhi ayaayeng.[8]

Before there were so many. They continued to trap. Yes [even in summer]. But they did not receive much. But then there was nothing they really wanted. Flour, [and] lard was all they ate [of the European-descended people's food]. I don't know about sugar. Also tea. Tobacco especially. That was all Anishinaabe people probably valued most a long time ago. That was why they did that [trap during the summer], to obtain tea, tobacco. Also because things were not too costly, was why they trapped during the summer. And more and more, until they began to acquire [any] number of

things. They are probably all gone now, the practitioners of
Anishinaabe ways, at least here where we are.

Throughout the first half of the twentieth century, families continued to
live mainly as they had in the past, trapping even when fur prices were low
and seeking relatively few wemitigoozhi European goods. This dadibaajim
demonstrates that despite colonial capitalism's invasion and increasing
arrogation of the homelands, Namegosibii Anishinaabeg desired to use
what the land provided and thereby preserve their autonomy and self-sufficiency. Avoiding wemitigoozhi's market economic philosophy while
still able to, they largely shunned its demands for needless and ongoing
consumption, its call for wastefulness and destruction.

Dedibaayaanimanook's dadibaajim describes a time of tremendous
transition, when wemitigoozhi's laws and economic system were rapidly
supplanting Anishinaabe lifeways. Due to the encroachment of wemitigoozhi's populations, resource development, and the creation of parks and
Crown land management, the noopimakamig aki boreal forests could no
longer provide for the Namegosibii Anishinaabe people's needs. The more
consumer goods they acquired, as well, the more they seemed to need.
In rapid succession, manufactured products replaced and made obsolete
many of the customary ways of producing and even conceptualizing life's
necessities and wants.

With no one still among us today who was familiar with the old
Namegosibii Anishinaabe traditions as she knew and practised them,
and in the face of her solitude Dedibaayaanimanook grieves the passing
of old ways and fellow practitioners. However, she communicates her
ongoing belief in the trustworthiness of the ancestral customs by sharing
her dadibaajim narratives. Few Namegosibii Anishinaabe people are left
to enact, speak, and uphold the customs of the old noopimakamig boreal
lands. As a consequence, dadibaajim narratives consist of a progressive
decline in the details of how traditional life was lived with each generation
that follows Dedibaayaanimanook's.

Retrieving Our Anishinaabe Selves

Namegosibii Anishinaabe narratives voice their speakers' abiding desire to mitigate wemitigoozhiiwaadiziwin's destruction of cultural ways. With her dadibaajim, Gwiishkwa'oo Eliza Angeconeb describes how she and her family determinedly and effortfully followed Anishinaabe customs. Her narratives speak to the adjustments they needed to make in response to the wemitigoozhiwag latecomers' arrival, as she concomitantly alludes to the gaps in her own Anishinaabe education:

> Jiibayi-zaagiing odizhinikaadaanaawaa, Jackfish Bay. Mewinzha i'imaa ingii' izhidaamin, Gweyesh, Aayizag, Bejii Betsy King, Jôjens, Ogin—gakina gaa'abinoonjiizhiwiyaang. Etago gaa' amwangidôko maangwag, giigooy. Wazhashkwag. Gaawn niin wiikaa ingii'amôsii [quietly laughs]. Ogii' baaswôwaa' amiish ezhi biindaabika'ôwaad. Bagida'ômin. Gaye maangwag niinawind ako, Jennie Giizhig. Babaamaakwagomoyaang Jôjens ako e' maangwa'gii'ani ziigwang, ani biboong. Dibi miina gaa-gii'izhaawaang. Gaawn ingikendanziin aapiji i'iwe. We were about eight years old indinendam. Gaawn ingii' gikendanziimin ji nitaa bimaakogomoyaang— [gestures] ingii' izhiweba'aamin [laughter]. Amiish ganabaj i'iwedi gii'ani izhaayaang, Vermilion Bay. Jôjensgaa' baatiinowag. Onjiiyaang Namegosibiing. Ingii' bimaakogomomin Red Lake, Vermilion Bay. Jiimis James Keesick. Gabe biboon gii' wanii'igewaad, ingii' nitaa wiijiiwaa ako Ja'iinsi e'agoodood naadagood izhi biboonishiwaad.[9]

They call it Jiibayi-zaagiing (Ghost Bay), Jackfish Bay. We lived there a long time ago, Gweyesh, Aayizag, Bejii Betsy King, Jôjens, Ogin—all of us children. We only ate loon, fish. Muskrat. I never ate them myself [subdued laughter]. They would dry them and then roast them in the oven. We set nets. We would also [catch] loons, Jennie Keesick and I. We went canoeing when Jôjens would [hunt for] loons during early

spring [and] in late autumn. I'm not sure where we went.
I do not know much about that. We were about eight years
old, I think. We did not know how to paddle—[gestures] we
swung it around this [laughter]. I think we made our way over
there to Vermilion Bay. There were many Jôjens children.
We were coming from Trout Lake. We canoed to Red Lake
[and] Vermilion Bay. [Also] Jiimis James Keesick. When they
trapped all winter, I used to accompany Ja'iinsi to set and
check rabbit snares where they spent the winter.

Gwiishkwa'oo describes travels throughout the Namegosibiing-
Wanamanii-zaa'iganing Trout Lake-Red Lake regions that began at
Jiibayi-zaagiing, where family and relatives customarily inaugurated the
trapping and hunting activities of the winter season. Although the location is now most commonly referred to as Jackfish Bay, Gwiishkwa'oo
insists upon the name Jiibayi-zaagiing (Ghost Bay) because its use
continually confirms the fact of the Anishinaabe people's presence.
The place name Jiibayi-zaagiing is at the same time a reminder of
specific events historically significant in the affairs of the Namegosibii
Anishinaabe community. Of genealogical importance is Gwiishkwa'oo's
mention of the names of family members and relatives, even though
most of the individuals are now deceased. Gweyesh Annie was her aunt,
and Aayizag Isaac, Bejii Betsy King, Jôjens George, Ja'iinsi, and Ogin
Jenny were first- and second-degree cousins.

Gwiishkwa'oo's dadibaajim demonstrates that families were still neigh-
bours, fellow hunters and fishers, travelling and dining companions, and
coworkers and friends who assisted and supported one another into the
early 1960s. She explains, for example, that she learned to snare rabbits
from her cousin Ja'iinsi during their stay in Vermilion Bay. Even though
it was increasingly necessary to modify aspects of the ancestral routes,
schedules, and activities in order to circumvent the wemitigoozhiwag,
Gwiishkwa'oo's narrative illustrates how two families continued to
follow the customs of travelling, hunting, and trapping synchronously
with the seasons. Some community members spent a winter in the
regions southwest of Namegosibiing, as far away as Vermilion Bay where
Highway 105 meets the Trans-Canada Highway (see Figure 4), rather
than in Namegosibiing and areas to the north, as the Giizhig ancestors had

done. These alterations coincided with the travel routes of Gwiishkwa'oo's paternal grandmother's people, those to whom the Indian Affairs pay lists referred as the "Otcheechackeepetangs" a century earlier. As indicated by both the oral dadibaajim and written records, the Otcheechackeepetang family had relocated from Biigaanjigamiing Pikangikum to the Gullrock region south of Red Lake at some time in the late nineteenth century. However, neither set of records gives any reason for their move. In choosing the route to avoid wemitigoozhi's incursions, Gwiishkwa'oo's father may have wished to reconnect with his maternal ancestors' routes by retracing portions of their journeys across the homelands, thus making the most of less than ideal circumstances.

The fragmentary nature of Gwiishkwa'oo's recollections is important to note. She may not have had opportunities to refresh her memories by revisiting and reliving the events and places of her early childhood. Due to the disruptive impacts of residential schooling and other such wemitigoozhiiwaadiziwin ways, including the need to find wage labour, she left her family at a very young age. The type of journey she discusses may have taken place only once for her, or other events in her life may have diminished her memories of them. One of my own childhood remembrances of Gwiishkwa'oo and her family was their seemingly abrupt departure in autumn when the shorelines were beginning to freeze, the mitigoog trees stood bare, and the skies were grey and overcast. Having had no personal experience with the seasonal travels of my aanikoobidaaganag ancestors, I did not understand that my cousin and her family were pursuing one of the most physically demanding yet culturally defining features of Namegosibii Anishinaabe identity.

Set during the early to mid-1950s, Gwiishkwa'oo's dadibaajim contains indirect references to the wemitigoozhiiwaadiziwin mindset and its effects on Anishinaabe cultural identity. She mentions, for example, that she learned to snare and skin a rabbit but that it was Ja'iinsi who taught her. During a time of greater social stability, she would have, unquestionably, learned from her mother, aunt, or grandmother rather than a cousin once removed. It is also worth noting that the latecomers' intrusions and interferences with traditional activities included provincial wiiyaasike-wininiwag game wardens who monitored Anishinaabe people's activities across the noopimakamig aki landscape. It was a time when customary economies were becoming increasingly unsustainable, supplanted by the new, market-driven order. When Anishinaabe people persisted with the aanikoobidaaganag's cultural ways wherever and however they could, the local wemitigoozhiwag disparaged—or pitied—them and cast them as the deservedly destitute or underprivileged.

Gwiishkwa'oo's next narrative describes several customary practices, tools, values, and spiritual principles associated with a successful moose hunt. Although able to watch her mother work, she herself had few opportunities for the direct, uninterrupted participation that leads to proficiency in many of the activities (for reasons she does not discuss):

> It's a big bone. Gaasha'igaade dash. Izhi agonjimaawaad
> nibiing. Nimaamaa gii' nitaa izhichige. Ingii'
> ganawaabamaa. Wiiyaas gaa onjiig. Amii' imaa
> gaa'onji ashamaawaaj animosha'—gegoon isago ogii'
> atoonaawaa', wiisagimanoomin, wiiyaas. Gaawn gegoon
> ogii'webinanziinaawaa' Anishinaabeg. Wiinge sago gakina
> gegoon ogii' aabajitoonaawaan. E-gii' agoodoowaad gaye
> mitigong gegoo jiigew. Makwa gaye gii nisaawaad. Gaawn
> gegoon ogii' webinanzhiinaawaa. Namanjisa wiin gaa'
> doodamowaagwen wiiyaas. Ribbons ogii' agoonaawaa'
> jiigew, gaa izhi neyaashiiwang. Blue, black, yellow—gakina
> sago—mitigong. Wegodogwen i'imaa ogii' atoonaawaa'.
> Makwa. Agoodoowaaj. Ingii' anoonigoomin goda ji
> izhichigeyaang. Amiish iko gaawn ingii'gagwedwesii
> gaawonji izhichiged Anishinaabeg.[10]

It's a big bone. And it was sharpened. They would soak it [moose hide] in water. My mother used to do that. I would watch her. Where the meat came from. And that was where they got what they fed the dogs—they would add something, [perhaps] rolled oats, [to the] meat. Anishinaabe people did not throw anything away. They used absolutely everything. And they also hung something on a tree by the water's edge. And also when they killed a bear. They did not throw anything away. I do not know what they did with the meat. They hung ribbons along the shoreline on a point of land. Blue, black, yellow—all colours—on a tree. They placed something there

for a bear. They hung it. Yes, we were requested to do the
same thing. But then, I would not ask the reason why people
did that.

Gwiishkwa'oo witnessed her mother working with specially crafted bone
implements for processing a moose skin. Winter being the best season
for such work, her mother submerged the hide under icy water, a procedure she refers to as "agonjimaawaad" (soaked it in water). It was far
from effortless work, requiring strength, patience, and a willingness to
work in frigid conditions. People nonetheless used the method because
it produced a well-crafted hide that was supple yet strong and pleasantly
tinged with the scent of smoke. A source of much personal satisfaction,
it was a signature of the artisan's identity.

Gwiishkwa'oo's narrative suggests that people adhered to protocols
that served spiritual purposes. Demonstrating their appreciation for the
moose spirit's gift, for example, they used special methods for disposing
of a moose's dewlap, and for the bear they hung ribbons on tree branches
to denote a successful hunt. They fed the dogs specific parts of an animal's
carcass to signify their relationship with them. These practices reflect a
belief system that imbues noopimakamig aki's everyday practicalities with
esoteric meaning.

It becomes apparent from this dadibaajim that parents instructed their
children on the importance of following customary practices to maintain
their Anishinaabewaadiziwin, or, as Dedibaayaanimanook would say,
Anishinaabewichigewin. When Gwiishkwa'oo was absent, either attending
boarding school or working for wages, she was deprived of the learning
opportunities that normally constituted a child's acquisition of cultural
values, principles, norms, practices, and sense of belonging. She alludes
to one teaching she clearly understood and respected: to avoid asking
questions directly. As Dedibaayaanimanook's omagakiig narrative about
the frogs has shown, the learner's main responsibility is to listen.

Narratives about returning to the ancestral customs become a
means for retrieving cultural identity. In the dadibaajim that follows,
Gwiishkwa'oo expresses a strong desire to recover from the cultural priva-
tions that wemitigooziiwaadiziwin inflicted upon her as an Anishinaabe
youth. She describes a visit she and her sibling, Jaani Charlie, once took
to their several places of home in Namegosibiing:

Baamaash bimaajaayaan [in] 1997 Trout Lake. Ingii'
wiijiiwaa i'iwedi Charlie wanii'iged [for] four years.
Amii'imaa bangii gaa' onji gikendamaan gegoon.
Gaawn wiikaa ingii' waabamaasii indede ji wanii'iged,
bakwanaad. Ingikenimaa gaye ge inizhag amik. Gaawn
wiikaa indede ingii' izhiwinigosii ji wanii'igeyaan. Gii'
ikidowag i'iwe, Anishinaabeg. Gii' gichi ikwewid ikwe
gaawiin i'iwe ji izhichigesig. Bakaan gewiinawaa ingii' izhi
bagidinigoosiimin ji izhichigeyaang.[11]

It was later, in 1997, I went to Trout Lake with Charlie when
he trapped [for] four years. That was when I started to learn
a few things. I never actually saw my father trapping, and
skinning an animal. But [now] I know how to skin a beaver
[after learning from Charlie]. My father never took me with
him to trap. Anishinaabe people said that when a girl became
a young woman, she should not take part in those activities.
There were other things for them [to do]. We were not
allowed to do those kinds of things.

When Gwiishkwa'oo mentions that she was never on a trapline with
either her father or male siblings, she alludes to a particular set of teachings. Anishinaabe custom required certain members of the family to
refrain from specific activities and avoid certain situations once a young
girl reached puberty. Instead, girls learned skills that prepared them for
adulthood from their mothers, aunts, grandmothers, and so on. If their
female mentors had knowledge associated with trapping and hunting—
as they did—it was they who taught them.

Gwiishkwa'oo intimates that wemitigoozhi-based activities interfered
with her acquisition of the complete set of traditional teachings that
was her birthright. Learning how to prepare a beaver pelt, for example,
happened much later in life for her. Had her cultural inheritance been
intact, she too would have had opportunities to achieve advanced levels
of learning in any number of disciplines, as one relative, Baswewe, had
done in medicine (see Figure 13). Gwiishkwa'oo too would have obtained
knowledge and developed skills to contribute to a healthy, socially stable,
and professionally balanced community. Instead, what her dadibaajim

narrative demonstrates is that families had to focus on developing individu-
alized ways of responding to the evolving and ever shifting circumstances
of domination and displacement.

Oo'oons John Paul Kejick's dadibaajim narratives address events that
contributed to the erasure of Namegosibii Anishinaabe people's physical
presence in the homelands. Of the same generation as Gwiishkwa'oo,
he indicates having no memory of living in Namegosibiing because his
parents, Naakojiiz and Gikinô'amaagewinini, had left Namegosibiing
before his birth. Instead, Oo'oons recalls how family members living in
the outskirts of Red Lake—Tomahawk Village, as the wemitigoozhiwag
latecomers referred to it—engaged with fragmented bits and adaptations
of the ancestors' land-based ways of life:

> [M]oonzoon e-gii' nisaawaad, baanizhaawed. Biindig
> ogii' michi agoodoon ji baatenig. Mashkimoding, pillow-
> case, ganabaj baabiina'ang gaa' izhi anoozhid. Michisag
> gii' atood [stamping his foot and laughing]. Wiinge
> gii'bigishkaa bakite'amowaad ezhi maamikawiyaan
> ozhitoowaad bimide.[12]

> [W]hen they killed a moose, they cut the meat. She simply
> hung it [thinly sliced meat] indoors to dry. Then she put it in
> a bag, a pillowcase, I think, then she would ask me [to stomp
> on the pillowcase]. She put it on the floor [stamping his foot
> and laughing]. They [also] pounded [bones] into tiny pieces,
> as I recall, for making fat.

Although the events of which Oo'oons speaks occurred after his parents
had moved into the oodenaang municipality of Red Lake, his family
continued to hunt moose and thus enjoy the benefits of wild meat. Their
ability to do so was due in part to the fact that they were members of
the Treaty 3 Lac Seul First Nation. With the luxury of outdoor spaces
now largely unattainable, people improvised by drying the meat to make
gaaskiiwag indoors and using pillowcases to make nooka'igan pulverized
dried meat. Oo'oons also mentions the practice of obtaining the fat of
cancellous bones by pounding them into a fine consistency. In one of her
more recent dadibaajim narratives, Dedibaayaanimanook stated that she

was a child when she watched her mother use an implement referred to as a "noojigane waagaakwad" to crush bones and extract osiganaanibimide fat. Persistence and patience were the main ingredients in this procedure.

Oo'oons's dadibaajim tells us that during the 1940s and 1950s Anishinaabe people still believed in the efficacy of traditional food and sought to retain the ancestral methods for its preparation. Despite increasing restrictions on hunting and trapping, they continued to find ways to access and use the homelands' resources as a means of holding on to their Anishinaabe cultural identity. Oo'oons chuckles in this narrative as he recalls how he danced on the pillowcase of gaaskiiwag dry meat to make nooka'igan. Perhaps he was thinking of how the latecomers regarded what they saw as the Anishinaabe people's bizarre ways.

In another dadibaajim, Oo'oons comments on a well-established custom that played a prominent and historically significant role in the landscape of Anishinaabe identity discourse. Discussing the odoo-demiwin method of recording lineal identity, he provides a glimpse of how Namegosibii Anishinaabe people conceptualized who they were as members of the larger Anishinaabe Nation. Oo'oons's mother had explained odoodemiwin to him, but he was still left with several questions:

> **Gaa-gii' onjisemagak iniweniwan, Anishinaabewaya'iin mewinzhago. Gaa-gii'omaamaayaan, Naakojiiz, ingii' dadibaajimogoo Anishinaabe ichigewin odoodem. Bebakaan aaniish aya'aawishan. Gonigesh gakina awiya Anishinaabeg odoodemiwag gaa-gii' onjiiwaad bebakaan ishkoniganing? Gonigesh wiinawaa inakey ikidowag e' odoodemiwaad aya'aaawishan?**[13]

> Where it [they] originated, those Anishinaabe practices of a long time ago [I do not know]. The one who was my mother, Naakojiiz, used to tell me about the Anishinaabe custom of odoodem. Of course there was a different animal [for each odoodem]. I wonder, do all Anishinaabe people have an odoodem, those from various reserves? Do they too speak in those terms of their totem being an animal?

Well aware of the major gaps in his knowledge, Oo'oons contemplates the nature and origins of odoodemiwin and whether all Anishinaabe communities and reserves still have such traditions. His specific mention of the reserves reflects the point of view of an off-reserve treaty Anishinaabe individual, intimating his awareness of the differential effects of treaties and the Indian Act on each community. Whether animals represented other groups and whether totems were in fact restricted to certain animal species may seem like rhetorical questions, but they are basic and fundamental for Oo'oons and his genealogical sense of self.

As with Gwiishkwa'oo and so many other Anishinaabeg of that generation, Oo'oons would have had this knowledge and he would have been able to pass it on to the younger members of the community had their cultural practices remained whole.[14] The subtext of Oo'oons's dadibaajim is a strong desire to recover the lost knowledges embedded in odoodemiwin and the sense of personal connectedness to the land and the animals that once characterized Anishinaabe communities. In a manner similar to the experiences of Dedibaayaanimanook and those of her generation cohorts, possession of that knowledge also acts as a counterforce to how wemitigoozhiiwaadiziwin's prevailing discourse spoke about the Anishinaabe people.

Other dadibaajim narratives present suggestions of how familial roles adapted within contexts of ongoing displacement. They are also expressions of longing for the compassionate, caring forms of relationship that held the community together. Martha Angeconeb Fiddler's (daughter of Aayizag Isaac Angeconeb) dadibaajim, for example, speaks of the fond memories she still holds for her paternal grandmother, Gweyesh. Approximately half a generation younger than Gwiishkwa'oo and Oo'oons, Martha was born and spent much of her younger childhood in Namegosibiing. She did not participate in the travels that so vividly delineate the early lives of elders such as Dedibaayaanimanook. Being around the same age as Gwiishkwa'oo, Martha's parents worked for a tourist camp in Namegosibiing throughout her infancy and childhood, compelling them to abandon the aanikoobidaaganag's travel customs. The need for wage labour is another example of how capitalism and its political power—the contexts of domination—worked to supplant Namegosibii Anishinaabe lifeways. From Martha's following dadibaajim, we learn how people nonetheless continued to pursue a number of cultural practices,

including the nurturing grandparent-grandchild relationship that typified family life:

> **Ingii' zaagi'ig, wiin ingii'dakobidaawason. Ingii'odaapinig.
> Eshkam i'iwedi ingii' nibaa. Gii' nitaa giizhideboonig
> cake. Amiish i'iwedi aapiji wii' izhaayaan, onzaam e'
> nitaa giizhide sweet stuff [laughter]. Ingii' wiipemaa gaye
> moonzhag. [E]' bimaakoshinoyaang, agwajiing gewiin osha
> ogii' waabandaan. She covered me up. She went and locked
> the doors.**[15]

She loved me, she, [when I was in] a cradleboard. She
delivered me. I would sleep there at times. She would bake me
cake. And that is where I would especially want to go, because
she baked sweet stuff [laughter]. I also slept at her place often.
[W]hen we lay in bed, [we looked] outside. She too saw it.
She covered me up. She went and locked the doors.

Gweyesh helped to deliver Martha and provided her with the security
of a dakinaagan cradleboard in accordance with the roles and responsibilities that typically came with gookomimaa grandmotherhood. As late
as the 1960s, when aspects of wemitigoozhiiwaadiziwin were becoming
entrenched in people's everyday affairs, Gweyesh was able to instill in
Martha the cultural teachings, values, and beliefs in which she herself
was so well grounded. Foremost of these was Anishinaabemowin, a gift
that continues through its use in Martha's dadibaajim narrative. The
ease with which she moves between two ontological systems of thought
indicates the efficacy of her grandmother's instruction, which, over and
above boarding school's impositions, she continues to speak today.

Many Namegosibii Anishinaabeg of Martha's parents' generation
who attended boarding school returned with an acquired belief in the
irrelevance of Anishinaabe cultural traditions and, worse, in the apparent
shamefulness of their Anishinaabeness. Hence, it was often the grandparents, those who never attended boarding school and were not personally
in contact with its negativities, who instructed children to value and
learn heritage languages and teachings. We can still heed the words of
Indigenous scholar Jo-Ann Episkenew, who points out that the causes

of cultural fragmentation lie in the pathologies of colonial structures, hierarchies, institutions, administrative bodies, "white privilege," racism, sexism, and ageism—not Anishinaabewiziwin Indigeneity.[16]

As the animated tone in her voice suggests, Martha was exceedingly appreciative of her grandmother's care while her parents worked. Important to note in her narration is the minimality of her description "agwajiing gewiin osha ogii' waabandaan" of what she and her grandmother once experienced. Amanisowin being an undesirable force in Namegosibii Anishinaabe cultural thought and practice, Martha remains consistent with traditional protocols by providing no detailed information about what it was they had both seen. This convention serves to prevent the risk of amanisowin's recurrence, and Martha's avoidance of even mentioning the word indicates her understanding of its use.

Born almost half a generation after Martha and much younger than Gwiishkwa'oo and Oo'oons, Riel Olsen had little exposure to Anishinaabemowin during his childhood and youth. Hence, he conveys his dadibaajim in English only as he describes the Namegosibii Anishinaabe customs that he came to know as one of Dedibaayaanimanook's urban-reared grandchildren. Although he spent brief periods of his childhood in the ancestral homelands, Riel's comments suggest a sense of regret in not having the language proficiency that imbues speakers with an in-depth understanding of Anishinaabe cultural thought. He discusses his relationship with Namegosibiing and his Anishinaabe relatives as follows:

For a while, me and him [his uncle, Harald] worked together as guides in the summer, in the winter. We'd spend a lot of the time in Trout Lake. It's not like we had any specific plans out there. We just subsisted off the land. [He] taught me how to set a net [for] fishes. [We] did a little bit of hunting. Unfortunately, now he's gone. I wish I learned a lot more. We went all over the place. He did tell me a lot about that stuff [place names, significances of places], over the years. Now that I look back on it, it seems like I either didn't ask enough questions or just simply wasn't taught a lot about the land and my connection to it and stuff like that.[17]

Riel alludes to the dearth of Anishinaabe cultural content in his life. When he was a youth barely into his twenties, when he lived with his maternal uncle Harald to learn about the land, their conversations were in English. Additionally, several years have gone by since Harald's passing. With so many senior elders and family members who were raised within the community no longer among us, a diminishing number of individuals are Anishinaabemowin speakers. Thus, Riel has had few opportunities to continue with his education from where his uncle's mentorship so abruptly ended. What is also apparent in Riel's dadibaajim is the profound appreciation he has for his Namegosibii Anishinaabe heritage. Despite an internship that was too brief to give him the solid grounding in Anishinaabe thought he seeks, the cultural learning he achieved provided him with exposure to hunting and fishing activities that helped to enhance his sense of relationship with the Namegosibiing homelands and his Anishinaabe ancestry. The traditional responsibility of mentoring and guiding a younger member of the family was a means for transmitting cultural concepts that made it possible for a learner such as Riel to acquire experiential knowledge. With its allusions to an uncle's companionship and willingness to teach, Riel's dadibaajim is a thought-provoking account about what constitutes Namegosibii Anishinaabe identity in today's contexts.

With each succeeding generation of dadibaajim, a diminishing ability to continue with ancestral practices becomes evident. Some narratives do not mention the underlying reasons for the disruptive changes in the traditional ways of life. Others make specific allusions to the interrelated factors of cultural and physical displacement, such as wage labour, that brought about the growing dependence on wemitigoozhi products and the fracture of land-based relationships. Martha's dadibaajim narratives, for example, indicate how the need for paid work prompted the sudden termination of traditional travel and identity-nurturing relationships with the land. These narratives describe how individual and family roles and ways of everyday living began to resemble those of the zhooniyaa-driven wemitigoozhiwag. Together, they all allude to the political economic contexts of what was for the Anishinaabe people wemiti-goozhi's relentless appropriation—and ongoing mismanagement—of the homelands.

Importantly, identity dadibaajim is about flexibility and adaptation—and loyalty to ancestral philosophies and values. For example, Anishinaabe people to this day persist in consuming traditional foods such as moose meat, duck, and fish whenever possible, and when they feast, no matter where they live, they create innovative ways for offering food to the aanikoobidaaganag ancestors. There are still senior elders among us whose narrative voices speak of protocols for proper relationships with the animal beings. They describe the special songs hunters and trappers used to maintain their affiliations. Some know and understand the symbolic meaning of spiritual names and remember the actual places where aanikoobidaaganag once lived, journeyed, and conducted ceremony. When elders who speak Anishinaabemowin continue to refer to the Cat Island of today's younger generations as Bizhiwi Minis (lynx island), to illustrate, they see the illogicality in naming an island after a domesticated feline when Namegosibiing's resident bizhiw lynx is a stridently independent being. Elders understand the importance of Anishinaabe names, preferring, for example, to conceptualize the Seagull Island of today as the Manidoo Minis (spirit island) of the ancestral vision seekers.

When we pay attention to what is important for the elders' narratives, we begin to experience them as the powerful tool for understanding, facilitating, and generationally transmitting Anishinaabe cultural content they once were. This is especially true when dadibaajim narratives speak from Anishinaabemowin ontologies and the land-based lifeways of trapping, hunting, fishing, and travelling. They explain that relationships, interactions, and a spiritual sense of connection to the homelands were key components of Anishinaabe self-identity.

When Anishinaabe people travelled synchronously with the seasons' cyclical patterns across vast distances of the boreal territories, they were maintaining a land-based sense of who they were. The outsider's sedentary perspective judged them as random, nomadic, irresponsible, and irrational, but the dadibaajim narratives speak unmistakably of the consistency, predictability, utility, coherence, and competence in how people organized and conducted their lives and travels. Dadibaaijm refers to the practicability and endurability of the people's methods for living responsibly on the earth. The senior elders' narratives also intimate that the notion of travel itself was fundamental to Namegosibii Anishinaabe cultural thought about and methodology for maintaining physical and mental health and robustness. They therefore allude to the marked contrast to wemiti-goozhiiwaadiziwin's settlement imperatives that push every human to permanently settle, overconsume, and irresponsibly accumulate material possessions, the kinds of activities that lead to the depletion of aki's ability to provide its inhabitants with contentment and good health. As well, dadibaajim shows that Anishinaabe customs served multiple purposes. The moose's dewlap placed on a tree branch was a gesture to honour the animal's gift. At the same time, it served as a form of the gikinawaajichigan method of communicating the hunter's presence and the nature of his/her activities in a manner that maintained respect for the natural environment and avoided its permanent damage.

By no means does this book claim to be an exhaustive description of the Namegosibii Anishinaabe cultural identity dadibaajim—were such a thing even possible. There are, for example, no male participants in this project who can speak directly and specifically from the frame of reference of a trapline that requires six days of travel from home. We may never hear Namegosibii Anishinaabe dadibaajim based on such experiences because, as Dedibaayaanimanook has frequently reminded us, individuals of that ilk have long left us. But, as we will see in the passages to follow, there are many other aspects of Namegosibii Anishinaabe culture-identity lifeways about which participants are well able to teach us.

Ni Noopimakamig-aajimomin
Our Boreal Narratives

Of the mentors who contribute to this work, the gichi-Anishinaabe senior elders are best positioned to articulate dadibaajim from which ancestral voices emerge to describe perspectives of life prior to the advent of wemitigoozhi's all-encompassing domination. They speak dadibaajim from contexts of culturally mediated landscapes that in many respects barely exist today. Even the briefest narratives allude to relationships that the ancestors cultivated with various elements of the boreal lands. When, for example, Dedibaayaanimanook describes the means by which her elders taught young children about appropriate conduct, she explains how the miishiijiimin skunk currant's typical characteristics act as a guide for respectful behaviour.[1] The pages of this chapter bring us into direct contact with the Namegosibii Anishinaabe dadibaajim narratives as the essence of the entire book. All the participants convey similarly grounded ideas and thoughts, although it is the dadibaajim narratives of the senior elders that speak most directly from noopimaka- mig aki's boreal frame of reference.

Noopimakamig Boreal Affinity

The people of Namegosibiig Trout Lake, as with most other Anishinaabeg, customarily expressed their identity in terms of noopi- makamig aki places of origin, anchoring their selves, their relationships, and their knowledges to the homelands. Taking place throughout the entirety of their traditional-use territories, the events of their dadibaajim clearly speak of close affinities with these spaces of home.

Namegosibiing's gichi-Anishinaabe senior elder Dedibaayaanimanook frequently reflects on her understandings and perceptions of what it once meant to live in noopimakamig aki, basing her comments on remem- brances, personal observations, and first-hand experiences that span nearly a century. At times, she makes contrastive allusions or even direct refer- ences to wemitigoozhi European presences as she shares her dadibaajim from the unique perspective of the one remaining elder who lived in and experienced much of the same traditional territories as the aanikoobidaa- ganag had done for generations before her.

Although she has not travelled the old routes in more than seven decades, Dedibaayaanimanook has little difficulty remembering place names and their associated significances. These recollections indicate that her attachment with the places where she spent her youth is still a part of how she sees herself and the world in which she was raised. Demonstrating the extent to which Anishinaabe people experienced the physical charac- teristics of the homelands, these conversations state that people gained knowledge from an early age about activities and events that were integral to their long-established journeys. Dedibaayaanimanook, for example, learned from the time she could first use a paddle that their spring travels took them down the river from Namegosibiing's oshekamigaang height of land. Important to note at this point, the discussions that follow are organized thematically rather than chronologically to better convey the narrators' lines of logic.

The maps in Figures 4 to 6 and Figure 27 convey panoptic information, presenting basic characteristics about these territories. As a set of
historical memories, the details contained in the dadibaajim narratives of
Dedibaayaanimanook and her fellow elders are able to infuse the flatness
of map diagrams with cultural historicity and bring their two-dimension-
ality to life.

In the next group of geographically related dadibaajim narratives,
Dedibaayaanimanook mentions the names of four places that members of her
family frequented. She begins with a discussion about where they wintered:

> Gaa-gii'izhi waasawang, Memegweshiwi-zaa'iganing,
> Jackfish Bay. Zaaga'iganiinsan. Mewinzha ogii'
> waawiindaanan shako indede gaa'izhinikaadamowaaj,
> wanii'igewaaj Jackfish Baykaang; maawaj
> Gaa-minitigwashkiigaag. Indedeko niwiijiiwaaban
> e'wazhashkwanii'igej. Ninitaa ando zhiigwanishiyaang
> e'akawaatoowaapan, Gichi-onigamiing. Jiibayi-zaagiing
> izhinikaade.[2]

> Memegweshiwi-zaa'iganing was a faraway place [from]
> Jackfish Bay. [There were] small lakes. A long time ago, my
> father would recite the names by which they were referred to
> when they were trapping from Jackfish Bay; especially [from]
> Gaa-minitigwashkiigaag. I used to go with my father muskrat
> trapping. We would go and spend early spring at Gichi-
> onigamiing waiting [for breakup]. It [Jackfish Bay] is called
> Jiibayi-zaagiing.

Dedibaayaanimanook speaks of the distant Memegweshiwi-zaa'igan,
northeast of Namegosibiing, where she became inexplicably ill in
early infancy. Although she herself never visited most of her father's
favourite trapping sites, she often heard him speak their names.
Gaa-minitigwashkiigaag, as the name implies, lies low and marshy (see
Figure 5). It is located on the eastern shores of Namegosibiing, a preferred
habitat for the wazhashkwag muskrats. Gaa-minitigwashkiigaag was
where the Giizhigs lived when winter first began and again in early spring
to trap for the wazhashkwag fur bearers.

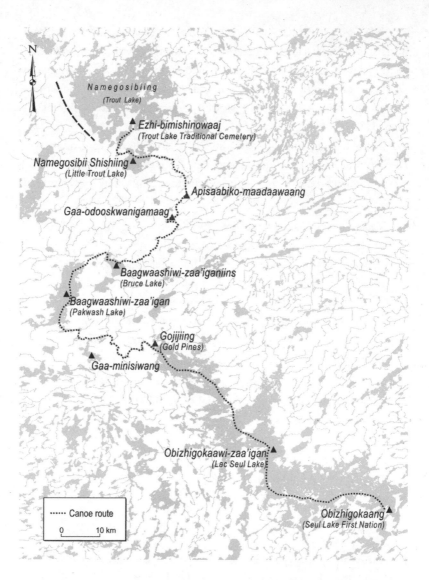

Figure 27.
Namegosibii Anishinaabe canoe route to and from Obizhigokaang Lac
Seul. Requiring stamina, endurance, organizational skills, and an indepth
knowledge of the homeland's physical features, these journeys took
approximately four days to complete.

Gichi-onigam, close to Gaa-minitigwashkiigaag, was a tiny body of water along the trappers' route to Ikwewi-zaa'igan and Swain Post, east of Namegosibiing. It is only just a speck barely visible on the map we are using, yet its location is readily identifiable for Dedibaayaanimanook, who is clearly more conversant with the land itself than the two-dimensional chart that leaves out the details still so familiar to her. Well aware that name changes function to erase Namegosibii Anishinaabe cultural identity and deny their historical presences in and expertise about the homelands, Dedibaayaanimanook points out that Jackfish Bay is actually Jiibayi-zaagiing (Figure 6). As previously noted, Anishinaabe place names are key components of the community members' identity discourse, sense of self, and connection to places of home. Dedibaayaanimanook alludes to the location and size of Gichi-onigam in the following segment:

Zaaga'iganiins ate gaa-gii'ayizhaayaang, Ikwewi-zaa'igan e-izhaayaang, George Swain. Ebimaakogomoyaang, akawaatoonaawaa ji zhaagigamiiwang Namegosib. Ingoding Gichi-onigaming. Gaawn wiin waasa, Namegosibiing osha bigo.[3]

There is a small lake where we used to go on our way to Ikwewi-zaa'igan [Woman Lake] [at the post of] George Swain. When we were on our canoe journey, while waiting for Namegosib to open. Sometimes [we waited] at Gichi-onigam. It is not very far, and is actually a part of Namegosib itself.

Her mention of Swain's post refers to spring visits to sell muskrat furs and purchase basic necessities needed for the strenuous journey to Obizhigokaang Lac Seul after the waterways had completely opened. In other conversations, she stated that George Swain was pleasant and appreciative of their visits, in marked contrast to many Hudson's Bay Company post personnel who historically viewed Anishinaabe trade as their entitlement and took it for granted.

Dedibaayaanimanook continues by describing a special place where she and her travel companions once stopped for the night. Here, she again demonstrates attention to detail when, with characteristic exuberance, she expresses appreciation for the aesthetic qualities of their surroundings:

Migiziwaabiko-ziibiing ingii' nibaaminaaban. Edadawe maawiin wenizhishing! Wawiinge bashkwaa. Gichi-mitigoog gaa-badakizowaaj gaa-izhi-nibaayaangiban Ikwewi-zaa'igan.[4]

We slept at Bald Eagle Rock Creek. It is truly a beautiful location! There was a clearing. It was edged with large trees where we slept, [on our way to] Woman Lake.

Although the name Dedibaayaanimanook mentions, Migiziwaabiko-ziibiing, prompts images of a bald eagle, a large rock slab, and a small creek that trickles into Namegosibiing, she does not explain it. Instead, she leaves us to wonder if a nearby rock resembled the shape of a bald eagle or whether it provided a convenient place for eagles to congregate and feast on fish. Perhaps it was neither—or both! As a gesture of honour, Anishinaabeg would choose a place name that reflected a particularly unusual quality about the land or commemorated an extraordinary event that occurred at the location. When a name related to an anomalous incident or situation, it became a historical record that served as a perpetual reminder, so long as it was in use. Generally, place names indicate the Anishinaabe people's cultural values, land and resources use, histories, social relations, and presences. Therefore, use of these names in itself can be regarded as a type of dadibaajim, telling us how Anishinaabe people thought about and assessed the land as a critical part of who they were. Unlike the European tradition, they did not usually name places after themselves or other people.

Dedibaayaanimanook also reveals extensive knowledge about the physical features of the homeland territories in terms of water flow, rivers, and watersheds. It is the same topographical knowledge that Treaty 3 negotiators used for fixing the boundaries of "surrendered" Anishinaabe land (see Figure 7). Dedibaayaanimanook outlines flow patterns as follows:

Gichi-ziibi, gaawn gegoon biizhaamagasinoon Namegosibiing. Amiigo etago'i Namegosib gaa-maajijiwang inakeya'ii Baagwaashiwi-zaa'iganiing. Ziibiinsensan etago bi-zaagidawijiwan gaye bezhigwan Waabamiko-ziibi

ogii'izhinikaadaanaawaa. Jackfish Bay someplace,
ziibiinsan. Gaawn wiin michaasinoonan maawiin,
Waabamiko-ziibi gaa-gii' izhinikaadang indede. Jiibayi-
zaagiing. Mii mayaa ezhinikaadeg. Gaawn wiin Jackfish Bay
izhinikaadesinoon. Bayizhi maamawijiwangin ini ziibiinsan
i'imaa.[5]

No large river enters Namegosibiing. There is only Namegosib
itself, and it flows out, into Pakwash Lake. Only small creeks
come flowing in. Also, one they called Waabamiko-ziibi [a
small creek]. Someplace in Jackfish Bay, small creeks [flow
in]. Probably it is not very large at all, Waabamiko-ziibi, as my
father called it. Jiibayi-zaagiing. That is the correct name. It
is not called Jackfish Bay. Those little creeks come flowing in
together there.

When Dedibaayaanimanook tells us that only small creeks flow into
Namegosibiing, she is confirming that it is a spring-fed lake. She calls
attention to nearby places where her father frequently trapped and
speaks of Waabamiko-ziibi, a creek that trickles into Namegosibiing
in the vicinity of Jiibayi-zaagiing Jackfish Bay (Figure 6). Importantly,
Dedibaayaanimanook's allusion to the lower elevations of Baagwaashiwi-
zaa'igan Pakwash Lake (Figure 27) suggests the breadth of her knowledge about the physical characteristics of the region. Here, she more
explicitly addresses the inaccuracy inherent in (using) the English name
Jackfish Bay—which she occasionally does for my benefit—rather
than Jiibayi-zaagiing. The heritage name (zaagiing) tells us that a creek
or stream empties into the lake at that location at the same time as it
reminds us about critical events (jiibay) in the lives and history of the
Namegosibii Anishinaabeg.

Figure 6 shows the first segment of the Namegosibii Anishinaabe
canoe route towards the southern regions of Namegosibiing, where they
visited ezhi-bimishinowaaj the community cemetery (Figure 6). As the
maps in Figures 6 and 27 indicate, they had chosen well when they sited
the cemetery directly along the route to and from Obizhigokaang Lac
Seul. The Giizhigs were able to visit the aanikoobidaaganag ancestors,
honour them with a feast, and maintain the grounds at least twice each

year with relatively little difficulty in terms of accessibility. Of immense significance in their lives, these visits allowed them to affirm their identity as the descendants of the Namegosibiing aanikoobidaaganag ancestors on a biannual basis.

At this point, it should be noted that the term "aanikoobidaagan(ag)" applies to either ancestors or descendants. When people spoke of a great-grandchild, great-great-grandchild, and so on, they used "aanikoo-bidaagan," a reference to the act of tying together. As a concept, it describes the genealogical nexus existing between a patriarch or matriarch and his or her set of descendants. A woman discussing either her great-great-grandchild or her great-great-grandmotherhood would use the phrase "niinzhwaa indaanikoobijige" (literally, I tie together twice), in reference to her achievement of having drawn that number of generations together.

Included with the Namegosibii Anishinaabe aanikoobidaaganag were Dedibaayaanimanook's paternal grandparents, Giizhig and Nookomiban Moonz(h)oniikwe. Although vital statistics records tell us that Moonz(h)oniikwe's English name was Mary, Dedibaayaanimanook almost always speaks of her paternal grandmother as Nookomiban (my late grandmother), not often as Moonz(h)oniikwe, and never as Mary. The information that the name Moonz(h)oniikwe is a reference to Nookomiban's moonz odoodem (moose totem) is part of Dedibaayaanimanook's Namegosibii dadibaajim.

Confirming her knowledge about specific details of the traditional terri-tories, Dedibaayaanimanook traces the first segment of the family's route south on Namegosi-ziibi (Trout Lake River). These discussions are some-what difficult to follow because the map—which Dedibaayaanimanook agrees to use in order to accommodate my lack of knowledge—is often more confusing than helpful for her.

After canoeing through the narrow passageway at the ezhi-bimishi-nowaaj cemetery at Gojijiwaawangaang (Figure 6), Dedibaayaanimanook indicates, they crossed Namegosibii Shishiing Little Trout Lake to arrive at the headwaters of Namegosi-ziibi Trout Lake River. She explains as follows:

Gii madaawa'amowaaj wedi Anishinaabeg gaa-gii'
ayaawaaj, Apisaabiko-maadaawaang. Ingoding gaa-gii'izhi-
nagishkawangidô e'madaawa'amowaaj gewiin ezhi
maadaawijiwang. Bizhiwininjii-baawitig izhinikaade

**baawitig. Amiish i'imaa bayizhi maamawijiwang
ziibiins, bezhigwan. Gichi-onigamiing gaawn aapiji
mangigamaasinoon. I don't know [laughter]! Maawiin
e'gichi gakiiwemog miikana e-gabadoong Gichi-
onigamiing, baawitigong gaagakiiwemogin dino. Mii'iwe
wenji izhinikaadeg Gichi-onigam, onzaam aabita
zaaga'iganiins.[6]**

When the Anishinaabe people from over there came down the
river. Apisaabiko-maadaawaang is where we sometimes met
up with them, on their down-river journey, where the river
merges [with Namegosi-ziibi]. A set of rapids [is] called Lynx
Paw Rapids. And that is where the one creek merges [with
Trout Lake River]. Gichi-onigam is not very large. I don't
know [laughter]! Perhaps because of the long portage trail
around Gichi-onigam, [it is] the kind that portages around
rapids. That is why it is called Gichi-onigam, because the lake
is only half the length of its portage trail.

Figure 27 represents the southern regions of the people's traditional-use
territory, describing one of the most important aspects of their identity
as it derived from their travels and the areas they circumnavigated on so
regular a basis. Before they stopped to rest at Apisaabiko-maadaawaang,
they manoeuvred through a series of three rapids. Dedibaayaanimanook
mentions Bizhiwininjii-baawitig (lynx paw rapids) without speaking of
the reasons for the name or the special dadibaajim narrative associated
with the site. Returning briefly to the subject of Gichi-onigam, she reacts
with amusement to my query about the apparent contradiction between
the name, Gichi-onigam (literally Big Lake), and the smallness of its
size. Dedibaayaanimanook explains that it was due to the length of the
portage trail, twice that of the lake.

When she speaks of meeting relatives from the east at the Maadaawaang,
Dedibaayaanimanook provides names of individual relatives. She incorporates details that include the size of a particular family as she wends her
way through the travel dadibaajim:

[W]edi maadaabimon, Gaa-waawaagaabikaag izhinikaade.
Gaawn maawn wiin niibiwa' bii izhijiwanzinoon Apisaabiko-
maadaawaang gaa-gii' izhi nitaa nagishkawangidô
Ikwewi-zaa'iganiing, Anishinaabeg. Ingoding ingii'
nagishkawaanaanig e'madaawa'amaang. Gebiyaaniman
Giiwegaabaw, Oojiiwasawaan. Miiwag igiweniwag
bebaatiinowaa' oniijaanisiwaa'. Ezhijiwang i'i nibi,
Manidoo Baawitigong. Migiziwag niisaya'ii gaa'ayaawaaj
gabadooyaangiban ako e' ando manoominikenaaniwang.[7]

It starts from over there, where it is called
Gaa-waawaagaabikaag. Probably not a lot of water flows
in at Apisaabiko-maadaawaang where we used to meet the
Anishinaabe people from Woman Lake. We would meet them
only sometimes on our voyage down the river. Gebiyaaniman
and also Giiwegaabaw, Oojiiwasawaan. They were the ones
who had many children. That water flows to Manitou Falls.
The bald eagles would gather beneath the falls when we
portaged as we journeyed to gather wild rice.

Dedibaayaanimanook first explains that the west-flowing river on which
the relatives travelled originates from Gaa-waawaagaabikaag, a name that
suggests a location with smoothly undulating rock surfaces. Recalling
the travels they took when she was a young child, she demonstrates how
thoroughly aware she was of the physical features around her and how
deeply ingrained they were in her memory.

Dedibaayaanimanook's dadibaajim alludes to Namegosibii Anishinaabe
relatives from the east who were similarly journeying to Obizhigokaang
Lac Seul. The reunions and gatherings they held confirmed their shared
ancestral origins as descendants of Jiiyaan and his six wives. Being cousins
of varying degrees, the Ikwewi-zaa'igan families were occupier-users
of the areas east of Namegosibiing. Gebiyaaniman's granddaughter,
to illustrate these interconnections, married Dedibaayaanimanook's
nephew, and Soons, of the Oojiiwasawaan family, later married
Dedibaayaanimanook's cousin's widow. Soons and his family made it
a point to visit Dedibaayaanimanook in Namegosibiing on numerous
occasions during the 1960s.

The travellers proceeded from Apisaabiko-maadaawaang, canoeing around a tight, elbow-shaped bend in the river appropriately named Gaa-odooskwanigamaag (the elbow place) (Figure 27). Replete with aquatic vegetation that attracted multitudes of migrating fowl in early autumn, Gaa-odooskwanigamaag was a veritable marketplace of fresh food. Dedibaayaanimanook has frequently mentioned that Manidoo-baawitig, north of Gaa-minisiwang, was a place of spiritual significance before its desecration by wemitigoozhiwag when they built a hydroelectric dam at the site. With her comment "that water flows to Manitou Falls," Dedibaayaanimanook speaks of the waters of Namegosibiing that merge into others and continue on a circuitous route to the west. She and her family canoed the relatively short distance past Manidoo-baawitig to Gaa-minisiwang for wild rice. In order to do so, it was necessary for them to portage around Manidoo-baawitig. Even today, after so many years, Dedibaayaanimanook is able to visualize the bald eagles that gathered to eat fish beneath the falls.

An interesting observation that Dedibaayaanimanook's mother brought to her attention exemplifies how closely attuned Anishinaabe people were to the features of their physical environment:

Adikamegwaaminikaaning, i'imaa wagijaya'ii, mii'imaa eko bakaaninaagwakiban ako nibi, wiinge e-waasegamig. Amiish i'iwe Namegosibii waabo. Wiinge maawiin mewinzha gii'naningosedog. "Mii' iwe Namegosibii waabo!" ako my mom indigoban bakaaninaagwak. Megwaa go e-bimaakwogomoyan mii' imaa onji bakaaninaagwak nibi. Maamakaazinaagwan. Miish i'iwe Namegosib![8]

Where the Whitefish Spawn, there, at the top, that was where the water had a different appearance. Because it was very bright and clear. That was Trout Lake water. I suppose it [the remarkable change in clearness] disappeared a long time ago. "That is Namegosib water!" my mom would say. Right there as you canoed along, the water suddenly changed. It was most amazing to see. Indeed, that [water clarity] is Trout Lake!

Dedibaayaanimanook discusses a remarkable phenomenon that revealed itself beneath them as they paddled up the Namegosi-ziibi Trout Lake River towards home. At a precise location above Adikamegwaaminikaaning (literally, where the white fish spawn) Whitefish Falls, an abrupt change in the quality and clarity of the water was evident. But Dedibaayaanimanook, as she contemplates the sublimity of what she saw during her childhood, is momentarily distracted by her thought that even this feature may not have escaped the far-reaching effects of wemitigoozhiiwaadiziwin's activities, which included degradation of water quality brought about by pollution from mining, road building, clear-cutting, and damming. Through her use of the phrase "gii'naningosedog," she evokes a sense of sadness not only for the probable fate of one of the natural wonders of the boreal world but also for how wemitigoozhiiwaadiziwin's many forms of disruptions have made it all but impossible for her—or anyone else—to travel the routes of the ancestors as they had done for several millennia. Her choice of terminology is highly contextual, reminding us that Anishinaabe people had no means by which to protect or preserve their homelands from what was, from their perspective, the latecomers' irrationality.

Dedibaayaanimanook then returns to the main thread of her narrative by quoting her mother, who pointed to the water with her paddle and exclaimed, "Miish i'iwe Namegosibii waabo!" (that is Namegosib water). Dedibaayaanimanook infers that her mother was referring to the water as both a physical and symbolic extension of the lake and its exceptional qualities. In this manner, dadibaajim is a voice of appreciation for noopi-makamig's extraordinary features that Anishinaabe people learned about from early childhood.

In the next segment of her dadibaajim, Dedibaayaanimanook remarks on the name changes that wemitigoozhiwag brought about. She mentions several, of which some are English translations of the original Anishinaabe terms and others are anglicized renditions, such as Pakwash Lake for Baagwaashiwi-zaa'igan (literally, shallow lake). In contrast, Baagwaashiwi-zaa'iganiins is now Bruce Lake, representing only an outsider's frame of reference, with nothing to do with its translated heritage meaning, little shallow lake. My use of Anishinaabemowin place names emphasizes what Dedibaayaanimanook understands but leaves unspoken, that each English name acts to deny the people's land-based identity and purge the land of their historical presence. Dedibaayaanimanook's dadibaajim narration is as follows:

> Namegosibii Shishiing; Namegosi-ziibi; Baagwaashiwi-zaa'iganiins; Gichi-baagwaashiwi-zaa'igan, [onzaam] Baagwaashiwi-zaa'iganiins e'ayaag; Gaa-minisiwang, bezhigwan minis izhi nitaa-manoomininikewaaj; Otawagi-baawitig; Gojijiing; Obizhigokaawi-zaa'igan, [gii']izhinikaadesinoon mewinzha. Gakina osha gegoon noongom bakaan odizhinikaadaanaawaan.[9] Zaagidawaang izhijiwan, ikidowag [the Arctic] ocean Gojijiing e-bi-ojijiwang nibi. I don't know about Biigaanjigamiing, bakaan ina wiin i'iwe?[10]
>
> Little Trout Lake; Trout Lake River; Bruce Lake; the large Pakwash Lake, named [because] there is the smaller lake, Bruce Lake; Gaa-minisiwang that has one island, where they used to gather wild rice; Ear Falls; Goldpines; and Lac Seul Lake, which is not what it was called a long time ago. Today people have different names for everything. They say that the water from Goldpines flows through Zaagidawaang to the [Arctic] ocean. I don't know about Pikangikum, is that different?

To clarify the recent history of Baagwaashiwi-zaa'iganiins Bruce Lake (Figure 27), Dedibaayaanimanook's dadibaajim states that it was the location of a small community cemetery where Dedibaayaanimanook's cousins, uncles, and aunts were buried, including Mooniyaans Thomas Keesick's wife, Maajiigiizhigook Mary.[11] When a mining company extracted iron ore within the immediate vicinity of the lake for approximately ten years, after-effects included the essential destruction of not only the area's natural characteristics but the cemetery of the Anishinaabe travellers.

Namegosi-ziibi empties into Baagwaashiwi-zaa'igan Pakwash Lake (Figure 27), where Namegosibii Anishinaabe people historically gathered various species of medicine plants on their journey home to Namegosibiing in autumn. However, it underwent a similar fate to that of Baagwaashiwi-zaa'iganiins when a hydroelectric dam flooded the lake and its islands, destroying natural shorelines, medicinal plants, and other floral species. Instead of mentioning that devastation, Dedibaayaanimanook refers to a map to identify Gaa-minisiwang, a lake further south along the route home. This was where the Namegosibii Anishinaabe people stopped to gather manoomin wild rice and conduct ceremony.

Dedibaayaanimanook displays her understanding of how the Namegosibiing water travels along its course towards the south and west, merges with others to flow west and north for hundreds of kilometres, and finally arrives at the Arctic Ocean via Hudson Bay. Although she poses her sentence as a question to elicit what my knowledge may be, she indicates her awareness that Biigaanjigamiing Pikangikum is not a part of the same water system as that of the Namegosi-ziibi Trout Lake River (Figure 9). Subsumed into Treaty 5 territory, the Biigaanjigamiing Pikangikum First Nation is located within the Berens River watershed. It becomes clear that Dedibaayaanimanook's knowledge derives from how she and her family and kin experienced the various characteristics of the Namegosibiing home-lands in terms of elevation, oshekamigaa height of land, and water flow.

The next dadibaajim details the activities associated with wild rice gathering at Gaa-minisiwang during the late summer–early autumn journey home. Dedibaayaanimanook specifies that her family and relatives performed manoominikem with care and devotion to detail, working only when the weather was suitable and taking only each family's estimated needs for the winter:

> Nitam gii'wiikongewaaj, ji-mino-izhiwebaninig ewii
> manoomanikewaaj. Bawaasin manoomin gii gichi-nooding.
> Biinish gaawiin gii'ani ayaasiiwag gii ani baatiinowaaj
> wemitigoozhiwag. Gii'minochigewag. Debweshi'i
> gaa'izhi-andawendamowaaj ji izhiwebaninig, mii' igo
> gaa'izhiwebaninig. Ji onji gaye gimiwanzinog gaawn gii'
> onizhishinzinoon manoomin, maawiin ombishkaa. Gaawn
> ginwenzh gaa' manoominikewaaj, niiwogon, naanogon.
> Gii'debisewaaj bebezhig mashkimodan. Gii'manaa
> dipaabaawe. Wiinge gii' ayaangwaamichigewag gegoon
> ji izhisesinog. Giishpin bangii dipaabaaweg gaawn gii'
> minwendanziiwag.[12]

They first held a ceremonial feast, for proper conditions for
gathering the wild rice. The kernels blow off when it is too
windy. Eventually, there were none of them left when settler
people increased in number. They [Anishinaabeg] did things
respectfully. They received as they requested, good weather
conditions. So that it would not rain because it was not good
for the wild rice as it might begin to ferment. They did not
take long to gather the wild rice, four [or] five days. Sufficient
for one sack each. It could not get wet. They were extremely
careful in order to avoid anything happening. If it became the
least bit damp, they were unhappy.

Emphasizing the attentiveness with which Namegosibii Anishinaabeg
carried out manoominikem, Dedibaayaanimanook reiterates the gath-
erers' sense of responsibility for how they approached each phase of the
work. If the winds were too strong, the manoomin was likely to blow
away. If the rice was even slightly damp, they were disappointed because
the crop was compromised. They knew it would likely ferment or
develop mildew. Importantly, a dampened crop signified that they had
not read the conditions correctly. These considerations all reflected the
mindset of spirituality with which the Namegosibii Anishinaabe people
approached their use of the homelands' natural resources.

Dedibaayaanimanook's dadibaajim demonstrates that manoominikem was an exchange based on the Namegosibii Anishinaabe people's
willingness and ability to remain vigilant about how they negotiated
their relationship with noopimakamig aki and its various other elements
and associated beings. Included among these were the winds, rain,
water, humidity, and constituent components and characteristics of the
manoomin itself. By her use of the phrase "bebezhig mashkimodan,"
Dedibaayaanimanook tells us that gathering wild rice was a community
effort in which all members participated. She uses the phrase "gii'debi-
sewaaj" to explain that people stopped gathering as soon as they reached
what they estimated they would need for the winter. Following the principle of avoiding unnecessary surpluses and the possibility of waste, the
families presided over an equitable division of the crop. They enacted
ceremony to symbolize and confirm their intent to conduct their affairs

with respect and to show their appreciation of the fact that their access to noopimakamig aki's largesse depended on fulfilling their obligations.

Dedibaayaanimanook's dadibaajim characterizes the attitude of care, humility, and thankfulness with which the Namegosibii Anishinaabe people utilized the resources of their noopimakamig boreal lands. That characterization is an oblique contrast to the massive destruction that the arrival of wemitigoozhiiwaadiziwin brought upon aki and Anishinaabe knowledge systems, skills, relationships, and manoominikewin itself, particularly when wemitigoozhiwag began to dam the rivers and extract noopimakamig's resources.

Perhaps the most memorable and evocative dadibaajim relating to the historical affairs of the Namegosibii Anishinaabe community depicts the people's final journey with Giizhig, their elder-patriarch. For maintaining and expressing Namegosibii Anishinaabe identity, the Namegosi-ziibi portage trails over which Giizhig and Nookomiban made their last travels are singularly meaningful. Dedibaayaanimanook describes what she remembers as follows:

> I don't remember gaa-gii'ani gagaakiiwe—amii' ishkôj
> gii' gopa' aangiban. Ingii' ani gagaakiiwe wiijiiwaaban
> ako e' gabadoonaaniwang nimishoomis zaginikenishij.
> Amiishi'ishkôj gii' gopa'angiban. Jibi wiin Gookomiban
> gaa' ayizhisheshiwigobanen [laughter]. Amiishi'i gewiin
> baamaa miinawaa e' ani dagwaagininig, amiishi'i gewiin gii'
> ishkwaa ayaaj Nookomiban.[13]

> I don't remember which way the portage trail went—it was his
> [my grandfather's] last portage journey. I would go with him
> as we made our way along the portage trails, as my grandfather
> held onto my arm. That was his last journey up the river.
> I wonder which way my late grandmother went [laughter].
> And then during the following autumn she too passed, my late
> grandmother.

This dadibaajim invokes the image of a small child and her aged grandfather assisting each other to negotiate a familiar course for what would be their last journey together. A testimony of longevity and the ironies of life, this dadibaajim is also about that same child who is now ninety-eight years old and herself in need of assistance.

Presaging a series of difficult closures, Giizhig passed shortly after their arrival home. Both he and Nookomiban were laid to rest at ezhi-bimishinowaaj the community cemetery (Figure 6). They spent their final days in Namegosibiing. With family members having lived under the guidance and direction of Giizhig's leadership for so many years, they mourned the passing of an era. This narrative by Dedibaayaanimanook suggests that the essence of relationship and identity is as much about events and places as it is about the memories people cherish and share through the dadibaajim practice. All of the land-related details of dadibaajim are expressions of how people perceive who they are as Namegosibii Anishinaabeg. Enhancing the Namegosibii Anishinaabe dadibaajim narratives, these details bear witness to the presence of the people throughout the homeland territories at the same time that they animate the insipid spaces of maps.

Guidances of the Ishpiming Heavens

By cultivating relationships along several dimensions, the aanikoobidaaganag ancestors emphasized their residency in the noopimakamig aki boreal homes. For example, they interacted with the entities who presided over Namegosibii Anishinaabe affairs from the astronomical distances of cosmology's remote wanangoshag stars.

Dedibaayaanimanook was a young child when her paternal uncle Naadowe embarked on his last journey to Namegosibiing in the winter of 1939. The visit included a ceremony to honour the heavenly being called Makoshkizh. Dedibaayaanimanook describes how Naadowe's tribute consisted of a song with which he requested a special blessing for his young niece:

Nimishoomenzhiban Naadowe ishkwaaj gii bi giiyoodepan
Namegosibiing, shkôj gii biizhaaj [1939]. Jiimis, Jôjens
gii bi giiyoode'aawaaj odedewaan. My mom gaa-gii'
ganoozhipan ji-ozhitooyaan bangiij onaabookaanens,
atooyaambaan minikwaaganens e-gii' miinag. Binamaa
e-gii' nigamopan. Miish i'iwedi gaa' izhi inootamaawizij,

ishpiming wanangoshag. Makoshkizh ogii'izhinikaadaan, ji
onji zhawendaagoziyaan. Gii'nigamo sa wiin igo.[14]

[It was] when my late uncle, Naadowe, visited Trout Lake for
the last time [1939]. Jiimis and Jôjens brought their father
home to visit. My mom asked me to make a small quantity
of wine. I poured some in a small cup and gave it to him. He
sang first. Then he directed his attention towards the stars of
the heavens. He referred to something as Makoshkizh, so that
I would be loved and cared for. Certainly, he sang.

This dadibaajim specifies how Anishinaabe people maintained special
relations with the stars and constellations of the night sky. Their close
association is evident from the Anishinaabe names of the beings and
from the deferential manner in which Anishinaabeg conducted their
interactions with all of the world. In view of the negative interpretations about how Indigenous people used alcohol, it is important to
note that Dedibaayaanimanook emphasizes the carefulness with which
her uncle used the wine. Onaabookaan (home-produced wine) was
a sacred component of a formal ceremony that represented respect,
honour, and deference. Using the phrase "gii'nigamo sa wiin igo,"
Dedibaayaanimanook underscores her uncle's use of song. Had Naadowe
misused the onaabookaan wine, he would not have been able to make
an offering, much less present a song of homage. Another important
detail is the mention of Jiimis and Jôjens's role in the event, directing our
attention to the care and concern that grown children showed towards
the well-being of elderly family members. In this case, they enabled
Naadowe's wish to visit his ancestral Namegosibiing for the last time and
arrange for Dedibaayaanimanook's blessing.

To help us understand the Namegosibii Anishinaabe people's identity
in terms of their relationship with the non-humans, we listen closely to
Dedibaayaanimanook's dadibaajim about how wanangoshag stars featured
in their lives. She tells us that people benefited in several ways from their
familiarity with the various stellar and constellational patterns and move-
ments across the spaces of the heavens:

Wiinge sago ogii' aabajitoonaawaa' odinaabanjiganiwaa' ishpiming wanangosha'. [O]gikendaanaawaa' ge-[a] ni-ayizhiwebak. Gaa-aanzigoodeg. Okwagoojinoog wanangoshag indede gaa-gii'nitaa-wiindan. Bezhig idash miina gii'agaasin i'i dino e'-okwagojinowaaj. Ojiiganang ogii'izhinikaadaanaawaan mii'iweni. Niibiwa' osha ogii' doodaanaawaa. Niibiwa' ogii'aabaji'aawaa' wanangosha' geni-izhiwebak.[15]

They absolutely used all that they calculated as they observed and studied the stars of the heavens. They knew what the weather would be. [They observed] Gaa-aanzigoodeg. It is a group of stars strung together [that] my father would always mention. Then there was a small cluster of them. They called that one Ojiiganang. They did many things. They used the stars in many different ways to know what the weather conditions would be.

By paying attention to the celestial beings and their mutual connectedness, Anishinaabeg received knowledge about how to navigate safely across their noopimakamig boreal homelands. They understood these relationships with wanangoshag to be reciprocal, as Naadowe's special ceremony to Makoshkizh shows. Using the term "odinaabanjiganiwaa," Dedibaayaanimanook states that people observed, studied, and meditated on the stars in order to arrive at their intended meanings. It is evident from the "aabanjigan" in odinaabanjiganiwaa' that dreaming was a component of this type of knowledge acquisition and that those with the power to dream were those who had undergone the ando-bawaa-jigem dream quest journey. Combining elements of the spiritual realm with their observational-intellectual skills, Anishinaabeg took on the responsibility of making accurate calculations about weather patterns and conditions to guide their travel plans and ensure a safe passage. These pursuits, of course, depended on being awake and outdoors during the night spaces of time throughout all seasons of the year.

An interesting feature of Dedibaayaanimanook's above dadibaajim is the apparent differentiation of constellations and stars as inanimate and animate that becomes evident from how she uses the language. By choosing the verb "wiindang" (inanimate) rather than "wiinaaj" (animate) for the constellation Gaa-aanzigoodeg, to illustrate, Dedibaayaanimanook explains that her father referred to something rather than someone. The name "Gaa-aanzigoodeg" (literally, what hangs upside down) itself alludes to what does as opposed to who does. Also, by using a verb phrase such as "ogii'izhinikaadaanaawaan" (they would call it) rather than "ogii'izhinikaanaawaan" (they would call her/him) in reference to the Ojiiganang Fisher constellation, Dedibaayaanimanook establishes its inanimacy. Anishinaabe people familiarized themselves with the identities of certain stars and constellations, their areas of influence, and the means with which to seek their assistance.[16]

The concept of identity formation secured in not only terrestrial but stellar and constellational systems of relationship draws on the role of celesial bodies that extends to dibiki-giizis, the night sun. Interestingly, Dedibaayaanimanook recently informed me that the sun is giizhigi-giizis (the day sun) while the moon is dibiki-giizis (the night sun). Similar to the stars, the dibiki-giizis moon and its many orientations and phases were critical providers of information. Dedibaayaanimanook gives examples of how the aanikoobidaaganag ancestors used their knowledge about the moon for organizing and tracking the passage of time:

Ayinishkaaj dibiki-giizis. Maamakaadendamaan noongom e'izhimikawiyaan, gaawn wiikaa gegoon e-gii'ayaasigô [calendar], gii' gikendamowaaj aaniin i'i e-gichi-anama'e-giizhigak. Daabishkoo gii'ikidowag gii'izhisej gii gichi-anama'e-giizhigak. Gaawn wiikaa gii' wanisesiiwag gaa'izhi-giiziswewaaj.[17]

How the moon changes its shape. When I think of it today, I am most amazed, that they never used one [a calendar], yet they knew when it was Christmas. It was as though, they said, it [the moon] positioned itself for Christmas. They never lost track of time with the method they used for telling time.

Dibiki-giizis, as Dedibaayaanimanook explains, presented itself to Namegosibii Anishinaabe people as an animate object that indicated when and how to carry out various activities, including travel plans, throughout the seasons across the boreal spaces. Hence, the people's proficiencies included the ability to identify the moon's distinct orientations at any time of the year as though it were a type of calendar. This, Dedibaayaanimanook muses in retrospect, was most remarkable, given that people had to recognize and remember not only the complex sets of patterns in which dibiki-giizis displayed itself in each of its numerous sub-phases throughout the year but also what activities each sanctioned.

The examples Dedibaayaanimanook gives in her next dadibaajim illustrate the method with which Namegosibii Anishinaabeg recognized, identified, named, and remembered each full moon of the year. Linked to a particular boreal phenomenon, each was named after a main seasonal development as it unfolded throughout the terrestrial homelands. Dedibaayaanimanook mentions some of the names of these major lunar alignments:

> **Migiziwi-giizis wa'a noongom gaa-oshkagoojing.**
> **Ge-agoojing, niki-giizis, miinawaash awasa'a mii' awedi**
> **maango-giizis, miinawaa awasa'a, omagakiiwi-giizis.**
> **Gaa-dakwaasigej wiin izhinikaazo wa'awedi noongom**
> **gaa izhisej [February]. My mom, animikodaadiiwi-giizis,**
> **gaaginôsigej gaye ogii' izhinikaanaan [January].**[18]
>
> This is the new moon of bald eagle moon. Next will be Canada goose moon, then the next one, loon moon, and after that, frog moon. The one who shines briefly is the one now [February]. My mom referred to animikodaadiiwi-giizis, which she also called the one who shines for a long time [January].

When the migiziwag bald eagles were returning in February-March, for example, the full moon was migiziwi-giizis. The next, when nikag Canada geese arrived from the south, was niki-giizis, and so on over the course of the year. Important to note is how the disruptions of wemitigoozhiiwaadiziwin become evident from Dedibaayaanimanook's mother's names for January and February. Animikodaadiiwi-giizis was a reference to New Year's celebrations, even though January is not the beginning of a new year in the ontological systems of the Anishinaabeg. Gaa-dakwaasigej (the one who shines briefly) alludes to the wemitigoozhi European convention of characterizing the month of February as shorter than the others when, of course, that lunar phase is of the same duration as the others.

Subsumed within Dedibaayaanimanook's allusions to the wemiti-goozhi's methods of calculation are implied references to the confusion they caused for the pre-existing notions of time and the naturally occurring events as a means for guiding decisions. Those who were able to stay on the land retained the ancestral way of time reckoning and the knowledge of how it directed their activities. Having to transition into the wemitigoozhi's ways of keeping track of time, people attempted to merge the two systems. But these efforts were often confusing and always distressing as people witnessed the land-based ways become meaningless for the generations who attended boarding school. For them, the moon, stars, and constellations were nothing more than distant objects to be studied in physics or astronomy.

Namegosibii Anishinaabeg made their observations from the unique perspective of the latitudes and longitudes of their noopimakamig aki land. Dedibaayaanimanook implies that when Anishinaabe people, herself included, no longer live in the ancestral homelands, they do not experience the return of migiziwag bald eagles and nikag Canada geese or even hear the voices of the maangwag loons and the songs of the omagakiig frogs/toads in the same way as the ancestors had because they are no longer within range of noopimakamig aki's power to enhance the effects of such phenomena.

In combination with their knowledge about the use of celestial equivalents to clocks and calendars, the people of Namegosibiing were eminently well acquainted with weather-related conditions. This system of mutually reinforcing knowledge, particularly critical when planning to travel across open stretches of water or frozen lakes, resulted from their familiarity with the events and affairs of the being they referred to as Zhaawan. Dedibaayaanimanook alludes to Zhaawan's role as follows:

Giiwedinong gii izhi miskwakwak izhi maajii miskwakwan gii' ikidowag zhaawanong inake gii izhi maaji miskwakwak. Mii'iwe e-giba'iganiwij Zhaawan. Miinawaa gwek inakeya'ii gii' izhi maajii miskwakwak, giizhoowayaa gii' ikidowag.

Niibiwa' gii' inôjige. Miish i'i debwe gaa-gii'izhiwebak.
Debwe sago wiinge bigo gii' izhiweban gegoon.[19]

When a red sky forms in the north, they said that the red
coloration begins in the south, when the red first begins to
appear. That is where it catches and stops Zhaawan. When
it began to get red in the opposite direction, it will be warm,
they would say. [An elder] had a lot of knowledge. And that
weather they predicted would occur. Indeed, what they
foresaw absolutely came about.

Understanding how Zhaawan's activities affected the skies throughout
the day in combination with knowledge of the ishpiming celestial night-
time beings comprised a portion of the Namegosibii Anishinaabe people's
body of traditional knowledge. It was the basis for their competency
in reading and accurately interpreting and predicting various weather
or land-based conditions and their effects. The efficacy of that form of
knowledge is evident in the dearth of dadibaajim about anyone being
lost, not knowing her or his directions, or dying from being caught in an
unforeseen situation. Rather, dadibaajim indicates how closely attuned
people were to the physical and spiritual characteristics of noopimakamig
and the ishpiming beings to which they were inextricably linked. For the
most part, these proficiencies are attainable only experientially by maintaining the kind of relationship with the land that is characterized by a
constant awareness of events and phenomena in all directions from all
parts of noopimakamig aki. And, as Dedibaayaanimanook asserts in her
dadibaajim, Namegosibii Anishinaabe knowledge is best achieved through
a lifelong relationship with the homelands.

Dedibaayaanimanook's dadibaajim also speaks on a broader level to
one of the fundamental components of Anishinaabe thought as it relates
to the responsibilities people needed to fulfill in order for the processes of
knowledge acquisition to begin. Here she alludes to the original cosmo-
logical order of Anishinaabe ontologies as it contrasted with that of the
wemitigoozhiwag Europeans:

Aaniish weweni gaye ogii' ganawendaan Anishinaabe
odakii. That's why it's so debwemagak gakina gegoon.
Gaawn gegoon ogii'gagwe nishiwanaajitoosiin odakiim.[20]

Indeed, as we well know, Anishinaabe people took care of
their responsibility to the land. That's why it's so true, all
of it. They never intentionally destroyed any part of their
homelands.

The Namegosibii Anishinaabe people were fastidious in preserving
deferential relationships with celestial and terrestrial dwellers alike. In
return, they received special kinds of knowledge, abilities, and skills. In
contrast, as the dadibaajim intimates, the wemitigoozhiiwaadiziwin way
of thinking and living disrupted the fine balance that led to knowledge of
how to live a sustainable way of life.

As Dedibaayaanimanook herself has often expressed, she was scarcely
able to spend sufficient time on the land with fellow Anishinaabeg to
acquire or remember the same level of knowledge about such natural
events as the comings and goings of Zhaawan as her parents and grandparents had done before her. Although she and those of her generation
now use wemitigoozhi inventions such as clocks and calendars, the
thought of having to abandon the knowledge systems that preserved
noopimakamig-based ways of life across so many generations is no less
unsettling for her as an Anishinaabe thinker than it would have been for
the aanikoobidaaganag ancestors themselves. Her allusive comparisons
are indirect references to the veracity of the former customs, and when
she seems to disparage the wemitigoozhi's way of thinking, she does so
for good reason.[21]

Dadibaajim outlines noopimakamig-Anishinaabe relationships that
present us with the identity of Namegosibii Anishinaabeg individually
and as a group. Speaking from and acknowledging it to be her personal
knowledge, senior elder Dedibaayaanimanook delineates the land of
her homeland territories and its characteristic qualities, which include
topographical features such the height of land, water quality, the flow

of rivers and streams, portage trails, rapids and falls, lakes and islands, relative distances, directions, and ishpiming's many dwellers. Although Namegosibiing was the base from which they pursued the various activities of life's seasonal patternings, Namegosibii Anishinaabeg regarded the entirety of the traditional-use regions as places of home. Always embedded within their dadibaajim is the sense of sanctity in the quality of how they interacted with the noopimakamig aki of their boreal home.

The ability to practise the Namegosibii Anishinaabe ways of life within the ontologies of the ancestors and learn their knowledges, however, quickly vanished with the displacements of wemitigoozhiiwaadiziwin. Most dadibaajim narratives include references to these forces of change and describe their effects from a Namegosibii Anishinaabe frame of reference.

Wemitigoozhiiwaadiziwin
Colonial
Identity

Although the Namegosibii Anishinaabe participants of this book do not use the term "wemitigoozhiiwaadiziwin," the all-encompassing phenomena of colonialism and capitalism are the critical backdrop of their dadibaajim. The narratives indicate that manifestations of wemiti-goozhiiwaadiziwin varied in mode, intensity, and blatancy. This chapter allocates dawisijigem spaces of decluttering for dadibaajim's discussions about wemitigoozhiiwaadiziwin's effects in the Anishinaabe people's lives and homelands. Spoken by the Namegosibii Anishinaabeg them-selves, dadibaajim is the most accurate and effective means for under-standing and describing how people conceptualized, described, and named the historical forces of domination that characterized the arrival of the latecomers.

Origin Of "wemitigoozhiiwaadiziwin"

Appearing so frequently in this dadibaajim-based work, the term "wemitigoozhiiwaadiziwin" requires elaboration. Attaching the "-aadiziwin" (the state of being/thinking a certain way) suffix to "wemitigoozhi" creates "wemitigoozhiiwaadiziwin." It is the term I as a Namegosibii Anishinaabemowin speaker use for the characteristic behaviours, attitudes, and systems of the colonizing settler immigrants and their descendants that Namegosibii Anishinaabe people have observed and experienced. In morphological terms, "wemitigoozhiiwaadiziwin" is a modification of the "zhaaganaashiiyaadizi-" that the Seven Generations Education Institute elders use for notions of thinking and being colonial.[1] The same group of elders expresses the concept of decolonization with "gego zhaaganaashiiyaadizisiidaa," a phrase that literally urges each of us to refrain from thinking and living "as a white person at the expense of being Anishinaabe."[2]

From a historical perspective, colonialism began for Indigenous peoples the moment wemitigoozhiwag—the Namegosibii Anishinaabe name for the British/European latecomers and, later, their descendants—set foot on the homelands. Wemitigoozhiwag were not simply the uninvited. Adept at constructing myths about themselves, Indigenous peoples, and Indigenous lands and resources, they were able easily to rationalize, accept, and live with acts of theft, violence, racism, murder, and genocide against the Anishinaabe people. The historical mindset that enabled colonialism is largely with us today in the form of the globalized capitalism of neo-liberalism. In the language of Anishinaabe people, "wemitigoozhiiwaadiziwin" refers to these malevolent forces.

"Wiiyaabishkiiwej," on the other hand, is a direct reference to the pale complexion of the Europeans (Dedibaayaanimanook, personal conversation, June 2013). "Wiiyaabishkiiwej" and "wemitigoozhi(wag)" were not derogatory, racially or otherwise, but they soon became associated with what was to the Anishinaabe people the latecomers' complete lack of rationality. In contrast to notions of worthiness, superiority, privilege, entitlement, and so forth still commonly linked to the English expression "white man" within dominant society, "wiiyaabishkiiwej" is a neutral word. It was and is not generally used by Namegosibii Anishinaabeg. Rather, they use "wemitigoozhi(wag)."

My approach to the English phrase "white man" derives from the Oxford dictionary, which states that "the term white has been used to refer to the skin colour of Europeans or people of European extraction since the early 17th century. Unlike other labels for skin colour such as red . . . white has not been generally used in a derogatory way."[3] It would seem evident, then, that the colonial British themselves constructed the English phrase "white man" in reference to how they saw themselves as they encountered and colonized Indigenous peoples. It is not an Anishinaabe invention. Neither does "wemitigoozhiwag" translate literally to white men or white people in the language of the Namegosibii Anishinaabeg.[4]

Phrases such as European settler people, European settler descendants, and so forth, instead of "white man/men/people" can be used to translate "wemitigoozhi(wag)" into English. Although cumbersome, they conceptualize groups from a geographical framework rather than the physical characteristics the colonizing settler people specifically chose for creating and ranking "races." This method, which I will continue to use until it too becomes racialized, may help to avoid engaging gratuitously or unnecessarily in the European settler people's colour-based, hierarchical discourse about what they perceive as worth.

Dedibaayaanimanook explains her understanding of how Namegosibii Anishinaabeg applied the term "wemitigoozhi(wag)" when referring to the European settler people and their descendants:

Wemitigoozhiwag gaa-izhinikaanaawaaj. Aaliz gaa-izhi-ayaaj, zhaaganaashiwag odizhinikaanaawaa.' That's the same thing, zhaaganaashiwag and wemitigoozhi[wag]. Mii bezhigwan maawiin izhinaagoziwag wemitigoozhiwag, gewiinawaa.[5]

What they called, the European settler people. Where Alice lives, they call them zhaaganaashiwag. That's the same thing, zhaaganaashiwag and wemitigoozhi[wag]. Perhaps it is the same with European settler people, that they too look like one another.

The first of the European foreigners to bring wemitigoozhiiwaadiziwin attitudes of colonialism into the homeland territories were the British. Dedibaayaanimanook notes that in the southern regions of Anishinaabe territory where her eldest child, Alice Olsen Williams, resides, people who include the Seven Generations Education Institute elders know these latecomers from Europe as "zhaaganaashiwag."

As Dedibaayaanimanook explains how Namegosibii Anishinaabeg use the term "wemitigoozhiwag," she suggests that wemitigoozhiwag probably share aspects of their physical appearance in common with each other in the same way that many Anishinaabe people still do with one another today. Her statements are not racial slights. Rather, they are accounts of how Anishinaabe people voiced their observations and experiences of the attitudes and behaviours they encountered with the arrival of the wemitigoozhi foreigners.

It became evident to the Anishinaabe people of Namegosibiing, as the number of arrivals increased, that other types of wemitigoozhiwag existed besides those whom they first encountered, the colonizing English. Dedibaayaanimanook explains that one of the most immediately obvious differences was how these people spoke zhaaganaashiimowin, language of the colonizer settler British:

Agwingosii-wemitigoozhi. Mii ini dino Njôy
gaa-gii'onaabemij. Agwingosii-wemitigoozhiwag
gii'izhinikaazowag. Baakwaay[i]shag. Gaawn
osha niinawind ingii' gikenimaasiwaanaanig
endaswewaanagiziwaaj. Miiwag eta igi gaa'gikenimangidô,
agwingosag, gaawiin gaye ingii'gikenimaasiwaanaanig.
Gaa-mayagwewaaj ogii'izhinikaanaawaa' nitam
gii-dagoshinowaaj. Gaawiinshwiin igidino Germany.
Gaa-mayagwewaaj gaa-izhinikaazowaaj. Miish i'i
gaa-izhinikaanaawaaj nisayenzag nitam gii-dagoshinowaaj.[6]

A Swedish European settler man. That was the type Njôy married. They were called Agwingosii-wemitigoozhiwag. The French. We of this area did not know about all the different types. We only knew of the Swedes, and we did not [yet] know [the Norwegians]. They referred to them as the ones

who sound foreign when they first arrived. And not those
[from] Germany. The ones who sound foreign, they are called,
as my older brothers called them [Norwegians] when they
first arrived.

Dedibaayaanimanook's discussion focuses on the processes by which
Namegosibii Anishinaabeg distinguished among and named the various
types of Europeans whom the English preceded. As they became more
familiar with the latest of the latecomers, they applied descriptors that
reflected their observations. Initially, they used hyphenated versions of
wemitigoozhiwag. French, for example, were "baakwaay[i]shii-wemiti-
goozhiwag," although Dedibaayaanimanook did not specify the meaning
of "baakwaaysh." The Swedes, with whom Namegosibii Anishinaabeg
first came into contact when a close family friend, Injôy, married one,
were "agwingosii-wemitigoozhiwag." As additional variations of strangers
appeared, Anishinaabe people dispensed with the "-wemitigoozhi" suffix.
The French, for example, became simply "baakwaay[i]shag."

Dedibaayaanimanook explains further by referring to a time when
people had no previously acquired information about immigrants from
Norway, Italy, Germany, Poland, and others who arrived in great numbers
after the Second World War. Immediately evident was that these people
from agaamakiing (the land across the ocean) Europe spoke zhaaganaashiimowin with their own distinct accents and peculiar ways of using the
language. Sounding markedly different from the English in their speech,
they were gaa-mayagwewaaj, the ones who sound foreign.

It is important to note at this point that sounds such as r, l, f, and th
are difficult to pronounce for traditional Namegosibii Anishinaabemowin
speakers. Hence, they find alternative ways for expressing themselves,
which is what Dedibaayaanimanook does when she uses the phrase
"Jônii dino" (the Jonny kind), in reference to a family friend who is
of Italian descent, in place of the word "Italian." To further illustrate,
Dedibaayaanimanook says "Irene ogozisan (Irene's son)" rather than
attempt to verbalize her grandson's name, Riel. Having both r and l,
that name is especially difficult for her to pronounce. The sound of the
letter r, moreover, is particularly challenging when it is the first letter
of a word. One way of dealing with non-Anishinaabemowin names is
to Indigenize them. Mary, for example, becomes Menii, and Andrew,

Aanjinoo. Charlie is pronounced as Jaani. How traditional elders refer to people is often about ease of pronunciation. Many of today's generations are, of course, easily able to articulate these English words and sounds because English is their first language. A non-Anishinaabemowin speaker would similarly have difficulty with the correct pronunciation of many Anishinaabemowin words. When my father first arrived in Namegosibiing, Dedibaayaanimanook states, his attempts to speak in her language were the source of much hilarity amongst members of her family.

It must also be noted that it was the Namegosibii Anishinaabeg who were encumbered with the challenges of learning another language, not the wemitigoozhiwag. It was they who needed to set aside their ontologies to accommodate and make room for those of the wemitigoozhiwag as they increasingly had to interact with them. When my mother, Dedibaayaanimanook, married my European-born father, she had to learn the language associated with commercial fishing in English. Owners of the airways, pilots, mechanics, MNRF officials, and so on all spoke in English, and the various policies, procedures, and equipment connected to the commercial fishing industry were defined and named in English by the wemitigoozhiwag. Even though Namegosibii Anishinaabeg had names for many of these in Anishinaabemowin, wemitigoozhiwag did not as a rule include them in their vocabulary.

Anishinaabe people came up with their own terms wherever none existed when conversing amongst themselves in Anishinaabemowin. They similarly had to be inventive when they communicated with wemitigoozhiwag during the earlier years of contact. Dedibaayaanimanook tells of a cousin who once went to the trading post to purchase supplies. Presuming it pointless to use the Anishinaabemowin word "zhigaagominzh," he thought for a moment and then requested "skunk potatoes." The amused post manager understood immediately that his customer wanted something with a strong scent and the approximate size of a potato. He brought out a bag of onions.

From an Elder's Perspective

Dadibaajim describes the Anishinaabe people's direct and immediate experiences with wemitigoozhiiwaadiziwin colonialism in terms of its impacts on their everyday lives. Their narratives are spoken in the

context of events arising from the latecomers' desire to extract and
exploit the homelands' natural resources. Reflecting their philosophies
and value systems, the wemitigoozhiwag's methodologies were highly
problematic for the Anishinaabe people and the healthy state of the
aki natural environment. As a young child at the time, for example,
Dedibaayaanimanook witnessed activities relating to the dam construction at Otawagi-baawitig Ear Falls (close to Gojijiing Goldpines, located
at the source of the English River) that began in the summer of 1928
when she was seven years old:

> **Namanj baakaj gaa' dashiwaagwen anokiiwaaj. Gii'**
> **ayinaakwagonjinoogsh mitigoog wedi wagijaya'ii baawitig.**
> **Namanjisa gaa' izhichigaadegwen. Niwaabamaabaneg isa**
> **wiin ako e' inaakwagonjinowaaj mitigoog.**[7]
>
> The number of workers was beyond counting. Logs were
> floating at the top of the falls over there. I do not know how it
> was done. But I used to see the logs all floating together.

Dedibaayaanimanook's memories and impressions about wemitigoozhi's activities invoke the word "baakaj" to convey incredulity and
dismay. Profoundly unsettling for the Anishinaabe eyewitnesses was the
spectacle of numerous workers balancing on logs floating in the water, as
the work of preventing the natural flow of the river began. With her use
of "inaakwagonjinowaaj," Dedibaayaanimanook describes the trees in a
prone, limbless state, stripped of their natural grace, beauty, and dignity.
What she saw was a strange submission to an equally strange violation.
Rivers, falls, forests, and trees were sacred entities worthy of deferential
treatment, according to Anishinaabe ontological thought. Hence, a dam
under construction was disturbing for the people of Namegosibiing on
several levels. Reflecting the wemitigoozhi's way of thinking and the
forces of colonialism, it suggested that the trees and the river and their
place in Anishinaabe ontologies were all expendable. It would seem that
the people and their interests were dismissed as non-existent by these
foreigner-interlopers.

Although she heard conversations about the building of the dam and
its associated activities, Dedibaayaanimanook herself was not old enough

to participate in them. However, she has stated in conversations with me throughout the years that her father once gestured to a large section of land near the construction site and told her that she would soon see the entire area inhabited by wemitigoozhiwag. Dedibaayaanimanook also remembers and tells of hearing her mother quoting various people, which included her cousin Omooday Paul, as they spoke of the effects of a dam:

> "'Da mooshka'an isa wiin igo,' Anishinaabeg
> wiin i'i gii' ikidowag," ako ikidooban my mom.
> "Wii'mooshka'oojigaade Obizhigokaawi-zaa'igan," maawiin
> gii' ikidowagako. Gaye ingii' noondawaa e-dazhindang,
> Omooday gaa-gii'ininj.[8]

> "'It will, at the very least, flood,' is what people would certainly say," is how my mom would quote other members of the community. "Lac Seul Lake will be flooded over," is what they would have probably said. And I also used to hear the one known as Omooday discussing it.

Quoting her mother's phrase "isa wiin igo," Dedibaayaanimanook tells us that the Namegosibii Anishinaabeg clearly understood the inevitable fact that Obizhigokaawi-zaa'igan Lac Seul Lake would become a reservoir. Namegosibii Anishinaabeg were trappers of beaver and knew how water responds to damming. They knew that when the river backed into Obizhigokaawi-zaa'igan, the shorelines, islands, and traditional water routes would all be altered by flooding. They were intently engaged in conversations amongst themselves about a dam at Otawagi-baawitig.

From an Anishinaabe perspective, it was characteristic of wemitigoozhiiwaadiziwin that state and corporate officials did not discuss the project with users of the Baagwaashiwi-zaa'igan-English River-Obizhigokaawi-zaa'igan water route (see Figure 27). Federal, provincial, and hydro decision makers proceeded with the project without any Namegosibii Anishinaabe participation in consultation, discussions, agreements, exchange of information, or compensation. Before building the dam, in fact, these wemitigoozhiwag had full knowledge of the immense damage Anishinaabe communities would suffer from the raising of the water level of Lac Seul Lake. The water would inundate trees, wild rice plants, and hayfields; drown the muskrats and flood their habitat; ruin homes, sheds, and gardens; destroy the cemeteries; and seriously affect people's livelihood.[9] It has taken several decades of legal challenges and negotiations with government and hydroelectric power company officials to determine what might be appropriate remediation for the wemitigoozhiiwaadiziwin's barbaric treatment of First People.[10]

It is important to remember that Dedibaayaanimanook's dadibaajim is a first-hand Anishinaabe account of a construction project that came with enormous negative consequences for the Namegosibii Anishinaabe people and their Obizhigokaang brethren. Their traditional territories, ability to travel and hunt, plant-gathering activities, and engagement in ceremony—not to mention their state of health and peace of mind—were all harmed. Dedibaayaanimanook's dadibaajim conversations are embedded in the social, cultural, economic, and environmental disasters that the wemitigoozhiwag inflicted. Namegosibii Anishinaabe people had to maintain a constant vigilance and state of preparedness for these types of events as they became increasingly common in their lives and homelands.

The dadibaajim I quoted earlier tells us that people who still lived in noopimakamig during the mid-twentieth century thought about and responded with apprehension to the notion of the wemitigoozhi and wemitigoozhiiwaadiziwin. Dedibaayaanimanook explains that her brother's intent was to play a practical joke during a journey to Ikwewi-zaa'igan in the 1930s:

> Nimaamikaw insayenziban, madaabiibatoopan.
> "Wemitigoozhiwag i'imaa ayaawag," indigonaan. Ezhi-gichi-
> zegiziyaang, Gweyesh. Anishaa e-ikidoj[11]

> I recall my elder brother, running down towards us. "There
> are European settler men over there," he said. Gweyesh and
> I were very fearful. But he meant it as a joke.

At the thought of coming into contact with wemitigoozhiwag, the young women were immediately overcome with fear, although Dedibaayaanimanook does not explain the reasons for their reaction. Despite individual friendships, the first response of Anishinaabe people was often stress, uncertainty, fear, and dread at the prospect of

encountering wemitigoozhiwag. Historically, they experienced wemitigoozhiiwaadiziwin as a force of destruction that took many forms, including schooling and religious proselytism as methods of assimilation.

Communicating the profundity of wemitigoozhiiwaadiziwin's effects
on Anishinaabeg, Dedibaayaanimanook's next narrative describes the
efforts of community members to preserve themselves as Anishinaabe
people. She outlines over the course of several conversations the events
surrounding the appearance of the gichi-dewe'igan great drum and its
ceremony in Namegosibiing that occurred at some time in the late 1930s
or early 1940s. Two significant factors suggest the intensity of the pressure
of wemitigoozhiiwaadiziwin on the Namegosibii Anishinaabe people to
change their ideas of who they were. One was their patriarch Giizhig's
instruction not to bring gichi-dewe'igan into Namegosibiing. The other
was the effort people expended to do just that. Beginning with the details
as she knew them from first-hand experience, Dedibaayaanimanook
describes and contextualizes how her own involvement came about:

> **Big dewe'igan insayenziban iidog ogii' ayaawaa', Gweyesh**
> **Namegosibiing [niimiwaaj]. Gweyesh gii-niingaanii.**
> **Aaniish ogichidaakwe izhinikaazo a'a dino gii**
> **niingaaniij awiya gichi-dewe'iganan. Miish i'i geniin gaa**
> **wii'izhi-igooyaan.**[12]
>
> The big ceremonial drum is what my late elder brother and
> Gweyesh had in Trout Lake [to hold a ceremonial] dance.
> Gweyesh took the lead. As you should know, that type [of role
> for a drum] is called ogichidaakwe, when someone leads in
> the presence of the great drum. I too was receiving coaching.

Dedibaayaanimanook stresses the identity of the large ceremonial drum
that came to Namegosibiing, differentiating it from the smaller, hand-
held version that Anishinaabe people use for recreational purposes and
establishing the spiritual nature of gichi-dewe'igan. Her use of the term
"ogichidaakwe," moreover, suggests the prominence of the great drum as a
ceremonial object throughout the region. Constituting the focal point of
the event, gichi-dewe'igan (an animate noun) may be regarded as having
been the agency through which the organization of the ceremony was

possible. Dedibaayaanimanook points out that her siblings Gweyesh and Jiibôt took a lead role in the arrangement. Having herself received training in the various aspects of the ceremonial proceedings, Gweyesh was able to guide Dedibaayaanimanook's participation.

Dedibaayaanimanook also shares details about the dance procession and ceremonial structure, something she refers to as "niimi'idiiwiga-migong" (the building where people dance). As we listen to her dadi-baajim, it is important to keep in mind the foreparents' instruction not to bring gichi-dewe'igan into Namegosibiing. Dedibaayaanimanook's narrative continues as follows:

> **Niingaan, ikwewag. Gweyesh gii' niingaanii, niin odaanaang Gweyesh. Indede, gaawn ogii minwendanziin gichi-dewe'iganan. Gaawn wiikaa gii' biindigesii. Agwajiing eta gii' ayaa e-ganawaabij, aanshinaa boodawewag gii dibikak. Ogii'minwendaan wiin e-ganawaabamaaj gaa niiminij niimi'idiiwigamigong. Waabanongshizhi ishkwôndemiwan, mitigoon shwaakaakidewan. Amiish i'imaa zhinoodaaganan waakaayichigaade-shi'imaa da niingaanii. [My mom] gii' biindige, gii'niimi.**[13]

> At the front, the women. Gweyesh led, and I behind Gweyesh. My father did not like the great ceremonial drum. He never went inside. He only watched from outside because they built a fire when it grew dark. He did, however, enjoy watching those who danced inside the structure. Its entrance is towards the east, with wooden poles placed upright in a circle. That is where the ropes encircle it, and that is where the lead dancer advances forward. [My mom] entered and danced.

Dedibaayaanimanook's detailed description of the niimi'idiiwiga-migong structure, including its shape, construction material, and direc-tion of entry, suggests that she too may have assisted with its assembly. Underscoring her father's disapproval of the ceremony, her description specifies that her mother entered the structure and joined the dancers but that her father watched from outdoors where the ceremonial fire burned.

Dedibaayaanimanook also explains that many relatives from neighbouring communities attended the ceremony:

Baabiizhaawaaj awiyag e' biniimiwaaj, Biigaanjigamiing, ya'aash gaye, Nishki'aa wiinawaa. Ininiwag eta. Gaawn wiin ikwewag. Onjida dash wiin igo gii'baatiinowag. Gaye gii' onjiiwag Aanzigo-zaa'iganing.[14]

People arrived to take part in the ceremonial dance, from Pikangikum, and also Nishki'aa and his family. Only the men, not the women. Still, many attended, coming from Otter Lake as well.

Even though practical reasons prevented women from coming, Dedibaayaanimanook states that a sizable number arrived in Namegosibiing. This dadibaajim hints at the logistical requirements for such an event. For the visitors from Biigaanjigamiing to be present meant at least two days of travel, and Ikwewi-zaa'igan and Aanzigo-zaa'igan Otter Lake are both at least a day's journey away. Participants from elsewhere and host community members alike all needed to plan for meals, accommodations, the venue for the event, and the accoutrements of the ceremony itself.

Given that the great drum is sacred and of great value, Gweyesh and her family had to have agreed, even if implicitly, to certain terms with its owner, who Dedibaayaanimanook surmised may have been Oziigaakigan of Lac Seul. Such an event required planning and organizing well in advance, perhaps when the people were still in Lac Seul and in contact with other Anishinaabeg. Even prior to the planning phases, the Gweyesh family had to have had discussions with community members and kinfolk in Biigaanjigamiing, Ikwewi-zaa'igan, Aanzigo-zaa'igan, and elsewhere. It is quite possible, in fact, that the event was fairly common knowledge throughout other Anishinaabe communities. However, it did not appear to have received any attention from the academic community, in contrast to the considerable interest researchers gave to the gichi-dewe'igan events among the Berens River Anishinaabeg.[15] Perhaps this lack of attention was the same general lack of awareness that helped to erase the presence of the Namegosibii Anishinaabeg and their identity as the people of the Namegosibiing homelands.

In the next part of her dadibaajim, Dedibaayaanimanook not only reiterates her father's antipathy toward the ceremony, but, importantly, she explains that the proscription had originated from her paternal grandfather, Giizhig. She also states the reason why other Anishinaabe people supported the great drum practice:

> **Indedesh gaawn gii' minwendanziin niimi'idiwin gaa-izhinikaadeg, dewe'igan gaa-mindidoj, nimishoomis gaye gaawiin. Ogii' minwendaanaawaan, gaawonji bimaadiziweya'ii izhichige, awiyag igo.**[16]
>
> My father did not like what is known as the great drum dance, nor did my grandfather. [But others] were in agreement with it, as a means of survival, all [of them] in general.

Dedibaayaanimanook's words suggest significant underlying reasons why the elders regarded the community's pursuit of the ogichidaakwe practice as troubling. Given that gichi-dewe'igan was not a part of their forebears' ceremonies, its presence in Namegosibiing seemed to say that the old spiritual traditions—those that had served them so well, safeguarding their philosophies, values, and unique identity across the generations—were at an end and that it was now the best way to counter wemitigoozhiiwaadiziwin in their lives.

To conclude the dadibaajim of a defining event in the affairs of Namegosibii Anishinaabeg, Dedibaayaanimanook alludes to the larger milieu in which these events were embedded:

> **Wiinge e-gii' minwendamowaaj aaninda, da-onji-bimaadizi Anishinaabe i'iwe izhichigej gii' ikidowag.**[17]
>
> Some people were most gratified, expressing their belief that it was the means by which they would be able to survive as Anishinaabe people.

As Dedibaayaanimanook's statement "da-onji-bimaadizi Anishinaabe i'iwe izhichigej gii' ikidowag" denotes, the circumstances surrounding her dadibaajim were a particularly daunting period of flux for all Anishinaabe people. The forces of wemitigoozhiiwaadiziwin began to fracture Anishinaabe-noopimakamig relationships. The increasing restrictions of Indian Act amendments and provincial policies on their ability to remain on the land and live as the ancestors had done purposely destabilized those relationships. In so many ways—spiritually, socially, culturally, and physically—the people's very existence as Anishinaabe communities was in peril. Dedibaayaanimanook's comment "da-onji-bimaadizi Anishinaabe," therefore, explains that those who arranged for gichi-dewe'igan's sojourn in Namegosibiing believed its practice would help Namegosibii Anishinaabeg to survive wemitigoozhiiwaadiziwin.

Although Gweyesh's role in the ceremony, including Dedibaayaanimanook's personal mentoring, appears to portray her as having abandoned the aanikoobidaaganag ancestral teachings, she was a practitioner of traditional ways who esteemed her elders. Taking on the responsibility of being his primary caregiver as he approached the end of his life, for example, Gweyesh was devoted to her grandfather Giizhig. Her seeming dissent undoubtedly indicates how few she saw her options were for resisting wemitigoozhiiwaadiziwin and its destructive forces in their lives as Anishinaabe people.

Understanding the fundamentality of spirituality in Anishinaabe identity and considering Gweyesh's affection for her elders, we can surmise that her decision to bring gichi-dewe'igan to Namegosibiing was neither trivial nor reckless. The timing of the gichi-dewe'igan events of this dadibaajim appears to align with the larger spiritual movement throughout the region during the early to mid-twentieth century wherein the great drum took on the role of lead protagonist. For the Namegosibii Anishinaabe elders, however, its inclusion deviated from their traditional custom of avoiding the use of large sacred objects and overtly visible forms of feasts and ceremonies. The preceding set of dadibaajim narratives tells us that wemitigoozhiwag did not often impact on Namegosibii Anishinaabeg in positive ways. In general, Dedibaayaanimanook's narratives allude to wemitigoozhiiwaadiziwin's inability to acknowledge its complete lack of respect for the natural environment and the Anishinaabe people's wish to continue with their customary land-based practices. But they also suggest that wemitigoozhiiwaadiziwin was not a uniform phenomenon among wemitigoozhi individuals and populations. Some wemitigoozhiwag were not as thoroughly and completely entrenched in an attitude of superiority, entitlement, racism, hostility, sexism, or condescension towards Anishinaabe people as others. These types of characteristics displayed themselves in varying degrees across time. In the following narrative, contextualized in the events of the hydroelectric dam construction at Otawagi-baawitig Ear Falls, Dedibaayaanimanook explains how her mother needed to use great care in managing something as seemingly straightforward as the purchase of a loaf of bread:

> **Ako gii' adaawena' bezhig, ogii-anoonaan ji-adaawetamaagoj, bakwezhiganan akiwenzii-wemitigoozhiwan. Indede sago ogii' wiijiiwaan. Miiwiin i'imaa gaa'ayaawaaj igi wemitigoozhiwag gii ano[kiiwaaj ji-giba'ig]aadeg i'i baawitig.**[18]

> She would buy one, asking an elderly European settler man to buy bread, to conduct the transaction for her. My father worked with him. That was where those European settler men stayed [while] working on the construction that shut off that falls.

Dedibaayaanimanook does not give reasons for why her mother asked an elderly wemitigoozhi, someone with whom her father frequently worked, to enter the store on her behalf. While this may appear to be an incident of no special significance, it shows that there were certain factors preventing an Anishinaabe woman from feeling free to walk into a store and make a purchase for herself. These conditions emanated from the historical overt expressions of racist-sexist attitudes. At the same time, however, Dedibaayaanimanook's dadibaajim shows that a certain degree of goodwill, trust, and friendship was possible on an individual basis. Importantly, this and others of Dedibaayaanimanook's narratives describe the efficacy of an astute woman who knew not only how to survive well in the noopimakamig homelands, but also how best to navigate the uncertainties and potential dangers associated with wemitigoozhiiwaadiziwin.

Red Lake's Refugees

Emerging from conversations with Namegosibii Anishinaabe elder Oo'oons Kejick is a portrayal of wemitigoozhiiwaadiziwin during the 1950s. These events occurred after those described in Dedibaayaanimanook's above dadibaajim. Laws and legislations that made it mandatory to obtain licences to hunt and fish having by this time denied the people their right to provide for themselves in Namegosibiing as the ancestors had done, various families and relatives began to settle in and around the municipality of Red Lake. They were able to find employment that was typically of low wages and poor health and safety standards. Oo'oons's dadibaajim alludes to one of the bitter ironies of wemitigoozhiiwaadiziwin in the following:

> Doodawindô Anishinaabeg aana gii ayaawaad, ingoji gii' izhinizha' windô. Ganabaj igiweniwag gaa-gii' andawenimaawaad Anishinaaben o'omaa ji-ayaasininij. They wanted to put the camp there. Mennonites osha odibendaanaawaan iniweniwan airplane hangar. Nashke i'iwedi gaa-gii' izhaawaad, nimishoomisiban. Amiishi'i bezhigwan i'imaa gaa' doodawindô. Ingoji i'imaa gii' izhinizha'indô.[19]

> This is how Anishinaabe people were treated when all they wanted was to live, they were forced out. Probably it was those who did not want Anishinaabe people to be here. They wanted to put the camp there. The Mennonites are the owners of the airplane hangar. Take, for example, over there where those including my grandfather went to live. There they were treated the same way. They were driven away.

Among the First People of the region were Oo'oons and his family, including his ailing grandfather Jiiyaan (Dedibaayaanimanook's paternal uncle) and other relatives who resided on the outskirts—the literal margins—of Red Lake. Some lived close to the water, as was the custom with Namegosibii Anishinaabeg. Although wemitigoozhiwag were also attracted to the shoreline, they regarded it as prime property and assessed its value in terms of zhooniyaa money. Oo'oons notes that it was also the missionaries who required lakefront property for the float planes they used to carry out theological humanitarian work among more remote Anishinaabe communities. Ironically, as is often the case in such endeavours, the missionaries' acquisition of land correlates to the displacement of its original dwellers, thus compounding the many forms of destruction that wemitigoozhiiwaadiziwin perpetrated upon those to whom they had come ostensibly to bring aid and comfort.

Oo'oons's dadibaajim tells us that wemitigoozhiwag, upon their arrival, evicted Anishinaabe people and demolished their houses wherever their quest for land took them. From the perspective of Anishinaabe people's experiences, wemitigoozhiwag in general perceived them to be in the way, needlessly occupying spaces that could be put to more productive (profitable) uses. This is the miiwishkaagem notion behind the ishkoniga-nan leftover system of reserves.[20] Land that settlers deemed to be of little or no value and sufficiently distanced and out of sight became reserves for Anishinaabe people, one of wemitigoozhiiwaadiziwin's methods of displacement. Oo'oons details the circumstances of how these dispossessions came about and how they directly affected members of his family:

Ingoji i'imaa gii'izhinizha'indô, Maagii Keesick. Ingii' ayaanaaban wedi. Nimaamikaw gaa-gii' bi ganoonindô Maagii, ingoji i'imaa ji onji izhaawaad. Gaaskaabooz gii' izhidaaban i'iwedi gii' biigwa'igaade owaakaa'igan. Mii'iwe gaa-gii' ikidowaad, "Gaawn ingoji nindoonji izhaasii. Mii-go omaa waa' ayaayaang," ogii' inaawaan.[21]

They were sent away from there, Maagii Keesick. I was over there. I remember when they came to tell Maagii and the others to leave. Gaaskaabooz was living over there when her house was demolished. What they had said was, "I will not move away from here. We choose to stay right here," is what they told them.

Oo'oons speaks as an eyewitness of the time local authorities came to the residences of family and kinfolk, among whom was his elderly grandmother Maagii Keesick, evicting them and destroying their homes. Not only did people not receive prior notice about appropriating their land, Oo'oons's dadibaajim makes no allusions to compensation for these instances of theft and mayhem. The phrase "ingoji i'imaa gii'izhinizha'indô" is more appropriate for dismissing a recalcitrant dog, but it precisely portrays the attitudes of presumption and entitlement and subsequent harsh treatment people encountered at the hands of wemitigoozhiwag. Important for identifying Namegosibii Anishinaabe community members, Oo'oons includes the name of his aunt, Gaaskaabooz.

When Anishinaabe families protested the orders to leave, they effectively placed themselves in the situation that wemitigoozhiwag refer to as "non-compliance," as Oo'oons explains in the following:

> **Naagaj miinawaa dakoniwewininiwag gaa-gii' biinaawaad. Ingii'ayaa aaniish geniin. Mii' gaa' ikidowaad, gaa-gii' inaawaad. Ingoji imaa ji-onji-izhaayaang, "ji-mikameg aandi ingoji gabeshiyaang izhidaayeg." Miish i'iwe gaa-gii' ikidowaad wemitigoozhiwag. "Giga mikaanan geyizhidaayan apartments." Amiish i'i wemitigoozhi gaa-gii' biizhaad i'iwedi.**[22]

> After a while they returned with police officers. I was there, too, after all. And that is what they said, what they told them. That we should remove ourselves from there, that "you find [your]selves somewhere else to live." And that is what the European settler-men said. "You can find apartments to live in." And that is how wemitigoozhi arrived over there.

Before presenting the details, Oo'oons uses "aaniish" to underscore the veracity of the description from his perspective as an Anishinaabe eyewitness. He then relates how authorities returned with reinforcements to ensure that people obeyed the order to leave. Alluding to the arrangements under which they would now be living, his use of the term "apartments" conjures cheaply constructed rental units, payments and due dates, rules, bylaws and regulations, landlords and janitors, and—without mentioning overt racism and hatred—various other complications that would henceforth be essential features of life. Oo'oons's dadibaajim highlights wemitigoozhiiwaadiziwin's increasing aggression against the personal autonomy and freedom of movement that once defined the everyday lives of Anishinaabe people.

Just as Oo'oons's dadibaajim contains no mention of prior notice about the intended land seizures, there is none about the people's having received, seen, or read letters or other similar documentation to inform them about the procedures of forced relocation about to take place. Indeed, people had long noted that it was generally routine for the wemitigoozhi-wag latecomers to disregard their human rights because one of the main tenets of wemitigoozhiiwaadiziwin was to imagine Indigenous peoples as less-than-human. The threat of physical violence as a means of seizing Anishinaabe lands typified the lack of justness that people faced on a daily basis as the realities of the wemitigoozhi-aadiziwin mindset settled upon the homelands and in their lives.

Before leaving Oo'oons's narrative, it is of interest to note the terminology he uses for presenting the events of their displacement. Oo'oons's Anishinaabemowin words are harsh because the language is reflecting, more so than describing, the callousness and cruelty of what happened. To explain that this is an example of how the Anishinaabemowin language in itself functions as an Anishinaabe value, people living traditionally would have had little need for language such as "ingoji imaa" when communicating formally with one another.

William King, another participant of this work, speaks Anishinaabemowin proficiently but uses it sparingly. That scarcity of Anishinaabemowin usage and other impacts of wemitigoozhi-aadiziwin in his lived experiences are evident when he mentions Balmertown as his place of birth and the Mackintosh boarding school of his childhood schooling:

William King, gaawn [an Anishinaabe name].
Balmertown. Ganabaj seven or eight, Mackintosh. Gaawn
aapiji [nimaamikawisii]. Once in a while [wanii'ige
Namegosibiing]. Ingoding, Trout Lake Lodge.[23]

[My name is] William King, I do not [have an Anishinaabe
name]. [I was born in] Balmertown. [I was] perhaps around
seven or eight [when I went to] Mackintosh [boarding school].

[I do not remember] very much. Once in a while [we trapped
in Trout Lake], at times [we lived at] Trout Lake Lodge.

William immediately informs us that he does not have an Anishinaabe
name, indicating that the traditional community in which elders
presented an infant with his or her dream-name no longer existed at
the time or place of his birth. Using the expression "gaawn aapiji," he
implicitly acknowledges a connection between the sketchiness of his
recollections and events associated with wemitigoozhiiwaadiziwin
such as boarding school attendance. That his dadibaajim does not name
people and places to establish his Namegosib heritage as forthrightly as
the others is undoubtedly linked to the ramifications of how Treaty 3
demarcated and defined each community. To explain, William's father,
Bezhigoobines Frank King, joined the Giizhigoog community when
he married Bejii Betsy and moved to Namegosibiing during the 1950s.
Although Namegosibii Anishinaabeg regarded him as a community
member, Indian Affairs insisted upon differentiating him as a member
of the Biigaanjigamiing Pikangikum community located within Treaty
5 territory. The same bureaucratic rationale carried over to William and
his siblings, with the result that access to their lineal inheritance of the
resources of Namegosibiing was fraught with uncertainty.

It is understandable that William neither explicitly proclaims his connections to Namegosibiing nor denies his Giizhig heritage, given the impossi-
bility of discussing the deeply injurious assault of wemitigoozhiiwaadiziwin
against ancestral knowledges, dadibaajim, and the choice to live freely on
the traditional homelands. The situation of William's family is an example
of how the historical irrationality of bureaucratic technicalities has served
to render identities ambiguous by ignoring the people's own methods for
describing themselves and their places of home. Community members
of Namegosibiing experienced these impacts of the wemitigoozhiwag
behaviours in their lives in Namegosibiing, Red Lake, and elsewhere.

When we survey the meaning of wemitigoozhiiwaadiziwin from
dadibaajim's Anishinaabe frame of reference, the Namegosibii
Anishinaabe people's presence and self-description begin to emerge. The

historical accounts of senior elders Dedibaayaanimanook and Oo'oons, for example, are a testimony of fear and avoidance of wemitigoozhiwag that were a result of the latecomers' attitudes, behaviours, and actions. Dedibaayaanimanook's dadibaajim about the great drum's visit, together with its circumvention of an ancestral teaching, suggests the stresses people encountered as wemitigoozhiiwaadiziwin became an increasingly recurring theme compelling them to turn to the unfamiliar as a means of holding on to their Anishinaabe sense of self. Having themselves lived the traditional customs of their aanikoobidaaganag ancestors, the elders speak from a place where they have an experiential understanding of contrasts that are evident in the juxtaposition of wemitigoozhiiwaadiz-iwin and Anishinaabe ontological thought.

Gaa Bii-izhi Gikendamang
Anishinaabe Rectitude

The dadibaajim of Namegosibii Anishinaabe participants at times gives voice to the conditions of wemitigoozhiiwaadiziwin colonialism. At other moments these concerns are expressed through silence. As a gift that the spirit of the ancestors carries across the generations and as a defining component of the people's identity discourse, Namegosibii Anishinaabe dadibaajim narratives articulate a commitment to survive the adversities of wemitigoozhiiwaadiziwin.

Shifting priorities and forms and patterns of wemitigoozhiiwaadiziwin over time required flexibility in how people were able to respond to the phenomenon of the wemitigoozhi. This chapter presents dadibaajim narratives that show how Namegosibii Anishinaabe participants think about the homelands and the teachings of the ancestors in the face of wemitigoozhii-waadiziwin's ubiquity. As the most senior elder of the community, for example, Dedibaayaanimanook speaks from the perspective of life lived through nearly 100 winters when she shares her thoughts about a partic-ular program ostensibly designed to teach ancestral methods of hunting and trapping. At the same time, her grandson Riel denotes the frame of reference of a younger generation when he alludes to the teachings that he may never hear because circumstances of wemitigoozhiiwaadiziwin denied him the contexts in which to learn.

Reflections of a Senior Elder

For Dedibaayaanimanook, the passage of time brings increasing evidence that the life she lived as a child in the noopimakamig aki boreal places of home is no longer possible. Values, priorities, and the every-day affairs of life have all undergone unimaginable changes as a result of wemitigoozhiiwaadiziwin. Reflecting her awareness of these inevita-ble and often distressing realities, she provides penetrating, insightful comments in the following dadibaajim:

> Gaa-gii' izhichigewaaj mewinzha aaniish gaawin
> da-izhichigesiiwag wemitigoozhi aaniish owanashkwe'aan
> Anishinaaben. Mii eta gegikendangiban. Gaawn ganabaj
> awiya noongom daa-doodanziin noopimiing ji-izhi-daaj.
> Noopimiing etago awiya izhi-daaj, wiikaa waabandazig
> oodenaang aapiji, maa'ang eta. Wedi dash dazhi
> oniijaanisiwaaj noopimiing—owiiwan – imbebiinsan
> ayaawaawaaj. Mii eta ge-izhichigepan, Anishinaabeg
> gaa-gii' bi izhichigewaaj. Aaniish inaa indebwe,
> gaa-biizhi-gikendamaan geniin bi-nitaawigiyaan, en. Mii'
> gaa-onji-gikendamaan.[1]

What Anishinaabe people did a long time ago they absolutely can no longer do because European settlers truly disrupted the Anishinaabe people. If they knew only that way of life, but probably no one now can live on the boreal land. Only if a person lived exclusively in the land, never seeing an urban environment except to acquire goods, and he and his wife raised their child on the land. That would be the only way of pursuing Anishinaabe lifeways from one generation to the next. I am correct, based on what I have come to understand from the time of my own birth. That is how I know.

From a perspective that extends across divergent ontologies, Dedibaayaanimanook's understandings are an outcome of having been born and lived her younger years within the boreal homelands among family and relatives. It was a time when the community of relationships informed, provided for, and maintained the socio-cultural infrastructures of an Anishinaabe world view. But, as Dedibaayaanimanook surmises, a return to the former ways of the aanikoobidaaganag foreparents would require a complete avoidance of oodenaang's urban influences and distractions because wemitigoozhiiwaadiziwin's values, principles, and beliefs increasingly undermine those that once sustained and guided Anishinaabe people's lifeways. She has always assessed the values and behaviours of an urban lifestyle and wemitigoozhiiwaadiziwin's endless pursuit of zhooniyaa profits in terms of the damage they perpetrate upon the aki earth, its resources, and Indigenous peoples across the world. Her dadibaajim narratives are about principles that are in alignment with the aki earth's demand for respectful treatment and therefore resonate with the carbon emissions and climate change discourses of today. This alignment, to Dedibaayaanimanook, results from clear, logical thinking.

Similar to the previous narrative, the next one speaks to competencies that have essentially disappeared and the larger contexts in which most of today's younger Anishinaabeg must live. Here, Dedibaayaanimanook notes that life on the land required specific types of skills and knowledge, and that there was a time when learning about these fundamentals of life in noopimakamig began at birth:

Gaa-oshkaya'aawiwaaj, gaawiin osha ganabaj awiya Anishinaabemosii noongom iwedi, noopimiing etago noongom iwedi. Noopimiing etago dazhi-izhi-daaj, his wife, amiidash i'iwedi dazhi oniijaanisij a'a ikwe noopimiing.

Ininiwag gii' odaapinaawasowag mewinzha. Omooday gii'
nitaa odaapinaawaso.[2]

The young people, probably none of them there [in Red Lake]
speak any Anishinaabemowin today, unless they lived on the
land. Only if [a man] lived on the land with his wife, and if she
birthed their children over there on the land. Men helped with
births a long time ago. Omooday was often there to help with
the delivery of a child.

At the centre of Dedibaayaanimanook's comments lies the significance
of Anishinaabemowin speech and the reasons for and consequences
of its non-use. She intimates that the off-reserve youths of today rarely
speak the language because there is no community in which dadibaajim is spoken in the Anishinaabemowin language. As a result, many
young people cannot fully capture aspects of an Anishinaabe world
view, including how births and places of birth relate to concepts of life
and selfhood.

To elaborate on the Anishinaabemowin term that Namegosibii
Anishinaabe people use for birth, "nitaawig-," it is the same intran-
sitive verb for "grow," as in a plant that begins to grow. Due to how
Anishinaabemowin is structured for making meaning, "nita-" associates
with the notion of "first." The language therefore conceptualizes birth
in the same way it depicts a plant's first indication of life by extending
roots into the noopimakamig aki earth-land. Drawing from the vitality
of noopimakamig aki in a similar manner, a person's personal and unique
relationship with his or her birthplace begins with the first moments of
birth when personhood commences.

Dadibaajim teaches that the roles and responsibilities for maintaining the many interconnections of life and dealing with their contin-
gencies required a wide range of skills. Demonstrating this principle,
Dedibaayaanimanook cites the case of her cousin Omooday as an illustra-
tion of how Anishinaabe people's value for life encompassed recognition
of and appreciation for the practice of male midwifery.

In other conversations, Dedibaayaanimanook frequently mentions the
inaccessibility of noopimakamig aki for today's Anishinaabe people. She
suggests, in fact, that it has undergone too many changes, brought about

by wemitigoozhiiwaadiziwin's neo-liberal philosophies and value system, to allow for a restoration of the noopimakamig wholeness she enjoyed in her childhood. Indeed, it is questionable that noopimakamig aki will ever be sufficiently vigorous and robust to support itself and the Anishinaabe way of life as it once did so eminently well.

Reclaiming Ancestral Identity

Despite the barriers of wemitigoozhiiwaadiziwin that preclude access to a permanent residence in the homelands, participants continue to identify with the ancestral lands. Oo'oons, for example, took opportunities when they arose to accompany relatives on brief visits to Namegosibiing. These outings were critical to Oo'oons, whose parents and relatives had already undergone the upheavals of displacement from Namegosibiing before his birth. He described a canoe trip down Namegosi-ziibi Trout River with fellow community members that clearly provided him with satisfaction:

> Gwanabisewaad, gagwe-bagwaanegamigokeyaang. Four days ingii' dazhiikaamin. Anishinaabeg mewinzha gaa-gii' izhi gabeshiwaagobaneg e-bimi-ayaawaad.[3]
>
> Their canoe tipped over [and] we were trying to set up the tents. It [the canoe trip] took us four days. [We went where] Anishinaabe people had camped a long time ago when they were travelling.

It is evident from his depiction of a canoe trip that enabled him to retrace portions of the ancient travel route that Oo'oons held the memory of his ancestors in high regard. Although the capsized canoe, drenched clothes, rain, and cool weather may not have been ideal, they seem to have enhanced his appreciation for the vigorous lifestyle of the aanikoobidaaganag. The expedition was, in fact, a profoundly meaningful reconnection to the memory of the foreparents and the noopimakamig homelands in which they lived and journeyed. At the same time, there is an intimation of sadness in the Anishinaabemowin words Oo'oons uses, "gaa-gii' izhi gabeshiwaagobaneg e-bimi-ayaawaad," which the English

version cannot fully capture. The sense of pathos in this dadibaajim lies
in the unspoken acknowledgement that the ancestors and their travels,
campsites, and many related activities could only ever be narratives and
memories for Oo'oons. However, reliving the canoe journey by sharing
its dadibaajim was an immensely uplifting experience for him.

Gwiishkwa'oo Eliza Angeconeb, too, expresses her longing to return to
Namegosibiing. Concomitantly, however, she indicates her understanding
that living alone on the land is not possible. She alludes to the illusoriness
of thinking that four sisters could live the ways of aanikoobidaaganag in
the absence of a complete community:

> **Moonzhag ninaanaagadawendaan, ambesh geyaabi
> izhi-daayaan wedi. Gaawn-sha awiya nimikawaasii
> ji-wiijidaamishij wedi, aazha gakina nishiimenzhag
> e-gii'maajaawaad. Ikwewag shwiin geyaabi bimaadiziwag.
> Awiya ji-manised. Bangii-sh wiin indaa gashkitoon ji
> maniseyaan. Aaniish moonzhag gaa' izhichigeyaan biinish
> eleven years old gii'daso-biboonweyaan maniseyaan ako,
> e-gii'naanaajidaabiiyaan.**[4]

> I often think, I wish I could still live over there [in Trout
> Lake]. However, I cannot ever find anyone to live with me
> over there, with all my younger [male] siblings gone. Only
> we women are still living. [We would need] someone to get
> firewood. I would be able to get a little wood myself, [as]
> that was what I often did up until I was eleven years old, that
> I would pull it home on a sled.

Gwiishkwa'oo describes the everyday chore of gathering firewood in
each of the phrases "awiya ji-manised," "ji-maniseyaan," and "maniseyaan
ako." By using words with the "manis-" stem, she underscores the criti-
cality of firewood to living in a noopimakamig boreal setting. "Manise,"
to explain, is the verb for gathering firewood, and the nouns for firewood
are "misan" and "manisaanan." Without the act or practice of manisem,
living on the land as the ancestors had done would be all but impossible.
This Gwiishkwa'oo understands, having acquired the knowledge of how

to assess the feasibility of living on the land in terms of manisem from her childhood task of bringing home the firewood.

With her comment that her male siblings have all passed and that only her sisters are still living, Gwiishkwa'oo intimates that life in Namegosibiing would not be sustainable on a long-term basis without a complete community to provide the many and varied proficiencies that such a way of life requires. To function off the grid, a community must consist of men, women, and children, not solely four grandmothers. This the foreparents understood. Yet her awareness of these logistical constraints does not suppress her stated yearning for the Namegosibiing homelands, even if only on the basis of brief, periodic visits. Her visits are the means by which she has been able to maintain contact with the places where she formed her Anishinaabe sense of self as a young child. Despite the financial costs of transportation, the demands of wage labour, and the uncertainties of shifting circumstances in the lives of her children and grandchildren, Gwiishkwa'oo has continued to visit Namegosibiing at least once every year.

Oo'oons Kejick's younger sibling, Niinzhoode Wilfred, immediately and unequivocally announces his Anishinaabe sensibility by introducing himself with his Anishinaabe name and identifying it as such. As with Oo'oons, Gwiishkwa'oo, Dedibaayaanimanook, and Martha Fiddler Angeconeb, Niinzhoode speaks from an Anishinaabe perspective by using his heritage language as follows:

> **Niinzhoode Anishinaabe [winikaaz]. Gaawn wiin aapiji ingii' ayaasii [Namegosibiing]. Onji intaawig Sioux Lookout. Sandy Beach i'imaa ate [ezhi-bimishinowaaj] a long time ago, gete ya'ii [amii' imaa ayaawag] indedeban, nimaamaaban, Paul Gikinô'amaagewinini, Naakojiiz.[5]**

> Niinzhoode is my Anishinaabe [name]. I was not [in Namegosibiing] for very long. I was born in Sioux Lookout. There is [a cemetery] over there by Sandy Beach. Long ago [there was] an old place [where] my late father and my late mother [are], Paul Gikinô'amaagewinini and Naakojiiz.

Niinzhoode Wilfred reaffirms his Namegosibii Anishinaabe identity
when he states that his father was Gikinô'amaagewinini Paul Kejick, a
grandson of the Namegosibii Anishinaabe people's patriarch, Giizhig,
and that his mother was Naakojiiz. By acknowledging his ancestral
connection to Namegosibiing and speaking in Anishinaabemowin, he
anchors his identity to the Namegosibii Anishinaabe community. He
also uses the phrase "gete ya'ii" to indicate his knowledge about the old
Namegosibiing dadibaajim narratives about specific places and associated events of physical, spiritual, ceremonial, and social significance
for him as a member of the community. Undoubtedly, this gete ya'ii
knowledge came to him from his parents, grandparents, personal observations, and experiences working in Namegosibiing. His knowledge
about sacred places includes the traditional cemetery of the aanikoobidaaganag, confirming that his Anishinaabe identity is grounded in the
Namegosibiing homelands.

Another identity narrative is that of William King, who expresses his
Anishinaabe heritage by making allusions to the place where he spent
time trapping with his family. The narrative (a portion of which I quoted
earlier) is as follows:

**Gaawn [I have no Anishinaabe name]. Once in awhile
[ingii' wanii'ige Namegosibiing], ingoding Trout Lake
Lodge [gii izhidaayeng], [gaye] inshiimenzhag.[6]**

No [I have no Anishinaabe name]. Once in a while [I trapped
in Trout Lake], occasionally [when we lived at] Trout Lake
Lodge [with] my younger siblings.

William, Dedibaayaanimanook's great-nephew, lived in several places
including Namegosibiing. Although he was born in Balmertown
and currently resides in Red Lake, he states that when he lived in
Namegosibiing during his youth, he could accompany his younger
siblings on the family's trapline as his parents were able to utilize it. As
an adult, William has reinforced a sense of connection with the land of
his maternal grandmother, Gweyesh, as a tourist guide, giving him a
legitimate way of spending time in Namegosibiing.

The dadibaajim narratives of younger generations incorporate allusions to factors that have tended to reduce their sense of affiliation with the Namègosibiing places of origin. Janae Fiddler, for example, intimates an indirect and more distanced connection to the traditional home of her mother, Martha, and maternal grandfather, Aayizag Isaac, than those of the more senior generations when she says, "I have never been to Trout Lake. Just that my mom grew up there."[7] Janae, a great-grandniece of Dedibaayaanimanook, was born in Thunder Bay, Ontario. Her statements suggest that her ideas of and association with noopimakamig lie in places other than Namegosibiing. The briefness, rather than the explicitness, of her remarks is also indicative of where she does see herself situated in regard to her ancestral place of home.

Adding her own sentiments about how she might have influenced her daughter's sense of identity and place of origin, Martha states the following: "I thought about them [her children] coming to visit and having a place there. I don't know if they'd want to stay there or live there because they're so used to that technology that we have today when there's nothing like that out there, just bush."[8] Had it been possible for her to keep a place of her own, Martha surmises, she may have been able to bring her children and grandchildren to Namegosibiing. Even though they were born and raised elsewhere, they would have had opportunities to develop a degree of that same closeness she continues to hold for Namegosibiing. Janae's comments, however, indicate that today's young people have a greater sense of affinity for other places and lifeways due to the circumstances of parentage, birth, and upbringing that draw them elsewhere.

Another youthful perspective is that of Riel Olsen, Dedibaayaanimanook's grandson. Referring to earlier experiences of living in Namegosibiing, he intimates a desire for greater knowledge about the history of his people and their relationship with the homelands as follows: "Of course, I pretty much consider it my home. My earliest memories are from out there. I haven't heard too much specifics in stories. I heard people's names, a general idea of how we ended up out there and a little history of our family going back to Sam Keesick, my great-great-grandfather. It's not only my mom; I've been out there and spent lots of time with assorted aunts and one uncle, Harald."[9] Riel notes that it was primarily the influence of his mother, who was born in Namegosibiing, and other family members that helped him to develop a distinct relationship with the place of his maternal ancestors.

There is, however, a tinge of regret in the tone of his dadibaajim narrative when he alludes to the Namegosibiing stories he has yet to hear. Acutely aware that Anishinaabemowin remains to be learned, Riel speaks English as his first language, mentioning Sam Keesick, the name by which he came to know about his great-great-grandfather Giizhig. Moreover, he regards Namegosibiing as having the power to draw family members together in order to visit, learn, and renew relationships.

In another segment of his dadibaajim, Riel elaborates on the activities he and his uncle pursued. He reaffirms the knowledge he gained from living on the land with his uncle Harald and learning about places and names of cultural significance for the Namegosibiing community. Reiterating his identity in terms of Namegosibiing as home, he also draws attention to the importance of continued homeland-based associations with family members and relatives as follows:

> In the winter we'd spend a lot of the time in Trout Lake. We subsisted off the land. [He] taught me how to set a net. [We] did a little bit of hunting. We went all over the place. He did tell me a lot about that stuff [place names, significance of places]. It's home to me. It always has been and always will be. And so it's not that I always think about it. I keep in touch with relatives. It's not too many of us left, so it's good to keep in touch, working [and] living out there. There's very few of us. [For] a lot of the family, that's the only place I run into them, when they come out to visit for a few days or a week, once a year. Actually, our branch of the family is probably the only ones that are out there fairly steady throughout winter and summer, Keesicks, Olsen-Keesicks, whatever. It's [the diminishing number of Giizhig's descendants in Trout Lake] been going on for a long time. Charlie [Jiins Angeconeb] and [N]ookom [Dedibaayaanimanook], I think, were pretty much the only ones that actually lived out there for most of the year, the last ones to. The way I see making money, you're always taking or using the land somehow, in a way that it shouldn't. Current society is at odds with the way we live. The two ways are almost not compatible anymore.[10]

Speaking from the perspective of his professional and personal life choices, Riel's dadibaajim demonstrates a strong desire to have his own Namegosibii Anishinaabe connections. Spending each summer in Namegosibiing as a guide was a means for pursuing and preserving his ancestral identity that concomitantly allowed him to earn an income. By critiquing wemitigoozhiiwaadiziwin as a value system that prioritizes pursuit of money without regard for consequences, however, Riel alludes to the irony of seeking a traditional land-based identity by engaging in wage labour that facilitates the larger money-driven system responsible for destroying the Anishinaabe people's noopimakamig homelands and lifeways. On the other hand, people who become successful in mainstream society accrue monetary wealth, financial security, and social status, but in so doing they usually lose contact with their ancestral homes. That there are no community members of any age living exclusively in Namegosibiing today is a consequence of that entire wemitigoozhiiwaadiziwin way of thinking.

Riel intimates his understanding that very few options are available for living in the manner of the Anishinaabe forebears. Furthermore, he reports that it is practically impossible to find anyone who is willing or able to exist without the luxuries and conveniences of the grid, stating that "everyone wants hair dryers, soap operas."[11] Riel implies that wemitigoozhiiwaadiziwin's laws and regulations force us to live in compliance with its notions of leisure, possession, ownership, bureaucratic management, and state control.

Riel concurs with his grandmother Dedibaayaanimanook's observations when he suggests that the feasibility of living on the land free of some form of wemitigoozhiiwaadiziwin no longer exists: "We just simply didn't have the so-called right to build houses on our land. I heard something about some three-person committee who decides the right for people who deserve to live out there. It's funny. Is that thing still going on? Like, this possession thing. I never really understood that. That's a total white man thing."[12] Riel's remarks about a committee are in reference to responses of the Ministry of Natural Resources and Forestry (MNRF) to court rulings of more recent times. These decisions direct authorities and officials of the MNRF to provide the community with greater opportunities for participatation in the management of the homelands. As is the usual case with bureaucracy, however, MNRF typically allows for some community input in minor areas such as how to implement the more encompassing decisions already determined by upper managers and officials. Often regarded by Anishinaabeg as little more than staged productions, these meetings with the MNRF tend to benefit and quell the voices of only a select few, thus causing harm to community relations and confusion among members. With a hint of irritation in his voice, Riel suggests that wemitigoozhiiwaadiziwin—for which he uses the phrase "a total white man thing"—lies behind the discontinuities in what was once a seamless connection to the homelands and a strong Anishinaabe identity. In contrast to the MNRF's methods, he implies, the aanikoobidaaganag ancestors welcomed access to the places of home as an inherited right.

Riel explains how he was able to meet his work needs and maintain a personal sense of relationship with Namegosibiing as follows: "I really don't need to look at it as work, going back out there. It's more like going back home for me. I'm able to spend half the time of the year out at Trout Lake because pretty much, like I said, I consider it my home. And when the season's over, it's time for me to leave. I would like to have a year-round presence out there someday."[13] With ambivalence, Riel mentions the end of the tourist season and the end of his summer-long visit home. He expresses determination to retain his sense of attachment to Namegosibiing by seeking ways for making it a permanent place of residence. As with Riel, Anishinaabeg today have not abandoned their desire to remain close to the land. Some use social media as modernized versions of their dadibaajim and mawadishiwem, which Riel also does when he shares thoughts about his Namegosibiing experiences with his family, friends, and homelands.

Namegosibii dadibaajim narratives indicate a strong commitment to hold on to or (re)discover the knowledges, teachings, and insights of the forebears; seek ways for strengthening and reinvigorating their relationship with the ancestral places of home; and maintain a Namegosibiing-linked identity. The narratives also illustrate how factors affecting parentage and place of birth and upbringing have shifted across the generations to influence their sense of self and to engender affinities to places other than Namegosibiing.

Like most other Indigenous peoples around the world, Namegosibii Anishinaabeg are experientially knowledgeable about wemitigoozhiiwaa-diziwin's unsettling forces of change. To help us better understand the historical events, conditions, and circumstances from which the dadi-baajim narratives in this book emerge, an examination of the izhibii'igem texts uncovers details about the names, dates, events, and lines of family relationships that were either unnecessary for how the aanikoobidaanag forebears lived or were destroyed when the wemitigoozhiwag arrived. These non-academic texts include corporate, state, and personal records about the people of Namegosibiing.

Gaa'izhibii'ig-aazoyang Mewinzha Historical Texts

Izhibii'igem written records that mention the Trout Lake Anishinaabe foreparents in terms of genealogies, specific individuals, and dates of events in their lives and activities do exist. In this chapter, I use Hudson's Bay Company (HBC) reports, treaty annuity pay lists, census data, and the published field notes of an interested private citizen, Gary Butikofer, to identify Namegosibii Anishinaabe individuals and their families, relational lines, and English and Anishinaabemowin names. In so doing, however, I specify that the need to use them arises from the disruptions that wemitigoozhiiwaadiziwin perpetrated upon the dadibaajim customs used by Anishinaabe people to retain information about who they were.

It is important to point out that certainty in identifying the ancestors by using izhibii'igem alone would be virtually impossible without the information provided by the narratives of senior elders such as Dedibaayaanimanook. It is the oral record that allows us to link the written information, often isolated or in scattered segments, into a meaningful coherence and chart individual lines of relationship. This chapter shows that dadibaajim explicates these relationships, allowing us to know the identity of our relatives and foreparents. Without the aggregative focus of the Anishinaabemowin dadibaajim narratives, moreover, the text records alone cannot recognize the Namegosibii Anishinaabeg as a distinct community. The family trees and roots that appear throughout the chapters of this book illustrate Namegosibii Anishinaabe ancestral relationships as based on the findings of both the oral and written records.

Often, the izhibii'igem text supplies anglicized versions as well as English names along with bits of information about calendar dates, births, deaths, marriages, and so on. Dadibaajim being the final authority in the Namegosibii Anishinaabe identity discourse, discrepancies within the written record tend to resolve themselves by deferring to the oral record. My placement of dadibaajim-derived names, where they still exist, in front of the English versions recognizes that oral record primacy. To remind ourselves, the senior elders' dadibaajim narratives are the most accurate source of knowledge about the Anishinaabe ancestors because they alone can speak contextually with subjective voices whenever their continuity has not been interrupted by wemitigoozhiiwaadiziwin. Also important to keep in mind, Dedibaayaanimanook frequently tells listeners that her dadibaajim is but her contribution to the Namegosibii Anishinaabe aweneniwiyang identity narrative. This work acknowledges that other families have their own unique contributions, perspectives, experiences, and emphases for a more complete self-description of who we are as the people of Namegosibiing.

Wemitigoozhi's Texts

The singular active verb "izhibii'ige" (she or he writes) derives from the noun "izhibii'igem" (text or writing); the passive form is "izhibii'igaade" (it is written). These Anishinaabemowin terms arise from an Anishinaabe ontological frame of thought that is based on the oral system of meaning conveyance. Given that the izhibii'igem written text contains certain bits of historical information (such as dates) that are not a part of the oral record, the search for Namegosibii Anishinaabe identity is likely to be most meaningful when we engage with the various texts from an Anishinaabe perspective. It is that perspective that allows us to gain access to the power of an elder's dadibaajim words in order to counter the often erroneous, unsettling notions about Indigenous peoples that comprise the izhibii'igem text.

Deriving from how Europeans thought about themselves vis-à-vis Indigenous peoples, written statements often reveal the pervasiveness of wemitigoozhiiwaadiziwin's destructive tendencies. HBC's Lac Seul post manager Charles Cameron, to illustrate, wrote Governor Simpson in 1830, explaining that "three families . . . 14 men entirely failed in their hunts. They spent the winter doing nothing."[1] While most would agree that a land-based lifestyle was a good way to live, they would also concur that it was not easy and that no one would have survived doing "nothing"— particularly during a severe winter. Cameron, of course, did not mean that Anishinaabe people literally did nothing but that they were not participating in activities that would effectuate the company's market ideology. But people may just as well have been doing nothing, when judged by the post manager of a profit-driven entity such as the HBC, if they were not bringing in the furs. Cameron's expression arises from the context of a British corporate imperative that measures the worth of anything in terms of profit, demonstrating why contexts are important to note when using historical records.

Of further contextual importance, Cameron's words are a reflection of wemitigoozhiiwaadiziwin myths about the non-existence of an Anishinaabe work ethic and about European standards as natural, normal, and universal. In fact, the ideology of Anishinaabe societies held that the physical environment and how people perform their work within it were of prime importance at the same time as it revealed the fundamental flaws in the principles of capitalism. Had the Anishinaabe fur producers been able to access dawisijigem spaces and voice their perspectives, they would surely have told a different dadibaajim by describing how hunters, trappers, and their families actually spent the winter.

In another example of wemitigoozhiiwaadiziwin's less than neutral inclinations, we move ahead by half a century to E.K. Beeston's HBC report of 1886 where he characterized Anishinaabe people as "quiet, very industrious, and generally well off."[2] The tone of this izhibii'igem sounds more accepting, but it exudes a sense of entitlement to make judgments about a people's character, thus denoting a perceived moral superiority. Again, the mythology about the universal applicability of European standards is clearly evident. These H B C excerpts illustrate wemitigoozhiiwaa-diziwin's inability to see or unwillingness to acknowledge its biases and consequential abuse of power.

One form of power misuse has been control of access to the means of izhibii'igem production. Without considering an Anishinaabe version of events, Cameron's 1830 report tends to depict the people as passive, helpless, indolent—and deserving of their own misfortune. Beeston's 1886 account, on the other hand, inclines to characterize the people as obedient, compliant servants who are eager to please the boss. Without overtly declaring it, historical izhibii'igem texts, including corporate records, treaty pay lists, census documents, Indian agency reports, and privately generated writings appear as statements of power, authority, control, superiority, expertise, and entitlement. Because the subtext of corporate and state records reflects particular historical practices, beliefs, values, behaviours, and frames of reference, these records require us to think critically about what they are actually saying.

The aanikoobidaaganag ancestors experienced certain texts as more than a display of benign visuals because lurking just behind them was an unfathomable, ever-evolving web of codes, laws, regulations, orders, policies, and administrative functionings. In their incomprehensibility, these izhibii'igem texts had the power to inspire fear. They were among wemitigoozhiiwaadiziwin's agents of control, and as trapping, hunting, and fishing licences—and eventually even wood-gathering, tree-cutting, and building permits—they represented countless intrusions into people's lives. Control over traditional Anishinaabe means of survival was embodied in wiiyaasikewininiwag, the uniformed game wardens from Ontario's M N R F to whom Oo'oons refers in the following dadibaajim:

> Onzaam ogoweniwag wenitigoozhiwag,
> wiiyaasikewininiwag, M N R ingosaag. Ingotaaj
> wedi ji-izhaayaan, ji-bi-andawaabamiwaad, aandi

ezhi-waakaa'igan ji-ozhitooyaan. Ji-izhiwaad, "Gaawn omaa
gidaa-ayaasii!" Daabishkoo ji-manaa ayaad awiya i'imaa.[3]

Because of these European settler people, the game wardens,
MNR, I am fearful of them. I am afraid to go there [Trout
Lake], that they will come looking for me if I build a house,
that they will tell me, "You should not be here!" It is as though
no one ought to be there.

Oo'oons's expression of fear relates to the events surrounding the eviction
of his family from their homes in Red Lake discussed earlier. Adding to
his anxieties were his experiences of the MNRF's use of game wardens for
enforcing provincial policies that regulated traplines and other land-based
activities. Fear is what Oo'oons mentions as the most fundamental obsta-
cle preventing him and others from living freely in the noopimakamig aki.
That disclosure accurately identifies the dissemination of terror through
text as an essential tool of wemitigoozhiiwaadiziwin's drive for compliance.

Particularly among gichi-Anishanaabeg who lived on the land—the
senior people who were skilled in orality rather than versed in reading,
writing, and speaking the English language and for whom writing did
not fit their oral way of communicating—the written text represented
foreign, usually threatening, concepts. It is understandable that (roman
orthographic) text appearing on licences and posted regulations became
reminders of possible or actual restrictions perpetrated by wemitigoozhiiwaadiziwin in land use, travel, spirituality, ceremony, and the sense of
autonomy characterizing Anishinaabe lifeways. Oo'oons provides an
example of how izhibii'igem symbolized and evoked memories of those
violences by wemitigoozhiwag by describing a visit he once made to a
place where Anishinaabe relatives once resided along the outer edges of
the Red Lake municipality:

I'iwedi babaa-izhi-daawag apartment izhi owaakaa'igan.
Gaawiin [log cabins] Anishinaabeg i'imaa gii' anokiiwag,
ji-waakaa'igewaad. Miish i'iwe naanaagaj i'iwedi
ina'adooyaan, there's a no trespassing sign, private
property, there's that big house. Miish enendamaan i' imaa

mewinzha gaa-gii'gwiiwizensiwiwaad, ani-akiwenzi[wag],
nashkesh noongom gwenawi-izhi-daawag aaninda.[4]

Over there, all around there, they were told to live in
apartment[s]. Not [in log cabins]. Anishinaabeg worked there,
building the houses. And further over there, as I was walking
along the road, there's a no trespassing sign, private property,
there's that big house. And that is what I thought there, those
who were young boys at that time, who are now old, some
have nowhere to live.

Oo'oons ponders the events and circumstances in which Anishinaabe
families with young children and old people alike had to leave the houses
they themselves had built, vacate the land, and move into apartments.
Describing a walk he once took along a back road, he recalls thinking
about the relatives who were once employed building homes for others
to live in and about the children who grew up to become old and home-
less—the street people of Red Lake. Oo'oons's dadibaajim is about
dispossessions that seemed to converge on the izhibii'igem sign warning
him not to trespass, advising him of displacement and forfeiture.

From the viewpoint of Namegosibii Anishinaabe oral tradition and
the lived experiences of the gichi-Anishinaabeg senior elders, language
ideology discourse mediates the terms "izhibii'igaade" and "izhibii'igem"
as symbols of wemitigoozhiiwaadiziwin. Understanding the contexts in
which historical texts are embedded and the role text has played in the
domination, terrorization, control, suppression, and forced assimilation
of Indigenous populations is critical.

Hudson's Bay Company Records

The journey into finding answers to the question of aweneniwiyang who
we are takes us on a search through the Hudson's Bay Company Archives
in Winnipeg, Manitoba. In addition to descriptions of corporate financial
affairs, reports remarked on details about the homelands, weather and
climate conditions, and aanikoobidaaganag individuals themselves. This
type of information, obtainable from wemitigoozhiwag's izhibii'igem
about how they perceived and described Anishinaabe people, includes

relationships in which the forebears engaged, the circumstances in which they lived and travelled, and so on, which help to identify the ancestors. As an example, Lac Seul post clerk Charles McKenzie stated that an Anishinaabe trapper named Geean traded with the HBC. Geean apparently acquired a gun, two capotes, a blanket, some thread, and a pair of horn combs in addition to an axe, a crooked knife, a file, and a quantity of tobacco in the autumn of 1846. Seven and a half months later, he and his companions returned for sewing needles, tobacco, a pair of leggings, and other items.[5] As becomes evident from other izhibii'igem sources, Geean was Jiiyaan, father of Giizhig (see Figure 14), who was the patriarch of the Namegosibii Anishinaabeg. Jiiyaan Geean was Dedibaayaanimanook's paternal great-grandfather, hence, my maternal great-great-grandfather.

It is interesting to note how Dedibaayaanimanook and other descendants followed in their great-grandfather's footsteps when they too visited the Lac Seul maamawichigewigamig—the term Namegosibii Anishinaabeg use for HBC posts, outposts, and stores—approximately a century later:

E-diba'amaadingiban ako, e-izhaayang adaawewigamigong, ni maamawiminaaaban, Niingaanaashiik, niin, idash Moshish, Ginôkoban, Shkwe, maamawichigewigamig e-diba'amaang.[6]

At Treaty Time we all went to the store together, Niingaanaashiik, and I, Moshish, the late Ginôk, Shkwe, to the Hudson's Bay store when we received our payments.

Dedibaayaanimanook and four of her cousin-siblings were teenagers in the mid-1930s when they too browsed the HBC trading post, now functioning more as a retail store than a trading post, during a visit to Lac Seul at Treaty Time. Although Namegosibii Anishinaabeg now had the convenience of using treaty money for acquiring goods, their pre-treaty aanikoobidaaganag had the freedom to travel, hunt, trap, barter, and purchase as they chose, unencumbered by izhibii'igem treaty terms that dictate where and how people may live and travel.

The merchandise that Namegosibii Anishinaabeg procured suggests not only the extent and nature of their participation in and exposure to capitalism's ideology of consumption, but also their preferences and

activities over time and across the generations as they reflected their abil-
ilty to maintain Anishinaabe philosophies and values. In her biographical
dadibaajim, for example, Dedibaayaanimanook mentions the Namegosibii
Anishinaabe fondness for plaid, or skaajimaniigin, the Scotsman's cloth, as
they called it (Figure 28). The greater their use of wemitigoozhi-produced
goods, the greater the erosion of traditional, land-based ways of living, as
Dedibaayaanimanook implies in her previously quoted dadibaajim, "Gaye
more and more, biinish gii'ani-ayaawag gegoon."

An important aspect of Namegosibii Anishinaabe identity as recorded
in the HBC documents relates to their traditional names, particularly
those written prior to the signing of the treaty and its adhesion. With
reports from across the homeland territories containing several names
that incorporate the word "giizhig," an explanation of its meaning and
usage is helpful for understanding the extent of its popularity among
the Anishinaabeg. "Giizhig," translating into English as day or sky, was
commonly combined with various word stems by using prefixes or
suffixes. HBC record keepers, for example, wrote the names in Roman
orthography as Nanah e Kejick Waish Kung, Show on ee Kijick, Mawbin
wai wai Kijick, Kaw Kai Kijick waish Kong, Kijick O, and Na na Kijick.[7]
These texts do not follow a standardized system of spelling, and without
actually hearing them pronounced by an Anishinaabemowin speaker—as
would happen within an oral society—it is difficult to decode their correct
meaning. The name Show on ee Kijick, for example, may have to do with
the southern sky where Zhaawan resides. Both Waish Kung and waish
Kong possibly refer to deer, caribou, or moose antlers, in which case it
would likely denote the person's odoodem totem. According to the written
record, these individuals were contemporaries of Jiiyaan Cheean, who,
as we have just noted, also traded at the HBC post in Lac Seul throughout the nineteenth century. It should be pointed that the HBC created
districts throughout the continent, with each having a main trading post.
The company's post at Lac Seul was situated within the company's Lac La
Pluie district in what is now northwest Ontario.

The name Giizhig, regardless of its spelling, plays a significant role
in the people's sense of identity. After the signing of Treaty 3 in 1873, as
the state and churches increasingly pushed for assimilation, Anishinaabe
people began to adopt the European convention of using family surnames.
Giizhig therefore became the surname of Giizhig's sons and their

Figure 28.
Skaajimaniigin in Namegosibiing (1930s). Dedibaayaanimanook (right)
wears a tartan skirt. Her cousin-sibling, Ginôk Eliza (centre), has on a tartan
blouse.

descendants. It has become symbolic of their shared heritage and sense of commonality, even as they retain adik odoodemiwaa as their caribou totem. Characterizing the oral custom, members of the Namegosibiing community would have pronounced Giizhig in more or less the same way. Today, however, Giizhig's scattered descendants give meaning to and conceptualize[8] Giizhig with varying spellings that include Kejick, Kesick, Keesick, Keesic, Kiishik, and so forth, depending on how government, church, and corporate officials wrote them down in their records.

Towards the end of the nineteenth century, several HBC documents make references to geographically based indications of the Namegosibii Anishinaabe people's identity. In his inspection report of 1890, for instance, E.K. Beeston mentions the death of the "Trout Lake Chief" as a reason for decreased profits. Although the record does not specify the individual's identity, it refers to Namegosibiing as "Trout Lake, about a 2 days canoe journey to the North up the Trout River from Mattawan."[9] In his 1899 summary report, Beeston wrote that "the trade with the Trout Lake Indians to the North" was a part of the post's regional activities, describing it to be "good Beaver and Otter Country."[10]

As noted earlier, the existence of an HBC post at Big Trout Lake in the Severn River region makes it important to establish the origin or location of each Trout Lake report. Any mention of Trout Lake as simply Trout Lake must relate to the Lac Seul post in some way in order to confirm its Namegosibiing identity. The above-quoted documents identify a Trout Lake that is recognizable as Namegosibiing because their description matches that of dadibaajim in terms of canoe travels along the Namegosi-ziibi Trout River through Maadaawaang Mattawa to and from Lac Seul. They present an accurate description of Namegosibiing's location.

While Namegosibiing is the Namegosibii Anishinaabe people's home, the place where the origins of their identity are rooted, the spaces over which they journeyed and conducted their activities stretched from Obizhigokaang Lac Seul in the south to memegweshiwi-zaa'igan north-east of Namegosibiing. Both HBC records and dadibaajim thus affirm the expansiveness of the people's travels and traditional-use territories.

In his 1890 report, Beeston listed the debts of the entire Lac Seul community together as "Lac Seul Indian Debts" in reference to the amount of cash that Anishinaabe people owed the HBC when they procured goods that they would later pay for with fur pelts. The names of the Namegosibiing forefathers were written in a subsection titled "Trout Lake, Indian Debts."[11] Recording Namegosibii Anishinaabe trappers as a group distinct from the others of the Lac Seul post implicitly acknowledged that they were a community in their own right.

For the same profit-related reasons of any corporation, the Hudson's Bay Company maintained meticulous records of each individual's debts, advances, payments, and purchases. In so doing, it inscribed the name of each trapper who traded with the company into the izhibii'igem archival record. The accounts receivables sheet titled "Trout Lake, Indian Debts" in Beeston's 1890 summary, for example, includes the names of several of the Namegosibii Anishinaabe aanikoobidaaganag. Akanakijik, George Angeconeb, John Angeconeb, Kysick, Naterway Kysick, Maskeshegan, Skandaga with Alex and Donald, and Peask[12] were trappers who were among the Namegosibii Anishinaabe ancestors, as Dedibaayaanimanook's dadibaajim confirms.

The eldest participants of this book were acquainted with some of these individuals personally. Both Gwiishkwa'oo Eliza Angeconeb and Oo'oons John Paul Kejick, for example, knew Naadowe Naterway Kysick and the two brothers, Maashkizhiigan Maskeshegan George Ashen and Oshkaandagaa Skandaga Charlie Ashen. Dedibaayaanimanook, of course, knew them well, but she alone knew Giizhig Kysick personally, being approximately seven years old when he passed. The others on Beeston's 1890 list, including Gichimookomaan George Angeconeb and Gaa-dadaakogaadej, were already deceased before any of the participants were born. Namegosibii dadibaajim tells us that Akanakijik and Peask were Eginegiizhig and Beshk, respectively. They too were relatives whose names were often mentioned in conversations that Dedibaayaanimanook heard among her elders.

Indicating that the HBC occasionally employed Anishinaabe individuals, E.K. Beeston's 1899 regional report mentioned that the "Trout Lake Indians to the North" traded at the Mattawan outpost and that "[a] few goods are sent there in charge of an Indian."[13] However, he did not indicate the person's name. Twenty-one years later, L.A. Romanet wrote a regional report that included a subsection titled "Trout Lake: New outpost of Pine Ridge."[14] His 1920 document also stated that Namegosibiing Trout Lake was the most strategic location from which to counter the activities of independent trader Swain, to whom he referred when he commented that a "small fur trader like Swain can upset the spirit of the old Company." Romanet noted that "we have an Indian, Chean Keesic, who is trading for the Company." His hand-drawn map of the region included a small circular mark captioned "H.B.C. trader" in the upper right quadrant of Namegosibiing Trout Lake.[15] This location is Jiibayi-zaagiing Jackfish Bay, where the families of both Jiiyaan (Oo'oons's paternal grandfather) and Dedibayaash (Dedibaayaanimanook's father) lived during the winter trapping season.

In the same 1920 report, Romanet noted that "the trader is not success-ful by any means," although "Swain's man established in the southern part of Trout Lake is making good."[16] It is understandable that Oo'oons's pater-nal grandfather, Jiiyaan Chean Keesic, was "not successful by any means,"[17] given that the work required him to be a successful trader at the expense of fur producers who were his siblings, cousins, nephews, and other kin. Jiiyaan's first loyalties were toward family members and relatives, not a profit-driven, foreign-owned entity, and in accordance with Anishinaabe protocol, he was respectful of their preference to deal with independent trader Swain. In response to my query, Dedibaayaanimanook stated that she never heard any discussions about an arrangement between Jiiyaan and the HBC, perhaps because she was too young a child to have formed memories of such conversations.

Anishinaabe trappers did prefer Swain to the "old Company," and as Dedibaayaanimanook's dadibaajim tells us and Romanet's 1920 report implies, he was a pleasant man. He was known to Namegosibii Anishinaabeg as "baamadaawe," a term that describes the trader's mobility, independence, and accessibility, which were in sharp contrast to the HBC's characteristic rigidity and lack of friendliness. In order to accommodate both the Namegosibii and Ikwewi-zaa'igan Woman Lake Anishinaabeg, baamadaawe Swain situated himself east of Namegosibiing, where Dedibaayaanimanook and members of her family travelled during the late 1920s and early 1930s. She describes a visit to Swain's post by first tracing the route they used:

Minitgwashkiigaag, Manoomini-zaa'igan, Gichi-onigamiing gaa izhinikaadeg. Zaaga'iganiins ateg gaa-gii' ayizhaayaang Ikwewi-zaa'igan e-izhaayaang, George Swain gaa-gii' izhinikaazoj. Agaawaa ingikendaan e-gii'

izhaayaangiban, indede, e-agaashiinzhiyaang, Gichi-jôj,
e-bimaakogomoyaang. Ingii' abinoonjiizhiwimin.[18]

Minitgwashkiigaag, Rice Lake, the one called Gichi-
onigamiing. There is a small lake where we would go, on our
way to Woman Lake, [to] the one named George Swain. I can
hardly remember that we went [with] my father, when Gichi-
jôj and I were little, that we would paddle. [Not us, because]
we were young children.

After her visit to the trading post, the young Dedibaayaanimanook
reported Swain's merchandise to be nowhere as appealing as she had
imagined. Although she visited baamadaawe's trading post no more
than once or twice, her father, brother, and other male relatives made
frequent journeys to replenish basic supplies and sell furs. Living in
Gaa-minitigwashkiigaag, her family found Swain's establishment to be
much closer than that of the HBC at Post Narrows on Red Lake.

Perusal of nineteenth-century samples of the HBC archives ascertains
that the company recognized Namegosibii Anishinaabeg as a discrete group.
Discussions about a strategic location for an outpost drew the company's
attention to the trappers' traditional-use territories and the distances and
direction of travel relative to the Lac Seul post. The company records
named individuals, usually writing down their Anishinaabe names as they
were able to spell them, but it is the dadibaajim oral record that can explain
who these individuals were as the Namegosibii Anishinaabe ancestors.

Treaty Annuity Pay Lists (1876–1897, 1910);[19] 1901 Canada Census[20]

Written records are useful in various ways for seeking Namegosibii
Anishinaabe identity. In their pursuit of maximum profits, for example,
the HBC carefully recorded and tracked the Namegosibii Anishinaabe
trappers, writing down their names in a secondary category of the
Lac Seul Anishinaabeg. This classification continued even after the
Namegosibiing community formally joined the Lac Seul Band in 1874.
Indian Affairs, on the other hand, did not make a point of differentiating
Namegosibii Anishinaabeg in terms of whether they lived in Lac Seul or

elsewhere. Rather, all payees' names appeared in alphabetical order under
the heading of Treaty No. #3, Lac Seul, Trout, and Sturgeon Lakes Band.

During the earlier years of record keeping, the Department of Indian
Affairs lacked a method for ensuring the accuracy of how they recorded
ages and dates of birth. One of its main concerns, once the treaties were
secured and the nation-building enterprise commenced, was to avoid
delaying or duplicating treaty payments to the Anishinaabe people.
Catherine Butler, a reference archivist at Library and Archives Canada,
explains that "lists were created in order to record the fulfillment of a
Treaty obligation and to ensure that the amount of payment made to
each household was accurate . . . [but] full nominal lists did not become
common practice until the 1930s."[21]

Treaty payment records provide sufficient information to map identities and places of origin, while dadibaajim describes lineal relationships.
Namegosibii Anishinaabe people primarily traced their kinship through
male family members, but in this book, I examine both male and female
lines of descent wherever possible. Biblical names, appearing with
increasing frequency in the written record, indicate the emergence of a
Christianized dimension to Anishinaabe identity at the turn of the twentieth century. As the Beeston report of 1899 noted, the church mission
was located close to both Treaty Point and the HBC post, effectively
creating a state-church-corporate sphere of control. Dedibaayaanimanook
and Oo'oons discuss how schools and churches effectuated changes in
Anishinaabe names and identities by means of the wemitigoozhiiwin-
ikaazowin European naming practices as follows:

O: O'omaa wemitigoozhi owiinzowin ogii' ayaasiin.
Bizhishig Anishinaabe. [Niin,] "Oo'oons." Baamaash
[wemitigoozhi owiinzowin gii' miinigooyaan] i'iwedi
gaa-gii' ganoonigooyaan.
D: "Ziiga'andaaso" gaa-izhinikaadeg gii
wemitigoozhiiwinikaazoj abinoonjiizh. "Ziiga'andaaso"
izhinikaade.[22]

O: Here, no one had a European settler's name. Only
Anishinaabe names. [I was] "Oo'oons." Only after [receiving
an English name], over there, I was spoken to.

D: What is known as water baptism, when a child is given a
European settler name. It is called baptism.

Oo'oons comments about a time when no one in his community was
without an Anishinaabe name, as he alludes to his own experiences. When
he left home, he was Oo'oons, but upon arriving at boarding school, he
was suddenly John Paul. Together with Dedibaayaanimanook's observation that children received European names at church baptismal ceremonies, his remarks show that schools and churches worked in concert
to erase Anishinaabe names and reformulate Anishinaabe people's identities to incorporate them into the European image. Pay lists and census
records replicated these changes.

Dadibaajim clarifies state-generated information by providing
Anishinaabe names—whenever they still exist—for the increasing number
of European-named individuals. By referencing English and anglicized
Anishinaabe (often barely legible) names along with the approximate
birth dates appearing on treaty pay lists and census data with Anishinaabe
names that dadibaajim mentions, a coherent identity description of the
Namegosibii Anishinaabeg begins to emerge. The census record, for
example, lists the name Keewassin "South Wind" (which includes the
quotation marks). It is Dedibaayaanimanook's dadibaajim, however,
that more fully identifies Keewassin "South Wind" as her paternal uncle,
Giiweyaas(h)in. This information may be of interest to the descendants
of Giiweyaas(h)in Keewassin "South Wind."

Interestingly, it was from Dedibaayaanimanook's dadibaajim rather
than the written text that I first learned Giiweyaas(h)in's Christian name
was William and that the Anishinaabe name of his eldest son was Aat(ch)
ayaa John Keewassin. Although he had passed before I was born, my mother's cousin Aat(ch)ayaa was a frequent focus of attention in her dadibaajim
during my childhood, often in humorous ways. Hence, I first heard of John
Keewassin as Aat(ch)ayaa and later learned that his father Giiweyaas(h)
in was William. The confusion I felt on realizing that Aat(ch)ayaa and
John Keewassin were one and the same person, however, could not have
remotely compared with Oo'oons's experience of having his identity so
abruptly and jarringly altered when he arrived at boarding school.

By keeping Namegosibii dadibaajim in mind while searching through treaty pay lists and the census records, it is possible to recognize and confirm the identities of key protagonists in the Namegosibii Anishinaabe narrative. I illustrate this method by focusing on five lead figures from among the forebears whose recorded information is the most legible: Giizhig Keejick, Angeconeb Ayangeequonabe, Otcheechackeepetang's mother (and Otcheechackeepetang himself, upon his mother's passing), Gaagige Abinoonjiizh Kahkeekaiabinoochee, and the person Indian agents referred to as Geean's widow. It remains unclear whether Geean's widow was Giizhig's mother, stepmother, or stepmother-aunt, given that Jiiyaan Geean had six wives. Four of these five individuals were among the group of 68 men, 82 women, 199 children, plus 10 others at the Lac Seul Treaty Time of 1876. The fifth, Otcheechackeepetang (also spelled Otcheechawkoopatung) and (or) his mother first received payments at Mattawan on the English River, then at Wabauskang, both located in Treaty 3 territory (see Figure 7). With guidance from dadibaajim, the documentation of these individuals in treaty pay lists and census information illustrates how ancestral lineages threaded themselves through various Anishinaabe communities and across the homeland territories.

Giizhig Keejick

Pay list Table 3 includes data of Giizhig and Moonz(h)oniikwe Nookomiban's children. The census record of 1901 accurately reflects Moonz(h)oniikwe Nookomiban's status as grande dame of the Namegosibii Anishinaabeg by identifying her as Okeemahcway (Chief Woman). In contrast, her 1930 death certificate refers to her as a "Home Maker" named Mary (Figure 29), recasting and erasing aspects of her pre-eminent Anishinaabe identity. In this study, I use her Namegosibii Anishinaabe name Moonz(h)oniikwe in honour of her memory as the community's matriarch and as Nookomiban to express her identity in accordance with the dadibaajim narratives of her granddaughter, Dedibaayaanimanook.

The pay list record shows Giizhig's only daughter to be in attendance for treaty payments in 1877, then again from 1879 to 1884. Dedibaayaanimanook has always maintained that her grandparents' only daughter passed in early infancy. Hence, the written record differs from the

Table 3.

Lac Seul Treaty Pay List Records of Giizhig Keesick and Moonzhoniikwe Mary's
Children (1876–1897)

DATE	DAUGHTERS	SONS	TOTAL
1876			6
1877	1	5	6
1878			8
1879	1	7	8
1880	1	7	8
1881	1	7	8
1882	1	8	9
1883	1	8	9
1884	1	8	9
1885		8	8
1886		8	8
1887		7[a]	7
1888		7	7
1889		7	7
1890		7	7
1891		6[b]	6
1892		6	6
1893		6	6
1894		6	6
1895		6	6
1896		5[c]	5
1897		5	5

Note. Dedibaayaanimanook's dadibaajim states that the Giizhigs' only daughter passed in early infancy.

a Giizhigs' son Giiweyaas(h)in William "South Wind" married Gibichigiizhigook Eliza and left the Giizhig family pay list.

b Mooniyaans Thomas was removed from the family listing when he married Maajiigiizhigook Mary.

c Naadowe Robert married Omashkiigookwe Sarah Goodwin.

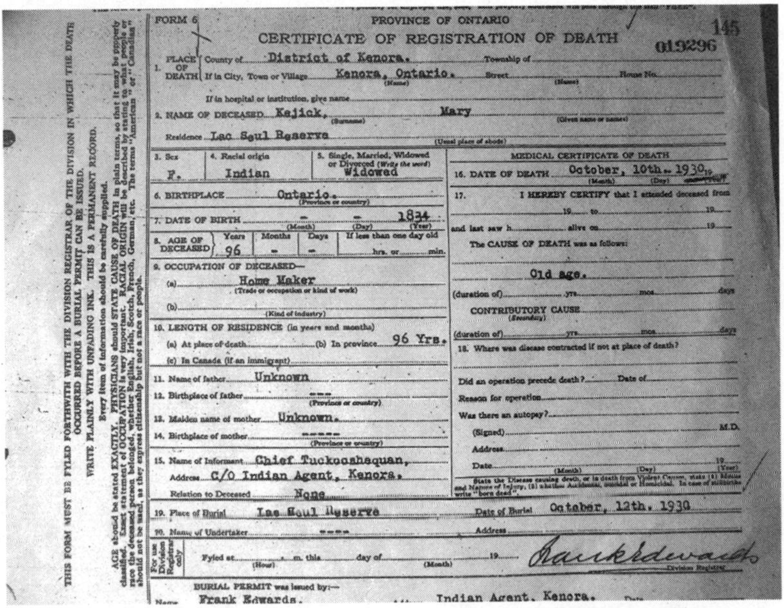

THIS FORM MUST BE FYLED FORTHWITH WITH THE DIVISION REGISTRAR OF THE DIVISION IN WHICH THE DEATH OCCURRED BEFORE A BURIAL PERMIT CAN BE ISSUED.
WRITE PLAINLY WITH UNFADING INK. THIS IS A PERMANENT RECORD.
Every item of information should be carefully supplied.
AGE should be stated EXACTLY. PHYSICIANS should state CAUSE OF DEATH in plain terms, so that it may be properly classified. Exact statement of OCCUPATION is very important. RACIAL ORIGIN will be described by stating to what people or race the deceased person belonged, whether English, Irish, Scotch, French, German, etc. The terms "American" or "Canadian" should not be used, as they express citizenship but not a race or people.

FORM 6

PROVINCE OF ONTARIO

CERTIFICATE OF REGISTRATION OF DEATH

145

019296

1. PLACE OF DEATH: County of District of Kenora. Township of
If in City, Town or Village Kenora, Ontario. (Name) Street (Name) House No.
If in hospital or institution, give name
2. NAME OF DECEASED Kejick, (Surname) Mary (Given name or names)
Residence Lac Seul Reserve (Usual place of abode)
3. Sex F. 4. Racial origin Indian 5. Single, Married, Widowed or Divorced (Write the word) Widowed
6. BIRTHPLACE Ontario. (Province or country)
7. DATE OF BIRTH – (Month) – (Day) 1834 (Year)
8. AGE OF DECEASED Years 96 Months – Days – If less than one day old ... hrs. or ... min.
9. OCCUPATION OF DECEASED—
(a) Home Maker (Trade or occupation or kind of work)
(b) (Kind of industry)
10. LENGTH OF RESIDENCE (in years and months)
(a) At place of death ... (b) In province 96 Yrs.
(c) In Canada (if an immigrant)
11. Name of father Unknown
12. Birthplace of father --- (Province or country)
13. Maiden name of mother Unknown.
14. Birthplace of mother ----- (Province or country)
15. Name of Informant Chief Tuckcoshequan,
Address C/O Indian Agent, Kenora.
Relation to Deceased None

MEDICAL CERTIFICATE OF DEATH
16. DATE OF DEATH October, 10th. 1930 (Month) (Day) (Year)
17. I HEREBY CERTIFY that I attended deceased from ... 19... to ... 19...
and last saw h... alive on ... 19...
The CAUSE OF DEATH was as follows:
Old age.
(duration of) ... yrs. ... mos. ... days
CONTRIBUTORY CAUSE (Secondary)
(duration of) ... yrs. ... mos. ... days
18. Where was disease contracted if not at place of death?
Did an operation precede death? ... Date of
Reason for operation
Was there an autopsy?
(Signed) ... M.D.
Address
Date ... (Month) (Day) 19... (Year)
State the Disease causing death, or in death from Violent Causes, state (1) Means and Nature of Injury, (2) whether Accidental, Suicidal or Homicidal. In case of stillbirths write "born dead".

19. Place of Burial Lac Seul Reserve Date of Burial October, 12th. 1930
20. Name of Undertaker ---- Address
For use of Division Registrar only: Fyled at ... m. this ... day of ... (Month) 19... Frank Edwards Division Registrar
BURIAL PERMIT was issued by:—
Name Frank Edwards. Indian Agent, Kenora. Date

Figure 29.
Moonz(h)oniikwe Nookomiban's death certificate. Dedibaayaanimanook's paternal grandmother's Anishinaabe name was Moonz(h)oniikwe. Courtesy of John Richthammer.

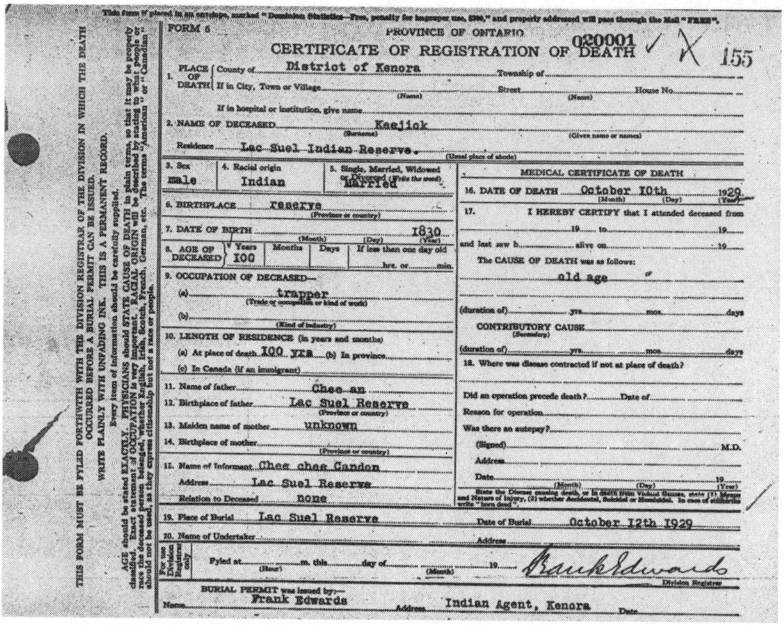

This form if placed in an envelope, marked "Dominion Statistics—Free, penalty for improper use, $300," and properly addressed will pass through the Mail "FREE".

THIS FORM MUST BE FYLED FORTHWITH WITH THE DIVISION REGISTRAR OF THE DIVISION IN WHICH THE DEATH OCCURRED BEFORE A BURIAL PERMIT CAN BE ISSUED.
WRITE PLAINLY WITH UNFADING INK. THIS IS A PERMANENT RECORD.
Every item of information should be carefully supplied.
AGE should be stated EXACTLY. PHYSICIANS should STATE CAUSE OF DEATH in plain terms, so that it may be properly classified. Exact statement of OCCUPATION is very important. RACIAL ORIGIN will be described by stating to what people or race the deceased person belonged, whether English, Irish, Scotch, French, German, etc. The terms "American" or "Canadian" should not be used, as they express citizenship but not a race or people.

FORM 6

PROVINCE OF ONTARIO

CERTIFICATE OF REGISTRATION OF DEATH 020001 ✓ X 155

1. PLACE OF DEATH: County of District of Kenora Township of
If in City, Town or Village (Name) Street (Name) House No.
If in hospital or institution, give name

2. NAME OF DECEASED Keejick (Surname) (Given name or names)
Residence Lac Suel Indian Reserve. (Usual place of abode)

3. Sex: male
4. Racial origin: Indian
5. Single, Married, Widowed or Divorced (Write the word): Married

6. BIRTHPLACE reserve (Province or country)

7. DATE OF BIRTH (Month) (Day) 1830 (Year)

8. AGE OF DECEASED: Years 100 | Months | Days | If less than one day old ... hrs. or ... min.

9. OCCUPATION OF DECEASED—
(a) trapper (Trade or occupation or kind of work)
(b) (Kind of industry)

10. LENGTH OF RESIDENCE (in years and months)
(a) At place of death 100 yrs (b) In province
(c) In Canada (if an immigrant)

11. Name of father Chee an
12. Birthplace of father Lac Suel Reserve (Province or country)
13. Maiden name of mother unknown
14. Birthplace of mother (Province or country)
15. Name of Informant Chee chee Candon
Address Lac Suel Reserve
Relation to Deceased none

MEDICAL CERTIFICATE OF DEATH

16. DATE OF DEATH October 10th (Month) (Day) 1929 (Year)

17. I HEREBY CERTIFY that I attended deceased from ... 19... to ... 19...
and last saw h... alive on ... 19...
The CAUSE OF DEATH was as follows:
old age
(duration of) ... yrs. ... mos. ... days
CONTRIBUTORY CAUSE (Secondary)
(duration of) ... yrs. ... mos. ... days

18. Where was disease contracted if not at place of death?
Did an operation precede death? ... Date of
Reason for operation
Was there an autopsy?
(Signed) ... M.D.
Address
Date (Month) (Day) 19... (Year)

State the Disease causing death, or in death from Violent Causes, state (1) Means and Nature of Injury, (2) whether Accidental, Suicidal or Homicidal. In case of stillbirths write "born dead".

19. Place of Burial Lac Suel Reserve Date of Burial October 12th 1929

20. Name of Undertaker ... Address

For use of Division Registrar only: Fyled at ... (Hour) ...m. this ... day of ... (Month) 19... Frank Edwards, Division Registrar

BURIAL PERMIT was issued by:—
Name Frank Edwards Address Indian Agent, Kenora Date

Figure 30.

Giizhig's death certificate. This document inaccurately identifies Giizhig's place of both birth and burial as a "reserve." In fact, he was born and buried in Namegosibiing Trout Lake, which was never a reserve. Namegosibii dadibaajim explains that there was one year between the deaths of Giizhig and Moonz(h)oniikwe. The izhibii'igem text document is correct in this regard. Courtesy of John Richthammer.

Table 4.

1901 Census Record and Dedibaayaanimanook's Dadibaajim of Mooniyaans Thomas and Maajiigiizhigook Mary's Children

DAUGHTERS	SONS	DATE OF BIRTH	RELIGION
	Omooday Paul	1893–1894	Anglican
Midaasogiizhigook Maud or Edith (?)		1894	Anglican
Naansii Nancy		?	Anglican

Note. Namegosibii dadibaajim tells us that these were not the only children of Mooniyaans Thomas and Maajiigiizhigook Mary (see Agger, *Following Nimishoomis*), who were both listed as "pagan."

Table 5.

1901 Census Record and Dedibaayaanimanook's Dadibaajim of Giiweyaas(h)in Keewassin "South Wind" and Gibichigiizhigook Eliza's Children

DAUGHTERS	SONS	DATE OF BIRTH	RELIGION
	Aat(ch)ayaa John	1887–1888	Anglican
	Anama'egaabaw James Ashen	1891	Anglican
	Oshkaandagaa Charlie Ashen	1893	Anglican
	Paul	?	Anglican

Note. Giiweyaas(h)in Keewassin "South Wind" and Gibichigiizhigook Petshay Keesheekook Eliza were both "pagan." Dedibaayaanimanook's dadibaajim provides the names of the rest of the Giiweyaas(h)ins' children (see Agger, *Following Nimishoomis*).

Table 6.

1901 Census Record and Dedibaayaanimanook's Dadibaajim of Naadowe Robert and Omashkiigookwe Sarah's Children

DAUGHTERS	SONS	DATE OF BIRTH	RELIGION
	Namegosibiiwinini Sam	1897	Anglican
	Nishki'aa Isaac	?	Anglican

Note. Both Naadowe Robert and Omashkiigookwe Sarah were listed as Anglicans. The rest of the Naadowes' children are discussed in Dedibaayaanimanook's dadibaajim (see Agger, *Following Nimishoomis*).

Table 7.

1901 Census Record and Dedibaayaanimanook's Dadibaajim of Dedibayaash William and Mary Ann's Children

DAUGHTERS	SONS	DATE OF BIRTH	RELIGION
	Waasegiizhig Donald	?	CC
"Lizza"		?	CC

Note. Both Dedibayaash and Mary Ann were identified as members of the "CC" church. Their daughter Gweyesh Annie does not appear in this record. Dedibaayaanimanook's dadibaajim explains the development of Dedibayaash's family after the passing of Mary Ann (see Agger, *Following Nimishoomis*).

Namegosibii Anishinaabe community's oral dadibaajim by approximately six years. Of interest, the pay lists indicate that Moonz(h)oniikwe was not present for at least eight payment gatherings. There are several possible reasons for her absence, all undoubtedly serious, but whatever they were, her non-attendance potentially diminished the family's total income for that period by the substantial amount of forty dollars.

Pay lists also show that Giizhig became a councillor on the passing of his Angeconeb relative in 1890, thus increasing his annual pay. Being involved in band council business, Giizhig would have had access to information about matters of interest or significance for the Namegosibii Anishinaabe community. Issues relating to treaty administration, Indian Act measures, plans to cut timber, the damming of rivers, and flooding of lakes across Anishinaabe lands were all critically important. According to the vital statistics record, Giizhig was born in 1830 and his death occurred on 10 October 1929 (Figure 30). Namegosibii Anishinaabe dadibaajim indicates that Giizhig lived longer than 100 years.

It is important to note the duplications in the Namegosibii Anishinaabe people's English names. To illustrate, Giizhig was Sam Keesick, his son Dedibayaash was William ("Bill") Sam Keesick, and his grandson Minzhinawebines was Sam William Keesick. Dedibaayaanimanook's partner (my father) resorted to using "Big Isaac" when referring to Naadowe and Omashkiigookwe's second child, Nishki'aa Isaac Keesick, as a means of differentiating him from another of Dedibaayaanimanook's cousins, Gwiiwish Isaac Keesick. These externally created names and changes, often confusing for both Anishinaabe people and latecomers alike, is reflected in data on religious affiliations appearing in Tables 4 to 7. For those who adhered to traditional spirituality, census enumerators wrote the letter "p" for "pagan" beside their names. It is evident that Christianity was becoming a noticeable force in Namegosibii Anishinaabe people's lives by the turn of the twentieth century, as fewer p's appeared beside names. As Dedibaayaanimanook's narrative above shows, Namegosibii dadibaajim recognizes the linkages between English names and the impacts of Christianity in their lives and Anishinaabe personhood.

During the year 1892–93, when Giizhig had already been a member of the Lac Seul Band Council as representative of the Namegosibii Anishinaabeg for two years, Ackewence, a councillor when Treaty 3 was signed, replaced the deceased John Cromarty, who was a signatory to the treaty adhesion of 1874. According to dadibaajim, Namegosibii Anishinaabeg heard about the chief who had, undoubtedly under considerable outside pressure, given his consent to wemitigoozhiwag's intent to harvest large tracts of on-reserve forest. People mentioned his name so frequently, in fact, that when Dedibaayaanimanook was a child, she and her playmates included him in their games by, ironically, naming the tallest tree after him. Information about events at the band level provide the larger, political contexts in which the aanikoobidaaganag ancestors lived. This helps us to appreciate the issues they faced.

The written records produce further information to augment Namegosibii Anishinaabe history. For example, Giizhig and Moonz(h)-oniikwe's son Naadowe Robert married Omashkiigookwe Sarah Goodwin, daughter of "Ossinaburg Indian" Pat Goodwin. See Table 6 (above) for census and dadibaajim information about Naadowe and Omashkiigookwe's family as it existed at the time. As mentioned above, Dedibaayaanimanook's dadibaajim tells us that the Naadowe and Omashkiigookwe family relocated to Oshkaandagaawi-zaa'igan Nungesser Lake, approximately two days' travel northwest of Namegosibiing, in the 1930s. Hence, izhibii'igem and dadibaajim together supply evidence that ancestral places of origin stretched from Oshkaandagaawi-zaa'igan Nungesser Lake to Osnaburgh, east of Namegosibiing.

Dadibaajim specifies that Mary Ann (see Table 7 above), first wife of Giizhig and Moonz(h)oniikwe's son Dedibayaash (Dedibaayaanimanook's father), and three of their children died under unusually tragic circumstances. Again, however, Anishinaabe convention does not allow us to discuss the details of these events outside the community. Canada's 1901 census record and dadibaajim list the children of Dedibayaash's second wife, Gaa-madweyaashiik Emma, and her first husband, Gichimookomaan George Angeconeb. Gaa-madweyaashiik's only child with her second husband, Dedibayaash, still with us today is Dedibaayaanimanook. While these relationships are complicated, it is necessary for descendants who seek to establish their identity to keep them in mind in order to understand these various lines of kinship and where they originate.

Jiiyaan Donald, another of Giizhig and Moonz(h)oniikwe's sons, and his first wife, Sarah Jeanne, were recorded as having no children at the time of the 1901 census. Dadibaajim tells of their daughter Moshish Mary, one of Dedibaayaanimanook's closest childhood companions, and her

Table 8.
Lac Seul Treaty Pay List Records of Ayangeequonabe's Family (1876–1897)

DATE	WOMEN	DAUGHTERS	SONS	TOTAL CHILDREN	TOTAL ATTENDANCE
1876	3			10	14
1877	3	3	7	10	14
1878	3	3	7	10	14
1879	3	3	9	12	16
1880	3	3	9	12	16
1881	3	3	8	11	15
1882	3	3	6	9	13
1883	3	4	6	10	14
1884	3	4	4[a]	8	12
1885	2	3	3	6	9
1886	2	3	3	6	9
1887	2	3	4	7	10
1888	2	2	4	6	9
1889	2	2	4	6	9
1890	2	1[b]	4	5	7[c]
1891	2	1	4	5	7
1892	2	1	4[d]	5	7
1893	2	1	3[e]	4	6
1894	2	1	3	4	6
1895	2	1	3	4	6
1896	2	1	3	4	6
1897	1	1	2[f]	3	4

Note. The spelling of Ayangeequonabe suggests that the original name in Anishinaabemowin is Aayaanjigwanaabe, the ongoing process of a bird's changing feathers, according to Butikofer's (Butikofer Papers) findings. This individual was probably Butikofer's "Old Angecomb."

a   A son, referred to as "Menwagujiqueb(?)" married and left the family listing to become #110 on the Mattawan pay list of 1884.

b   A daughter left the family to marry #14 of Wabauskang.

c   Ayangeequonabe passed in the winter of 1889–1890.

d   The eldest son, referred to as "Ayangeequonabe's son," replaced his deceased father as #4 and was listed as head of the family.

e   A son left the family to marry the daughter of #21 and become #169. He was Gichimookomaan George Angeconeb, Gwiishkwa'oo's paternal grandfather.

f   Ayangeequonabe's son "W" was deceased.

Table 9.

Mattawan Treaty Pay List Records of Otcheechackeepetang's Mother and
Otcheechackeepetang (1876–1897)

DATE	MEN	WOMEN	SONS	DAUGHTERS	TOTAL CHILDREN	TOTAL ATTENDANCE
1876	1	1			1[a]	4
1877	1	1		1	1	3
1878	1	1		1	1	3
1879	1	1		1	1	3
1880	1	1	1	1	2	4
1881	1	1	1	1	2	4
1882	1	1	1	1	2	4
1883	1	1	1	2	2	4
1884	1	1		2	2	4
1885	1	1		3	3	5
1886	1	1		3	3	5
1887	1	1		2	2	4
1888	1	1		3	3	5
1889	1	1	1	3	4	6
1890	1	1	2	3	5	7
1891	1	1	1	3	4	6
1892	1	1	1	4	5	7
1893	1	1		1[b]	1	3
1894	1			1	1	2
1895	1			1	1	2
1896	1			1	1	2
1897	1					1

Note. Indian Affairs did not provide Otcheechackeepetang's mother's name.

a   The "other" may have been Otcheechackeepetang's mother. If so, it is unclear why the record identified
her as the head the family in 1876. She disappeared from the record thereafter and was replaced as the
family head by her son Otcheechackeepetang.

b   Two female children were deceased during the winter of 1892–1893 while a daughter left to marry
Ayangeequanabe's son, who subsequently became #169 of Lac Seul (see Table 8). She was my maternal
grandmother, Gaa-madweyaashiik Emma.

younger sister, Moshishens. Giizhig and Moonz(h)oniikwe's two youngest
children, Netawibiitam John and Jiimis James, do not appear in the 1901
census. But dadibaajim records them for us. Dedibaayaanimanook explains
that the children of Netawibiitam John and his wife, Minogaabawiik,
or (as her grandchildren, great-nieces, and great-nephews all called
her) "Gookomens," included Detaginang Frank and Manzinigiizhig
James. Netawibiitam and Minogaabawiik and their family remained in
Namegosibiing for most of their lives. Giizhig and Moonz(h)oniikwe's
youngest son, Jiimis James, and his family, as Dedibaayaanimanook has
also stated, did not return to Namegosibiing from Lac Seul. With one
or two exceptions, all of Jiimis and Akandoo's approximately fourteen
children attended boarding school.

The pay lists and census records of that period did not usually contain
birthdates, although they frequently included individuals' ages. As previously noted, the year, month, day, and hour of an event were not part of
dadibaajim because Namegosibii Anishinaabe people adhered to their
traditional system of demarcating the time of events through the use of
contextual information. When people reported the birth of a child, they
included details that made it possible to infer the season of his or her
birth. Dadibaajim, to illustrate, states that Dedibaayaanimanook's sister
Gweyesh gave birth during their journey up the river to Namegosibiing.
This indicates that Aayizag Isaac (father of Martha Angeconeb Fiddler)
was born in late August or early September. Even closer attention to the
specifics of Dedibaayaanimanook's dadibaajim reveals information about
the location of Aayizag's place of birth by her mentioning the portage trail
that family members assisted Gweyesh to navigate.

In other cases, an unusual or rare event might have coincided with a
birth. Giiweyaas(h)in's grandson, Babiikwaakojaab, for example, was born
during a giizis eclipse. Such details make it possible to identify precise
dates if that is the information sought. During the time people lived a
traditional Anishinaabe way of life and events such as births, deaths,
illnesses, and so forth took place within the community, devices such as
clocks and calendars were not necessary. In my own family, four siblings
were born in Namegosibiing, with our maternal grandmother and aunts
acting as midwives. With watches and calendars in common use by then,
my father recorded the time and date of birth of three siblings in order
to provide a "legitimate" reporting to the appropriate authorities. Indian

Table 10.

Lac Seul Treaty Pay List Records of Kahkeekaiabinoochee's Family (1876–1897)

DATE	WOMEN	DAUGHTERS	SONS	TOTAL CHILDREN	TOTAL ATTENDANCE
1876	1			5	7
1877					
1878					
1879					
1880	1	2	5	7	9
1881	1	2	4	6	8
1882	1	1	5	6	8
1883	1	1	5	6	8
1884		1	5	6	7
1885		2	4	6	7
1886		2	3	5	6
1887		2	3	5	6
1888		2	4	6	7
1889		2	4	6	7
1890		2	5	7	8
1891		2	4	6	7
1892	1	2	4	6	8
1893		2	4	6	7
1894		2	4	6	7
1895		2	3	5	6
1896		2	2	4	5
1897	1	2	2	4	5

Note. The family appears not to have attended diba'amaadim for these three years. Whether they ever received payment for this period is unclear.

agents and the 1901 census enumerators did not obtain such specifics from their Anishinaabe participants.

Angeconeb Ayangeequonabe

We may infer from both the Indian Affairs izhibii'igem record and Dedibaayaanimanook's dadibaajim that Ayangeequonabe was a contemporary of Giizhig (see "Old Angecomb," Figure 24). Because polygyny was still fairly common at the time, the three women who accompanied Ayangeequonabe for the first several payments may have been his wives (see Table 8). The pay lists, without any details, show that Ayangeequonabe was employed by the Lac Seul Indian agency from 1879 to 1884, after which he became a Lac Seul Band councillor. Upon Ayangeequonabe's death in the winter of 1889–90, his son became #4 on the pay list, in accordance with what was apparently the recording convention of giving a number to the head of each family. In 1892–93 another son, Gichimookomaan George Angeconeb, married the daughter of Otcheechackeepetang, #21 of Wabauskang. We know from dadibaajim that she was Gaa-madweyaashiik Emma (zhashagi odoodem pelican totem), Dedibaayaanimanook's mother and my maternal and Gwiishkwa'oo Eliza's paternal grandmother.

Otcheechackeepetang's Mother; Otcheechackeepetang

Treaty pay lists, the census record, and dadibaajim are also helpful for tracking the Namegosibii Anishinaabe people's ancestry through Gaa-madweyaashiik Emma. In 1876, her grandmother, Otcheechackeepetang's mother, attended diba'amaadim at Maadaawaang Mattawan (see Table 9). Situated at the convergence of the English and Chukuni rivers, approximately 100 kilometres northwest of Obizhigokaang Lac Seul, Maadaawaang Mattawan was where another HBC Lac Seul outpost was located. It was a convenient location for the Anishinaabe people to collect their treaty payments and where the HBC expected to obtain those payments either by selling goods or collecting on outstanding debts.

Namegosibii dadibaajim states that Gaa-madweyaashiik Emma and her family originated from the Biigaanjigamiing Pikangikum community on Berens River in what would become Treaty 5 territory. Later, when she was still a young child, they relocated to Gull Rock and Two Island Lakes, immediately south of Red Lake. It was the reason why the Otcheechackeepetang family collected treaty payments at Maadaawaang. Gaa-madweyaashiik married her first husband, Gichimookomaan George Angeconeb, in 1892–93, according to the written record, thus gaining status with the Lac Seul Band while losing her membership in the Otcheechackeepetang family. According to the written record for the same year, a daughter of the family was deceased. This may have been the individual Dedibaayaanimanook once referred to when she stated that one of her maternal aunts had drowned.

Dedibaayaanimanook's dadibaajim speaks of illnesses that affected community members in ways that inevitably would have prevented them from attending treaty payment gatherings. Giiweyaas(h)in's fifth son perished when he caught a virus while attending to business at Post Narrows on Red Lake. By choosing not to attempt to return home, however, he prevented further losses in lives. Dadibaajim also suggests that harm was sometimes the result of onjinem or "bad medicine." To reiterate, however, these types of events are waawiimbaajimowin topics about which details must remain within the Namegosibii Anishinaabe community.

Dadibaajim explains that there were other ways by which the Namegosibii Anishinaabe ancestry traces to Otcheechackeepetang. Dedibaayaanimanook stated that Gichimookomaan George Angeconeb and Gaa-madweyaashiik Emma's daughter Annie had a daughter, Gwejech (Dedibaayaanimanook's niece), who married Giizhig and Moonz(h) oniikwe's grandson, Maashkizhiigan. Of interest, it was Jiimisens, a son of Gichimookomaan and Gaa-madweyaashiik Emma's daughter Agnes, who helped Dedibaayaanimanook locate her parents after she flew to Sioux Lookout for the hospital birth of her second child. At that time (1946), Dedibaayaanimanook's parents still adhered to the custom of spending several weeks of summer in the Obizhigokaang Lac Seul region.

Kahkeekaiabinoochee (Child Forever)

Kahkeekaiabinoochee Lac Seul #57 and his family were absent from Treaty Time for three consecutive years, but there is no information to suggest reasons for their non-attendance (see Table 10). Of pertinence to the

Namegosibii Anishinaabe community, Kahkeekaiabinoochee's daughter married Giizhig and Moonz(h)oniikwe's eldest son, Mooniyaans Thomas, Lac Seul #165, in 1890–91 (see Table 3). The record referred to her as Mary, but dadibaajim states that Giizhig gave her the name Maajiigiizhigook to denote her entry into the Giizhigoog house. It was Maajiigiizhigook who, just hours before her passing, gave a special blessing to Dedibaayaanimanook.

Jiiyaan Geean's Widow Meequeneke

Pay lists referred to our fifth individual of significance as Cheean's widow from 1876 until 1882, when the record more specifically identified her as #22 Cheean's widow Meequeneke. Usually, pay lists did not include the name of a widow, wife, mother, or child. Rather, a female individual was listed as so-and-so's widow or mother. Beginning in 1882, however, the records began to include the names of women who arrived for payments as heads of households. In 1883 and 1884, #22 Cheean's widow Meequeneke was again on the list but the word "dead" was inscribed in the remarks column for each of the two years. Finally, in 1885 and thereafter, Cheean's widow Meequeneke was not on the list and #22 was no longer in use. With regard to the Lac Seul pay lists in general, it appears that recorders added additional details about individuals and events as time progressed. The names of women who arrived alone for their payments began to appear on the lists, even though the names of male individuals to whom they were previously associated were also listed.

As a charter member of the Jiiyaan family, Meequeneke played a lead role in the creation of the Namegosibii Anishinaabe identity narrative, whether she was Giizhig's mother or stepmother. Her continued presence at the treaty gatherings was an embodiment of the Jiiyaan house. Historically significant in the dadibaajim record of the Namegosibii Anishinaabeg, Meequeneke retained her Anishinaabe name and her own personhood-humanness in the annals of the wemitigoozhiwag.

Wemitigoozhiiwaadiziwin is evident in how the written record identified and documented Anishinaabe people. Treaty annuity pay lists, for example, reflected underlying ideologies and systems of forced assimilation that had enormous negative impacts on the people's personal, familial, and community lives. How Namegosibii Anishinaabeg conceptualized the notion of treaty is therefore worthy of note. Dedibaayaanimanook shares the following observations:

> **Onzaam bangii e-gii' miininj Anishinaabe zhooniyaan, mewinzha. Wiinge osha ogii'majendaanaawaa. Ogii'dazhindaanaawaa'. Gaawn misawaa daa-gii' debwetawaasiiwag aana andooshkamowaapan e-izhichigaadeg. Ogii' gikendaanaawaa' e-gii' makamindô odakiimiwaa'.**[23]

> Because they did not give enough money to Anishinaabeg right from the start. They had no confidence in it whatsoever. They would discuss it. Besides, no one would have listened had they asked. They knew that their homelands had been taken from them by force.

Dedibaayaanimanook was a child when she heard her elders discuss what they saw as the travesty of the treaty and its implementation. Some of the most senior elders of her childhood, including her grandfather Giizhig, Nookomiban Moonz(h)oniikwe, and older great-uncles and great-aunts who attended Treaty Time from 1876, would have been able to provide dadibaajim about first-hand experiences with how the Indian agents and other officials conducted the business of treaty.

In the elders' estimation, the wemitigoozhi's treaty-making and treaty-payment systems were an ersatz version of debwetam-inaakonigem, belief in the truthfulness of an agreement and how best to fulfill its terms. Namegosibii Anishinaabeg were well aware of the inadequacies of wemitigoozhi's diba'amaadim. They knew that the payments they received could in no way compensate for the homelands and resources, autonomy and self-sufficiency, and identity that wemitigoozhiwag attempted to erase from their lives through wemitigoozhiiwaadiziwin's acts of theft, seizure, deception, and duplicitous treaty making across the territories of their home. Using the term "makamindô," Dedibaayaanimanook presents a precise, accurately defined characterization of the violent, destructive nature of wemitigoozhi's actions. She points out that Namegosibii Anishinaabeg lived through these experiences with the knowledge that their protests would go unheeded because another of wemitigoozhiiwaadiziwin's realities was that Anishinaabe concerns were rarely, if ever, given attention. As we assess the historical record in conjunction with dadibaajim, it becomes evident that wemitigoozhiiwaadiziwin's ultimate goal was genocide, to rid the landscape of Anishinaabeg and Anishinaabewaadiziwin.

In another conversation, Dedibaayaanimanook and Oo'oons Kejick delve more deeply into the notion of diba'amaadim and its payments. Although both elders seemed bemused by the rationale for such a practice, it is evident by their comments that they are critiquing the fundamental irrationality of the wemitigoozhi's treaty-making methods:

O: Noondaagesii aaniin mayaa gaa-gii' izhichigaaniwang i'iwe treaty. Amiish etago gaa' izhi noondamaan, "Aazha wii' diba' amaadim."

D: Obizhigokaang gii' dazhi diba' amaadim treaty. "Zhooniyaa ogimaa gii' dagoshin," gaa' idamowaaj.

O: Noongom gaa izhinikaadamow[aaj], wedi, baamaa diba'amaad[ing].

D: Gaawn ingii'noondawaasiig.

O: Wegodo[gwen] etago naanwaabik gaa-gii' onji miinin[eng].

D: Namanj gaa' inanokiiyaan.

O: Amii maawiin i'iwe, awegwen iidog mayaa gaa-gii' inanokiigwen, gaa-gii' ikidogwen gaye, ini Anishinaabeg ji-doodawindô. Ji miinindwaa zhooniyaa, naanwaabik, dibi gaa'onji-doodawindô. Gaawn ingii' noondawaasii. Miish iko geyaabi wa'a apii niinzhwaaso niishtanashi bezhigo biboon eyaan, geyaabi naanwaabik nimiinigoo.[24]

O: [I never] heard the precise rationale for that treaty. The only thing I ever heard was, "Payments are going to take place."

D: The treaty payments took place at Lac Seul. That was what they meant by, "The money chief has arrived."

O: [That is] what they refer to today, over there, when they are getting paid.

D: I did not hear them [explain it].

O: I wonder about why we received only five dollars.

D: I wonder what work I did.

O: Perhaps that is it, for the work, whoever exactly did it, and because of what someone decided should be done with Anishinaabe people. That they be given cash, five dollars. I wonder why they were dealt with in that way. I have never heard him [Indian agent] explain it. And even now when I am seventy-one years old, I am still being given five dollars.

With his remarks, Oo'oons voices an observation that comes with a lifetime of experience with the diba'amaadim peculiarity. He states that he himself never worked specifically for the money he receives each year, and as he wonders what the work was and who may have done it, he questions why no one ever provided him with a sensible explanation for the payments. Similarly, Dedibaayaanimanook asks what she could have possibly done to earn the same paltry sum. Based on the Anishinaabe work ethic and debwewin truth's sense of integrity, Oo'oons concludes that the diba'amaadim payments are not a reimbursement at all. Dedibaayaanimanook, on the other hand, does not engage extensively with the narrative stream, not because she has nothing to contribute, but precisely because there is so much to be said.

Spoken in Anishinaabemowin and derived from an Anishinaabe frame of reference, the two elders' probing remarks are in fact a figurative treatment of the complex wemitigoozhiiwaadiziwin phenomenon. Their succinctly worded interrogation of the nature of treaty strikes at the fundamental issues of intent, interpretation, and implementation. Directed at the historical nature of wemitigoozhiiwaadiziwin's interchange with Anishinaabe people, their comments suggest that wemitigoozhiiwaadiziwin's idea of relationship usually embodies zhooniyaa as low wages in exchange for manual labour and the exploitation of Anishinaabe bodies, minds, knowledges, lands, and resources.

Hence, the elders' dadibaajim indicates that their experiences belie the Anishinaaabemowin term "diba'amaadim," and that the historical arrangement referred to by the English word "treaty" was rooted in an attitude of deceit. As he speculates whose wemitigoozhiiwaadiziwin mindset may have instigated the idea of engaging with Anishinaabeg in that manner, Oo'oons ponders the reasons for the treatment. He draws our attention to the fact that he never heard a reasonable explanation for the diba'amaadim practice. Relying on the evidence of their experiences, Anishinaabe people must conclude that wemitigoozhi's notions of diba'amaadim defy logic because wemitigoozhiiwaadiziwin has never proven to be rational, generous, or morally ethical toward them or their homelands. Despite these insights, Oo'oons and Dedibaayaanimanook are far from fixated on the subject because they understand and speak to the truthful meaning of wemitigoozhi's treaty as a particularly problematic case of wemitigoozhiiwaadiziwin.

Although the Namegosibii Anishinaabeg were expanding in population, their access to the spaces of home was rapidly diminishing as ever-increasing wemitigoozhi populations displaced them. They had long sought reserve status, but their requests met with silence, confirming what they already knew. Wage labour and relocation were eventually the only options for those of Martha Angeconeb's parents' age group. If they chose to remain in the Namegosibiing territories and work for the lodges as guides, dock hands, waiters, cooks and cooks' helpers, dishwashers, laundry and maintenance staff, and general labourers, they faced the legal uncertainties of living in their own homes on Crown land or living on lodge property where the proprietor deducted their board and room expenses from their wages. These were among the challenges and apprehensions that wemitigoozhiiwaadiziwin's arrival brought to the people as they proceeded through the twentieth century.

Butikofer Papers

Gary Butikofer was associated with the Mennonite Northern Light Gospel Mission[25] of Red Lake from 1970 to 1990. During that twenty-year span, he learned Anishinaabemowin and carried out numerous

interviews with local Anishinaabe community members, including
Waabachaanish Gerald Bannatyne, a wiisaakodewinini relative of the
Namegosibii Anishinaabeg. "Wiisaakode" is a term that refers to an individual of mixed heritage, of Anishinaabe and European parentage. Being
a wiisaakodewinini or wiisaakodewikwe, a man or woman of mixed
heritage, was a significant factor in how Anishinaabe people experienced
and were able to navigate wemitigoozhiiwaadiziwin. People of mixed
heritage usually associated with their Anishinaabe kin, who accepted
them as members of the community. Often enacting a range of inter-
cessory roles, they seemed, in general, better positioned to interact with
wemitigoozhiwag. Alexander Morris, for example, dispatched wiisaakodewinini Charles Nolin and other Métis men to the Anishinaabe chiefs
with the expectation that they would be able to "give them friendly
advice" because, as "men of their own blood,"[26] they could use "the influence which their relationships to the Indians gave them, to impress them
with the necessity of their entering into the treaty."[27] Waabachaanish
Gerald's work with Gary Butikofer was that of a wiisaakodewinini who
functioned as a liaison between the wemitigoozhi interviewer and his
Anishinaabe respondents. Having himself learned Anishinaabemowin,
Butikofer did not need Waabachaanish to translate or interpret for him.

My gratitude for Gary Butikofer's contribution towards the exploration of Anishinaabe identity is complicated by my recognition, from a
Namegosibii Anishinaabe perspective, that the *Butikofer Papers* are the
product of an "outsider" who arrived with the wemitigoozhi's cultural
practices, values, and belief systems.[28] The case of Butikofer presents the
conundrum that the forces of wemitigoozhiiwaadiziwin that actively
sought to replace the Anishinaabe people's spirituality were also those
that actively sought to document their identity dadibaajim. Nonetheless,
the dadibaajim of all of Butikofer's interviewees, including Waabachaanish
Gerald himself, contributes important and interesting details to the larger
Namegosibii Anishinaabe identity narrative. For the most part, the
contents of the *Butikofer Papers* and the facts of Namegosibii dadibaajim
are in agreement.

To explain Waabachaanish Gerald's connection to Dedibaayaanimanook,
his niece Gichi-jii Agnes married Dedibaayaanimanook's cousin
Jiimis James (see Figure 34). As close friends, Gichi-jii Agnes and
Dedibaayaanimanook enjoyed Anishinaabemowin discussions about

the historical knowledges contained in Namegosibii dadibaajim. Both were aware of Waabachaanish Gerald's habit of writing quantities of notes about historical events as he had heard of them. Unfortunately, all were destroyed in a house fire.[29]

Butikofer writes of Waabachaanish Gerald as having personally known Jiiyaan Chiian's son Giizhig. Explaining that the HBC "appointed old Chiian as chief trapper or head trapper,"[30] Butikofer describes Waabachaanish Gerald's account of the protocols surrounding the fur traders' exchanges with Jiiyaan Chiian and his entourage:

> They would make a big feast for Chiian. The HBC gave him a silk hat and a sword and a coat and a flag. They would expect Chiian any day, but they didn't know when. They would all wait with the feast until Chiian came. That was before the treaty. All the Indian people gathered at the HBC store for this feast. When Chiian arrived all dressed up with his sword hanging down, they would go to meet him and then open up their storehouse of goods to trade with him. After the trading was over, the HBC would treat everyone to a big feast. Nothing would happen until Chiian arrived. (I suppose Gerald means the HBC would not begin trading with anyone until after Chiian arrived.)[31]

Demonstrating a desire to use what they perceived to be his position of influence across the homeland territories, the HBC's designation of Jiiyaan Chiian as head trapper was undoubtedly an acknowledgement of his pre-existing leadership role as the head of a large extended family (Jiiyaan having had six wives). It was a time when Anishinaabe people's expertise and labour in the fur business were critical to the company's operations. The HBC's dependence on their participation in the fur trade initially compelled traders to show a measure of respect towards them and treat them as colleagues rather than employee-subordinates or worse. Importantly, Butikofer specifies that the events occurred before the treaty and its adhesion (1873–74), when Anishinaabe people were autonomous, free to make choices about where and when to travel and trade. The balance of power had not yet shifted.

Butikofer adds other details about Jiiyaan Chiian's identity and his association with the H B C, specifying that he was Giizhig Kiishik's father: "Gerald heard a lot about Chiian from his son Kiishik. Kiishik still had a big metal medallion that the H B C had given Chiian to wear around his neck. I think Gerald saw it. The coat Chiian was given was dark with big shiny buttons. It was not a red coat."[32] This passage is a glimpse into the Anishinaabe-H B C interface, showing that the company's coat and medallion were symbolic of how the company perceived the value of cultivating a friendly relationship with not only Jiiyaan Chiian but, by extension, the community he represented. For his part, Jiiyaan Chiian was a territorial lead trapper who would have been well acquainted with the meaning and significance of trade arrangements and the role of goods and gifts as incentives and as a means of providing for his community. These relationships enable our understanding about the H B C's use of such "institutional practices" to encourage trappers' loyalties as it attempted to thwart the baamadaawe independent traders.[33] With Jiiyaan Chiian's acceptance of and participation in these customs, it is evident that a balanced relationship was possible between the two parties during that period.

Dedibaayaanimanook speaks of having seen a medallion during her youth, stating it belonged to her grandfather Giizhig. Hung with a red ribbon, it was kept by her parents in a special box. Gwiishkwa'oo and Dedibaayaanimanook both remember that it remained in the possession of the Dedibayaash and Gaa-madweyaashiik family and that Gwiishkwa'oo's parents then kept it briefly, after the passing of Dedibaayaanimanook's parents. As some later speculated, it may have been cached somewhere in Namegosibiing or stolen.

Butikofer's writings are largely able to add clarity to the identities of various relatives and ancestral lines. He states, for example, that the English name of Ojoozhimimaa Ochoshimimaa ("Everyone's Nephew," adik odoodem caribou totem) was John Animal Sr.[34] But he also seems to indicate that the same individual was William Spence of Lac Seul. Butikofer writes that Ojoozhimimaa Ochoshimimaa's father was Gichi Inini Kihchi Inini, without specifying the identity of the latter's father. We know from Namegosibii dadibaajim that Ojoozhimimaa Ochoshimimaa was either Dedibaayaanimanook's father's first cousin or first cousin once removed. Based on how dadibaajim speaks of the ancestors, however, it is likely that Gichi Inini Kihchi Inini's father was Jiiyaan (see Figure 24), which would make Dedibaayaanimanook Ojoozhimimaa Ochoshimimaa's first cousin once removed. Dedibaayaanimanook's Namegosibii dadibaajim has remained silent on Ojoozhimimaa's English name, perhaps because there was never a need to use it.

Butikofer and Namegosibii dadibaajim both indicate that "old Angecomb," the original Angeconeb, was one of Jiiyaan's sons.[35] If so, then today's Angeconebs also trace their ancestry to Jiiyaan. Gwiishka'oo Eliza, to illustrate, would be a Jiiyaan descendant through her paternal grandfather, Gichimookomaan George Angeconeb. She is also a descendant through her father's stepfather, Dedibayaash. Butikofer further states that "old Angecomb" and his wife Goome Koome were the parents of Jakaabesh Chakaapes, another relative of Dedibaayaanimanook's father Dedibayaash (see Figures 24 and 25).[36] Apparently, Goome Koome had at least two children, Jakaabesh Chakaapes (who never married) and his sister, whose name Waabachaanish Gerald did not know. Jakaabesh Chakaapes was therefore another cousin of Dedibaayaanimanook's father, but quite possibly not a full cousin, considering that his grandfather Jiiyaan had six wives.

Of relevance, Butikofer notes that Jakaabesh Chakaapes spent winters in Namegosibiing and Ikwewi-zaa'igan Woman Lake and summers in Obizhigokaang Lac Seul, as were the cultural customs and travel patterns of the Namegosibii Anishinaabeg. Furthermore, Dedibaayaanimanook's dadibaajim seems to recognize Jakaabesh as a relative by how her father spoke of him. In this manner, details from both the written record and Namegosibii dadibaajim allow us to make plausible speculations about the relational bonds that existed among Namegosibii Anishinaabeg.

Providing an additional layer to the identity dadibaajim of the Namegosibii aanikoobidaaganag is Butikofer's account of Dedibaayaanimanook's maternal ancestry. He includes a 1982 interview with Dedibaayaanimanook's brother Jiins Charlie Angeconeb, who informed him that their maternal grandmother was named Gaachim Kaachim (see Figure 31). Jiins Charlie translated their grandmother's name into English as Crying all the Time[37] and clarified the English meaning of Angeconeb to be Changing Feathers of a Bird.[38] Furthermore, according to Butikofer, the uncle of Gaa-madweyaashiik Kamatweyaashiik Emma was Waasekamigigaabaw Waasekamikikaapaw,[39] #39 of the Wabauskang Band. As such, he was Dedibaayaanimanook's maternal great-uncle. In his

Figure 31.
The likely maternal ancestry of Dedibaayaanimanook.
Dedibaayaanimanook's mother, Gaa-madweyaashiik Emma, was first
married to Gichimookomaan George Angeconeb. Hence, Jiins Charlie and
Dedibaayaanimanook were half-siblings.

GAA-DADAAKOGAADEJ KAHTAKATOKAATE
("SHORT LEGS") AND MS. THOMAS

MAJOOJSHWANAAWAGAN
MAAHTOTOSWAN-AAWIKAN
JOHN ANGECONEB (MARRIED
GOJAANJII CAPAY)

CLARA

MINJIMOOYE MINTIMOWIYE
(MARRIED ALEX CAPAY)

JIIMIS JAMES ANGECONEB
(FIRST MARRIED MARY BULL,
THEN MARY QUOQUAT)

Figure 32.
Gaa-dadaakogaadej and the Community of Namegosibiing.
Dedibaayaanimanook intimates that the Angeconeb ancestors were
prominent actors in the Namegosibii Anishinaabe historical narrative
(Agger, *Following Nimishoomis*). Butikofer's findings suggest that "Old
Angecomb" was a sibling of Giizhig.

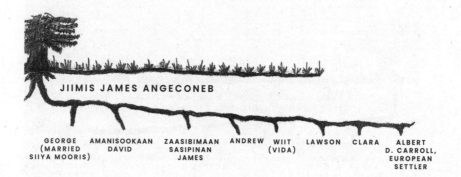

JIIMIS JAMES ANGECONEB

GEORGE   AMANISOOKAAN   ZAASIBIMAAN   ANDREW   WIIT   LAWSON   CLARA   ALBERT
(MARRIED   DAVID   SASIPINAN   (VIDA)   D. CARROLL,
SIIYA MOORIS)   JAMES   EUROPEAN
                                                                                    SETTLER

Figure 33.
Namegosibii Anishinaabe relationship with Zaasibimaan James Angeconeb.
When we visited Zaasibimaan several years ago, Dedibaayaanimanook's
knowledge explained the patterning of our shared lineage. Her use
of the Anishinaabe system of knowledge preservation, dadibaajim,
confers understanding about relationships in ways that are relevant in an
Anishinaabe frame of reference.

Figure 34.

Interconnection between Angeconebs and Giizhigs. Dedibaayaanimanook's cousin Jiimis James, son of Naadowe Robert and Omashkiigookwe, married Agnes Bannatyne, whose father's brother was Waabachaanish Gerald Bannatyne.

1981 interview with Dedibaayaanimanook herself, Butikofer quotes her
as saying that her mother's name, Gaa-madweyaashiik Kamatweyaashiik,
translates as the Sound of Trees in the Wind.[40] Dedibaayaanimanook's
own dadibaajim notes that it was a gift from Giizhig.

Continuing with the Angeconeb branch of the Namegosibii
Anishinaabe ancestry, Gaa-dadaakogaadej Kahtakatokaate[41] ("Short
Legs") was first married to a Thomas, according to Butikofer (see Figure
32).[42] Several years ago, Dedibaayaanimanook, Gwiishkwa'oo, and I visited
Jiimis James Angeconeb's son, Zaasibimaan James, in Winnipeg where
he spent his final years (see Figure 33). At that time, however, I had little
knowledge about how we were related. Butikofer's information may be
of special interest to those who know Garnet Angeconeb, whose ancestry
derives from this line.[43]

Butikofer lists Gaa-dadaakogaadej Kahtakatokaate's children with his
second wife, Mooska'osi Mooska'awisi, which translates into English as
Bittern (see Figure 34). Namegosibii dadibaajim states that Gichi-jii's
mother was Gichi-ikwezes, but whether she was the Kwesens Butikofer
mentions is not known. If they were one and the same individual, then
Gichi-jii's grandfather was Gaa-dadaakogaadej Kahtakatokaate. The last
of Dedibaayaanimanook's close friends of her generation, Gichi-jii had a
deeply grounded understanding of the historical content of Namegosibii
Anishinaabe dadibaajim and undoubtedly recognized the importance of
her uncle Waabachaanish Gerald's work.

Of special interest here is Butikofer's inclusion of certain phrases
that his Anishinaabe interviewees express as "ingii' waabamaa(ban)"
(I saw her/him/it), "gaawiin ingii' waabamaasii" (I did not see her/him/
it), or some other similar phrase. For example, he writes that "Gerald
never saw Wawiye but he did see Amo and Kichi Miskwe."[44] Similarly,
Dedibaayaanimanook speaks in terms of having seen or not having seen
someone or something. In one part of her dadibaajim, for example, she
mentions that she saw a relative of her father's, thus testifying that the
individual was still living during the time of her childhood.

This customary form of Anishinaabe speech indicates the speaker's
role as an eyewitness who gives a first-hand account about an event. As
a method of substantiation, the custom was necessarily based on the
reliability of an individual's word. Anishinaabe people as an oral society
were fastidious about establishing and maintaining a reputation of

trustworthiness in order for their dadibaajim to be accepted as Anishinaabe knowledge. Once an individual was discovered to be a fabricator of stories, on the other hand, she or he was ascribed a standing in the community with the phrase "nitaa giiwanimo" (he or she habitually speaks untruths) and perceived as untrustworthy.

In summary, Butikofer's work contributes Anishinaabemowin and English names and their meanings, as well as information about who were the children of whom, details of events, and forms of expression. He does not, however, have the means with which to arrange the information he gathered into a genealogical coherence. Dadibaajim and its embedded meanings make it possible to integrate information from izhibii'igem written texts, such as those of Butikofer, the HBC archives, and state records, into a comprehensive, more complete arrangement of Namegosibii Anishinaabe genealogies and identities.

My use of izhibii'igem, as I have indicated previously, is in no way meant to suggest that the dadibaajim oral system of record keeping and information retrieval, including odoodemiwin and aadasookewin, are deficient. Within the Anishinaabe cultural context, dadibaajim fits perfectly with a travel-based lifestyle that works optimally with few rather than many physical possessions. Dedibaayaanimanook has already pointed out that the essential tools of orality are thought, memory, and recall, as all elders have understood. In the following dadibaajim, she illustrates how this system kept events in chronological order by referring to a time when they were living in a particular place in Namegosibiing:

Amiish i'i wedi gaa'izhi-ani-goziyaangiban e'giigooyikewaaj Jiins. Amiish i'imaa gaa' izhidaayaangiban. That's the same time, gewiinawaa i'iwedi gii'izhidaabaneg gii' biijigoziibaneg Oshkaandagaawi-zaa'iganiing, Gichi-jii. Minôtesh gii' dakobizo i'i apii.[45]

And then we moved over there when they [and] Jiins were fishing. And that was where we lived. That's the same time they too were living over there, they had moved from

Oshkaandagaawi-zaa'iganiing, Gichi-jii. Minôte was in a
cradleboard that time.

As Dedibaayaanimanook's dadibaajim moves spontaneously along, it
picks up details which then become prompting devices for further information. Rather than attempting to recall dates, Dedibaayaanimanook
explains the time factor by associating an event with an incident or situation through her use of the term "apii," at the time when. Her dadibaajim
consists of a set of recollections, including a particularly endearing image
of the infant Minôte in her dakinaagan cradleboard, thus demonstrating
how the time frame of an event is established in terms that are meaningful
for the community. In this dadibaajim, Minôte embodies the immensely
significant event of an addition to the Namegosibii Anishinaabe community's population.

In another example, Dedibaayaanimanook similarly denotes the
time of an event by using two key components of her narrative that work
together to explain when it took place:

**I [was] really young that time. Ya'iish gaa-gii' onji
wiijiiwiwaaj—Aayizag osha dakobizooban.**[46]

I [was] really young that time. That was why they had me
come along—you see, Isaac was in a cradleboard.

Her description of a journey with family members uses the same
method, associating a time in her youth with the particular spring
when her nephew was still in a cradleboard, "Aayizag osha dakobizooban." Dedibaayaanimanook's narrative explains how an object, such as
the dakinaagan cradleboard, can not only serve a primary purpose but
enact a symbolic role in how Anishinaabemowin speakers conceptualize
and organize events for dadibaajim. Record keeping in which an event
is linked with an especially cold or snowy winter, someone's birth or
passing, an important visit, and so on indicates an oral society's system
of information storage and retrieval for the purpose of communicating
with debwewin truth accuracy. There was no need for the writing practices and implements of literateness among Namegosibii Anishinaabeg.

Foundational to a society based on the existent voice, dadibaajim functions most effectively through constant use, reinforcing and refreshing memory and maintaining the speaker-listener relationship. But, as noted earlier, it also depends on the ethic of debwewin truthfulness. To illustrate, Namegosibii Anishinaabeg did not associate the English word "treaty" with notions of debwetam-inaakonigem. They understood early on that Treaty 3 was not honourable in either its izhibii'igem written content or its administration because a true balance of power did not exist between wemitigoozhiwag and Anishinaabeg. Being neither naïve nor gullible, Namegosibii Anishinaabeg were acutely aware of the power differential and thus focused on the heart of the matter: compensation for theft of homelands, resources, and self-determination. The notion of diba'amaadim, as it applied to treaty payments, was a source of deep skepticism for the Namegosibii Anishinaabe elders, as historical experiences contradicted the confidence and trust-based ideals implicit in the debwetam-inaakonigem of an ethical treaty-making process conducted in good faith.

My use of the izhibii'igem text to recover information about identities by tracing through recorded genealogies reflects the need for substantiation by documentation. Yet the reliability of izhibii'igem's information is itself only as accurate as the soundness of the recorder's listening and recording skills, processes, procedures, and interpretational accuracy. In a telephone communication in March 2006, Library and Archives Canada reference archivist W. Russell stated that an Indian agent was responsible for at least three copies of data, one being his own set to update on an ongoing basis throughout the year. Information varied when inconsistencies arose from clerical errors, discrepancies between an agent's working copy and information gathered at Treaty Time, and varying ability to hear and/or spell what Anishinaabe people were telling them. Particularly given the use of Roman orthography without a standardized spelling system in place, the illegibility of some Indian agents' handwriting, and the state of deterioration of certain texts—even when typewriters came into use—that made them difficult to read, dadibaajim plays the lead role in searches through izhibii'igem for information that augments Namegosibii Anishinaabe identity.

Of importance in this exploration of the Namegosibii Anishinaabe ancestry, Butikofer's notes unmistakably identify Chean of izhibii'igem as Jiiyaan of dadibaajim, father of the Namegosibii Anishinaabe people's patriarch, Giizhig. The description of Jiiyaan's visits to the H B C, as spoken by Waabachaanish and recorded by Butikofer, suggests the value that fur traders placed in maintaining positive relations with Jiiyaan and his family and community. By recognizing Jiiyaan's influence and seeking his goodwill, in fact, the company acknowledged the identity of the Namegosibii Anishinaabeg, their work ethic, reputation, integrity, and, by extension, the homelands that birthed them and sustained their lives. Concomitantly, Anishinaabe people undoubtedly knew that the H B C's gestures of friendship would exist only for as long as the company needed their cooperation to remain profitable, as the option still existed for them to take their furs to competing traders in the region. Butikofer's work is of further value for having included people's odoodemiwin totem.

Butikofer's record adds details that help us regain what wemitigoozhii-waadiziwin's encumbrances have attempted to destroy. He states, for example, that "Mayinkaan and Moosonihkwe were brother [and] sister,"[47] indicating that Ma'iingan Mayinkaan (wolf) was Dedibaayaanimanook's father's maternal uncle, that is, Nookomiban's brother. As well, information about how names translate into English provides us with ideas about the ways in which our forebears thought about themselves and their relationship with the world around them. As a result, it is very likely that our efforts to recover the identity of our ancestors will change our understanding of them as our knowledge improves.

The people of Namegosibiing were a discrete group of Anishinaabeg, the "Trout Lake Indians," whose ancestral territories extended to Biigaanjigamiing Pikangikum and Oshkaandagaawi-zaa'igan Nungesser Lake in the northwest, Maadaawaang Mattawan and Obizhigokaang Lac Seul to the southwest and south, respectively, and Ikwewi-zaa'igan Woman Lake to the east. Giizhig, whom today's descendants refer to as their patriarch, was born in Namegosibiing, as was his father, Jiiyaan. With summer visits to the Lac Seul region usually lasting less than two months, the Namegosibii Anishinaabeg spent most of the year in their Namegosibiing places of home. Some individuals decided to stay in Obizhigokaang Lac Seul while others relocated to the Red Lake area during the early to mid-twentieth century. For Giizhig and Moonz(h)oniikwe's three sons, Dedibayaash William, Netawibiitam John, and Jiiyaan Donald and their families, Dedibaayaanimanook's dadibaajim explains, Namegosibiing remained their place of home.

Today's descendants of the Namegosibii Anishinaabe aanikoobidaaga-nag are scattered. Some live in Winnipeg, others in Victoria, Edmonton, Red Lake and Balmertown, Sandy Lake, Dryden, Thunder Bay, Curve Lake, Toronto, and elsewhere. As each succeeding generation moves further from their Namegosibiing roots, descendants become affiliates of other communities, places, and ancestral lineages. An example is the youngest participant of this book, Janae Fiddler, who is five generations removed from Giizhig and expresses her ancestry in terms of her father's Sandy Lake community. Taking on other identities, she and those similarly situated are less likely to be familiar with their Namegosibiing progenitors and their dadibaajim narratives. Nonetheless, they too share the Giizhigoog lineage and the option to claim Namegosibiing as their homeland.

Zagakibii'igem
Conclusion

Dadibaajim narratives play a critical role in addressing questions about the identity of Namegosibii Anishinaabe people. With the capacity to describe the daily realities of dispossession and physical removal from the land of the forebears, they are a means by which to interrogate the denial of the Anishinaabe people's experiences that has had the effect of erasing their identity and preventing their return to the ancestral places of home. Participants have engaged with dadibaajim to describe relationships among community members and the noopimakamig aki, historical events, wemitigoozhiiwaadiziwin's many forms of maltreatment, and the necessary adjustments that have had a great impact upon the Namegosibii Anishinaabe community.

As the most senior community elder, Dedibaayaanimanook speaks to a time span of several generations. The subject matter of her dadibaajim reaches back no fewer than 200 winters to the late eighteenth and early nineteenth centuries when her great-grandfather Jiiyaan was living. She uses dadibaajim to portray the height of land across hundreds of square kilometres of Anishinaabe aki land, demonstrating her extensive experience of life in the homelands. One of the most remarkable features of the Namegosibii aweneniwiyang dadibaajim of Dedibaayaanimanook and the other contributing elders is its portrayal of a lineage that has attached to the same geographical spaces for so long a period of time. Importantly, all of the participants' dadibaajim narratives describe how the forces of wemitigoozhiiwaadiziwin have used such mechanisms as land use and occupation policies to obfuscate Anishinaabe people's efforts to remain within the Namegosibiing spaces of home.

Generationally closest to the aanikoobidaaganag ancestors, the senior elders express a strong affiliation with Namegosibiing, affection for the ancestors, and a deeply held trust in the veracity of their elders' teachings. They can still describe the land-based customs that people practised before the advent of wemitigoozhiiwaadiziwin. But they also speak their dadibaajim from contexts of hardship brought about by changing social, economic, and political conditions and their related uncertainties. They are realistic in how they assess the prospects for Anishinaabe survival as a people in view of wemitigoozhiiwaadiziwin.

The next generation of participants continues to use Anishinaabemowin. Their cultural grounding helps them to maintain a Namegosibiing-imprinted identity as they explore the possibility of returning home, even if only for brief visits. The dadibaajim of the youngest participants suggests that the type of challenges experienced by their predecessors has largely changed. Born, raised, and living within the urban milieu of Western thinking, they must navigate an economic system that demands their participation in order to survive. They often come face to face with wemitigoozhi's prejudices and the paucity of opportunities to pursue ancestral ways of life and thought. As such, their access to and familiarity with Anishinaabemowin and the dadibaajim narratives are limited. Factors relating to age, place of birth and childhood, parentage and family lifestyle, schooling, and time spent in the homelands have all influenced the participants in terms of their ability to communicate from the Namegosibii Anishinaabe ontological position of the foreparents. By sharing their thoughts and insights, they contribute to the dadibaajim identity narratives of the Namegosibii Anishinaabeg, even though they use few Anishinaabemowin words.

The dadibaajim narratives teach us that valuable knowledge resides with all who are of the community, no matter how the hierarchical schemes of the dominant society ranks them and no matter that their insights may not often reach the dawisijigem spaces of mainstream discourse. For those who navigate the various disciplines of Western knowledge production and look only to privileged groups as the authority and source of legitimacy, dadibaajim reminds us that knowledge resides in unexpected places, whether the land, the wanagoshag of the night skies, the omagakiig frogs and their mists of rain, or each of us as Namegosibii Anishinaabeg. Importantly, when the elders communicate dadibaajim from Anishinaabemowin's ontological frame of reference, respect for the debwewin truth that the natural environment of aki earth offered our ancestors throughout the ages emerges as a fundamental teaching.

Anishinaabemowin dadibaajim is of value to all who are concerned for the well-being of the only aki earth that we have to nurture and educate us. Dadibaajim presents the Anishinaabe philosophies that ensured aki would continue in the state of healthiness that the European latecomers found so irresistible. In so doing, it challenges the contradictory mythologies that the homelands were empty spaces of wilderness devoid of human populations. Dadibaajim makes it clear that the lands were not unpopulated, that they were "wild" only in the sense that the ancestors respected the natural environment and refrained from activities of exploitation, development, or cultivation on the large-scale industrial basis now so common.

Dadibaajim explicates the principles that inspired Anishinaabe people to manage their relationships with the natural environment and its innumerable components in ways that allowed them to survive successfully as communities and polities for thousands of years, without the carbon footprints or socio-economic disparities that exist across the world today. While dadibaajim explains that conditions throughout the homelands became impossible for the presence of one group, the Anishinaabeg, but accommodative for another, the wemitigoozhiwag, it also explains that we must respect the aki earth if we want to live sustainably.

Participating in this journey into the exploration of Namegosibii Anishinaabe identity teaches us that dadibaajim is a fundamental epistemological institution for Anishinaabemowin-speaking people. At the same time, it teaches that searching for the meanings embedded in Anishinaabemowin dadibaajim and its cultural contexts is an inter-ontological endeavour that requires careful listening and reflection. To illustrate, I once spoke in zhaaganaashiimowin English to ask my mother what I presumed to be the straightforward question of what plants are in terms of how Anishinaabe people categorize them. When Dedibaayaanimanook asked for clarification and I responded by switching to Anishinaabemowin, wegonesh iniweniwan plants gaa-izhinikaadegin, I soon discovered my inability to describe what I meant by even the English word "plant." Simply rephrasing myself, wegodogwen ini plants, was not helpful. Instead, I had to reorient my approach to the whole notion of what is a logical question from an Anishinaabemowin speaker's perspective. It became evident that my query must have suggested the lack of a sound mind to my mother, who knew I knew what a gitigaan plant is. My ill-conceived attempt to find Anishinaabemowin words corresponding to the Western classificatory system of knowledge construction demonstrates the peculiarities and challenges of working from two distinct ontologies.

From the perspective of a Namegosibii Anishinaabe community member and with the guidance and direction of dadibaajim's insights, I have come to understand that our most reasoned response to wemitigoozhiiwaadiziwin is to return to the spiritual-intellectual landscapes of Anishinaabewaadiziwin. This is where the essence of accommodation and reconciliation resides. Access to the knowledges of dadibaajim however, requires the time, opportunity, and language to hear them.

This kind of work indicates that our ontological origins inhere within the Namegosibii Anishinaabe dadibaajim narratives. They are able to resolve questions about dilapidated cabins and collapsing cemetery cribs and explain the identity of Namegosibii Anishinaabe tourist guides and their relationship with those who rest at the ezhi-bimishinowaaj cemetery. The dadibaajim narratives about the ancestors' philosophies have the power to expose wemitigoozhiiwaadiziwin's myths, flaws, and evils. Revealing the foreignness of wemitigoozhi's systems that were imposed on the Namegosibii Anishinaabeg and their homelands, the dadibaajim narratives concomitantly offer a way home for Namegosibii Anishinaabeg and lay out a path to re-education and learning for non-Anishinaabe Canadians. They are part of a growing body of Anishinaabemowin voices taking their rightful place within the dawisijigem spaces of Canadian discourse.

Acknowledgements

Gichi miigwech to all who demonstrated their belief in the value of this work through their interest and inclusivity. Among these are members of my family who include my mother and senior mentor Dedibaayaanimanook Sarah Keesick Olsen, spouse Garth Agger, daughter Leslie Agger, granddaughter Ikwezens Emilia-Helen Maple, and elder-sister Alice Olsen Williams; research participant-mentors Gwiishkwa'oo Eliza Angeconeb, Martha Angeconeb Fiddler, Janae Fiddler, Niinzhoode Wilfred Kejick, Oo'oons John Paul Kejick, William King, and Riel Olsen; and long-time family friend, historian-archivist John Richthammer, who has so generously given of his time, energy, and expertise in support of my endeavours to document some of the Namegosibii Anishinaabe identity narratives. Much thanks to the University of Manitoba Press editors for their patience and tolerance. I also want to thank Roger Roulette for contributing his knowledge of how Anishinaabemowin functions when written. Finally, I wish to acknowledge the memory of Dr. Renate Eigenbrod, who saw the relevance of this kind of work and cleared the way for many similar endeavours.

Notes

Preface

1   For an example of this, see Peacock, "Teaching as Story."

2   Nichols and Nyholm, *Concise Dictionary*, ix–xxviii.

3   "Dadibaajim" is Anishinaabemowin for oral narrative, the content of a narrative, or the practice or process of oral narration. This term evokes the ongoing nature of Namegosibii Anishinaabe narration across the generations, while the closely   related term "dibaajim" refers to a narrative about a specific subject of a more limited scope and duration.

4   Nichols and Nyholm, *Concise Dictionary*, ix–xxviii.

5   Ibid.

6   This was brought to my attention in a personal conversation with P. Ningewance in 2014.

Bezhig / One: Ninamegosibii Anishinaabewimin / We Are the People of Trout Water

1   Dedibaayaanimanook states that one of her favourite scents is that of the giishkaatig cedar.

2   Gehl, "Debwewin Journey."

3   Johnston, *Th!nk Indian*, 39.

4   Ibid., 78.

5   Simpson, "Land as Pedagogy," 7.

6   Ibid.

7   Agger, *Following Nimishoomis*, 155.

8   Vizenor, *Manifest Manners*.

9   Bird, *Telling Our Stories*.

10 Butikofer, *Butikofer Papers*, 76–96.

11 Many of these records are designated as B.107/d/1 (pp. 9–20) and are housed at the HBC Archives in Winnipeg, MB.

12 For a succinct rendition of these historical events, see Doherty's article at http://www.bac-lac. gc.ca/eng/discover/politics-government/canadian-confederation/Pages/northwest-territo-ries-1870.aspx.

13 Richthammer, "Memento Mori," 57, 64, 80, 90.

14 Nicholas, "Decolonizing the Archaeological Landscape."

15 Schultz, Lavenda, and Dods, *Cultural Anthropology,* 167.

16 Herzog, "Invisibilization and Silencing."

Niinzhin / Two: Wenji Gikendamang / How We Know

1 Clark, "Mawadishiwewin," 74.

2 Guédon, "Dene Ways"; Kovach, "Conversational Method."

3 009ADO2013, 1. For efficiency, I numbered the mentor-participant audio tapes from 001 to 021, with each labelled side A or B. Each pair of parentheses includes the tape number and side, first letter of the narrator's first name (Anishinaabe, where one exists), year of the conversation, and the transcript page number. For example, 008ABR2013, 2 indicates that the tape number is 008, both sides of the tape contain the dadibaajim, the participant is Riel Olsen, the meeting date is 2013, and the transcript page number is 2. The system that I use to identify each participant is to capitalize his or her first name in the following manner: Dedibaayaanimanook, D; Gwiishkwa'oo, G; Janae, J; Martha, M; Niinzhoode, N; Oo'oons, O; William, W; and Riel, R.

4 A similar conversational exchange might occur when a student searches for the right term while conversing with a professor whom he greatly respects. Not wanting to ask her directly, he says, "Now, I wonder what that is called" or, "I'm trying to think how that goes," and waits for whether or not the professor will see fit to provide him with the correct word.

5 011BDO2012, 3.

6 001AD2012, 3.

7 Richthammer, "Memento Mori", 4.

8 001BDO2012, 4.

9 014AD2010, 8.

10 Erdrich, *Books and Islands,* 82.

11 Matthews, "Repatriating Agency."

12 Dedibaayaanimanook explained these forms of the word "oninj" in a personal conversation in June 2016.

13 Kulchyski, "Bush Culture."

14 014BD2010, 8.

Nisin / Three: Wenji Inendamang / Subjectivity

1 Hopkins, "Relational Flow Frames," 177.

2 Cruikshank, *Life Lived Like a Story,* 2–4.

3 Eigenbrod, *Travelling Knowledges,* 44.

4 Kovach, "Conversational Method," 45–46.

5 Eigenbrod, *Travelling Knowledges.*

6   Geniusz, *Our Knowledge*, xi.

7   Absolon, *Kaandossiwin*, 73–74.

8   Ibid.

9   Kulchyski, "and," 321.

10   Eigenbrod, *Travelling Knowledges*.

11   Johnston, *Th!nk Indian*, 58.

12   Absolon, "Indigenous Wholistic Theory."

13   Oo'oons John Paul Kejick passed on 4 March 2017.

Niiwin / Four: Ezhibii'igaazoyang / How We Are Written

1   Mignolo, *Darker Side of Renaissance*, 29.

2.   Mignolo, "Delinking," 451.

3   Baca, "Te-ixtli," 1–2.

4   Memmi, *Colonizer and Colonized*.

5   Johnston, "One Generation from Extinction," 14.

6   Bender, "Reflections on What Writing," 177.

7   Cushman, "New Media Scholarship," 65.

8   Steinbring, "Saulteaux of Lake Winnipeg."

9   Bishop, "Emergence of the Northern Ojibwa," 48.

10   Rogers and Taylor, "Northern Ojibwa."

11   Ibid., 232.

12   Bishop, *Northern Ojibwa*, 226n73.

13   Bishop's first map appears in *The Northern Ojibwa*, page 2; his second map is in "The Emergence," page 41.

14   Rogers and Taylor, "Northern Ojibwa," 237.

15   Hallowell, "Bear Ceremonialism."

16   Ibid., 138.

17   Hallowell, "Some Empirical Aspects."

18   Ibid., 401.

19   Hallowell, "Incidence, Character, and Decline."

20   Ibid., 253.

21   Hallowell, "Spirits of the Dead."

22   Ibid., 37.

23   Brown and Matthews, "Fair Wind."

24   Landes, *Ojibwa Woman*.

25   Peers and Brown, "'There Is No End," 549.

26   Agger, *Following Nimishoomis*, 51–52.

27   Steinbring, "Saulteaux of Lake Winnipeg."

28 Agger, *Following Nimishoomis*, 19–20.

29 See Smallman, "Spirit Beings, Mental Illness."

30 Kulchyski, "Anthropology in the Service."

31 Jenness, "'Blond' Eskimos," 259.

32 Brown and Peers, *Pictures Bring Us Messages.*

33 Brown and Grey, *Memories, Myths and Dreams.*

34 Ibid.

35 Dunning, *Social and Economic Change.*

36 Richthammer, "Memento Mori," 75.

37 Eastman, *From the Deep Woods.*

38 Copway, *Traditional History.* https://archive.org/details/traditionalhist00bookgoog.

39 Ibid., 128.

40 Warren, *History of the Ojibway*, 71.

41 Peers and Podruchny, "Introduction," 1.

42 Daniels-Fiss, "Learning to Be a Nêhiyaw," 240.

43 Ballard, "Flooding Sustainable Livelihoods," 233.

44 Borrows, "Listening for a Change."

45 Borrows, "Indian Agency," 18.

46 Borrows, *Drawing out Law.*

47 Ibid., 103.

48 Ahenakew, *Wâskahikaniwiyiniw-âcimowina.*

49 Debassige, "Re-conceptualizing Anishinaabe Mino-bimaadiziwin."

50 Debassige, "Building on Conceptual Interpretations."

51 Young, "Anishinabemowin."

52 Ibid., 105.

53 Johnston, "One Generation from Extinction," 11.

54 Ibid., 10.

55 Ibid.

56 Ibid., 12.

57 Simpson, "Construction of Traditional Ecological Knowledge."

58 Pitawanakwat, "Anishinaabemodaa Pane Oodenang."

59 Eagle, "Wenji-ganawendamang Gidakiiminaan."

60 Clark, "Mawadishiwewin."

61 Treuer, "Ge-onji-aabadak Anishinaabe-inwewinan."

62 Ibid., 88.

63 Ibid., 87.

64 Treuer, *Anton Treuer, a Linguist.*

65 Simpson, "Anti-colonial Strategies," 380.

Naanan / Five: Wenji-Anishinaabewiyang / Our Anishinaabe Selves

1   014AD2010, 2.

2   018AD2010, 2.

3   Agger, *Following Nimishoomis*.

4   002BD2012, 4.

5   016BD2010, 12.

6   This brief description about aadasookewin is not itself aadasookewin and is therefore not a violation of the Namegosibii Anishinaabe proscription.

7   012BD2011, 3–4.

8   014AD2010, 22.

9   013AG2013, 2.

10 Ibid., 5.

11 Ibid., 4.

12 004ADO2012, 2.

13 001BDO2012, 3.

14 Bohaker, "Reading Anishinaabe Identities."

15 007AM2012, 1.

16 Episkenew, *Taking Back Our Spirits*, 7.

17 001AR2013, 1.

Ingodôso / Six: Ni Noopimakamig-aajimomin / Our Boreal Narratives

1   The English name for this perennial creeper tends towards a negative connotation by drawing attention to the odour it releases when disturbed. "Miishiijiimin," on the other hand, is a neutral term that refers to the edible fruit's bristly surface. One of the first berries of the boreal forest to appear after the snow has melted, miishiijiimin was evoked by elders and parents as a lesson for children—conveyed in the expression "baamaa giin, miishiijiimin"—to respect their elders by refraining from pushing ahead of them.

2   005AD2012, 2–3.

3   001AD2012, 2.

4   Ibid., 3.

5   006BD2013, 2–3.

6   Ibid., 3.

7   Ibid.

8   010ADGO2013, 1.

9   001AD2012, 2.

10 005AD2012, 3.

11 Agger, *Following Nimishoomis*, 41–42.

12 015AD2013, 1.

13 016AD2010, 3.

14 002BD2012, 2.

15 Ibid., 3.

16 For Michael Wassegijig Price's teachings on Anishinaabe astronomy, see his web page at https://michaelwassegijig.com/star-knowledge.html.

17 005AD2012, 1.

18 002BD2012, 2.

19 Ibid., 3.

20 Ibid.

21 I once attended an academic seminar where the main presenter acknowledged that he had intentionally excluded women from his research project. Without an explanation of why he was interested only in the knowledge of the community's male members, his methodology for mapping and ground-truthing seemed odd.

Niinzhôso / Seven: Wemitigoozhiiwaadiziwin / Colonial Identity

1 Wendy Geniusz uses the phrase, "Gego wemitigoozhiiyaadizisiidaa," quoting the elders who work at the Seven Generations Education Institute (see http://www.7generations.org/).

2 Ibid.

3 See http://www.oxforddictionaries.com/definition/english/white under "Usage."

4 Dedibaayaanimanook has never heard what "wemitigoozhi" means, although one community member stated that it refers to a man extending a piece of wood.

5 009AD2013, 3.

6 Ibid.

7 016AD2010, 8.

8 Ibid.

9 See Library and Archives Canada RG 10, Vol. 7585, File 6144-7 for correspondence among Indian Affairs in Ottawa, the Minister of Ontario Department of Lands and Forests and the department's surveyor, the Department of the Interior in Ottawa, and the Indian agent.

10 The issues of compensation have yet to be completely resolved for the Lac Seul First Nation. For a brief description of the First Nation's efforts to achieve a just settlement, see https://www.firstpeopleslaw.com/index/articles/453.php.

11 001AD2012, 3.

12 010ADG2011, 3.

13 021AD2013, 1.

14 010ADG2011, 3.

15 See Brown and Matthews, "Fair Wind," 62.

16 019AD2010, 2–3.

17 014AD2010, 10.

18 016ABD2010, 8.

19 001BDO2012, 5–6.

20 This refers to the notion of being in the way of, or a hindrance to (as in the case of Red Lake), settlement, progress, development, etc. Belief in this idea was a factor foundational to the Red Lake "frontier" mentality that drove efforts to rid the landscape of Anishinaabe populations after the discovery of gold in the 1920s. I am grateful to language specialist Roger Roulette for bringing the "miiwishkaagem" term to my attention.

21 001BDO2012, 6.

22 Ibid.

23 003AW2012, 1.

Nishôso / Eight: Gaa Bii-izhi Gikendamang / Anishinaabe Rectitude

1   001AD2012, 1.

2   Ibid.

3   009ADO2013, 2.

4   013AG2013, 1.

5   003AN2012, 2.

6   003AW2012, 1.

7   007AMJ2013, 2.

8   Ibid.

9   008AR2013, 1.

10 Ibid.

11 008BR2013, 2.

12 Ibid.

13 Ibid.

Zhaangaso / Nine: Gaa'izhibii'igaazoyang Mewinzha / Historical Texts

1   B.107/d/1, Hudson's Bay Company Archives, hereinafter HBCA.

2   D.25/1 fo. 158, HBCA, 21.

3   001BDO2012, 4.

4   004ADO2012, 1.

5   B.107/d/1, HBCA, 9–20.

6   014BD2010, 6.

7   B.105/e/9, HBCA.

8   Along a similar line of logic, I would argue that bell hooks is conceptually different from Bell Hooks.

9   B.107/e/7, fo.2, HBCA, 7.

10 B.107/e/8, HBCA, 9.

11 B.107/e/7, HBCA, 16.

12 Ibid.

13 B.107/e/8, HBCA, 9.

14 A.92/19/11, HBCA, 21.

15 Ibid., 9–10.

16 Ibid., 21.

17 Ibid.

18 001ADO2012, 2.

19 Pay list information is located at Library and Archives Canada, Ottawa, on reels C-7135 to C-7137, vols. 9351 to 9368 and vols. 9370 to 9373 of the RG 10 series and online at http://heritage.canadiana.ca/view/oocihm.lac_mikan_133552.

20 Canada 1901census information is available online at http://www.bac-lac.gc.ca/eng/census/1901/Pages/about-census.aspx.

21 Email communication, 25 June 2015.

22 011BDO2012, 4.

23 018AD2010, 1.

24 011BDO2012, 3.

25 Further information about the Mennonites' missionary work in the region may be found at https://ontariomennonitehistory.org/tag/northern-light-gospel-mission/.

26 Morris, *Treaties of Canada*, 49.

27 Ibid., 51.

28 Butikofer, *Butikofer Papers*, 76–95.

29 Dedibaayaanimanook, personal conversation, 2013.

30 Butikofer, *Butikofer Papers*, 77.

31 Ibid., 77–78.

32 Ibid., 79.

33 Promislow, "One Chief, Two Chiefs," 69.

34 Butikofer, *Butikofer Papers*, 81.

35 Ibid., 83.

36 Ibid.

37 Ibid., 89.

38 Ibid.

39 Butikofer offers "Bright Land to Stand On" as a translation. It can also be "Stands (or Standing) on Bright Land." The name Waasekamigigaabaw may be the reason why Gaa-madweyaashiik Kamatweyaashiik Emma's surname has been identified in English as Bright (personal conversation with J. Richthammer, 2008). Dedibaayaanimanook, however, knew her mother's surname to be Strang. This is an example of how church and state impositions have caused confusion with Anishinaabe names and identities.

40 Butikofer, *Butikofer Papers*, 88.

41 The misspelling of Kahtakatokaate can be corrected by interchanging the second k with the second t.

42 Butikofer, *Butikofer Papers*, 85.

43 Garnet Angeconeb received an Order of Canada for his work in cultural tolerance.

44 Butikofer, *Butikofer Papers*, 80.

45 016BD2010, 15.

46 001AD2012, 3.

47 Butikofer, *Butikofer Papers*, 84.

Glossary of Namegosibii Anishinaabemowin Terms

Note: This word list is specific to how Dedibaayaanimanook and her fellow land-instructed elders use the language to reflect a Namegosibii Anishinaabe frame of reference.

aadasookaan(an). Narrative(s) attached with certain prohibitions. Note that this is an inanimate noun.

aadasookewin. Act or practice of telling special narratives.

-aadizi. Is or thinks a certain way.

aaniin. How?; in what way?; why?; how are you?

aanikoobidaaganag. Literally, those who tie or are being tied together; ancestors; descendants. Dedibaayaanimanook confirmed that aanikoobidaaganag is understood to be inclusive of the genders (personal communication, January 2017).

aantagiin. Now how does (such and such go)?; now in what way (is such and such)?

adik. Caribou. Adik is the odoodem of the Giizhigoog house. In her conversation with Oo'oons, Dedibaayaanimanook surmises that Giizhig's father, Jiiyaan, must have been of the adik odoodem.

agaamakiing. The land that lies across the ocean, sea, or large lake, i.e., a large body of water.

aki. the earth; soil; land.

amanisowin. A premonition, warning, or alert, often in the form of an unnatural event that serves to warn of something ominous. As a practice, it was a means to frighten, forewarn, or produce fear. It could be association with "bad medicine."

anama'aawin. (The practice or organization of a) religion that includes prayer. Among the Namegosibii Anishinaabeg, it is used in reference to Western religions, never to the ceremony or spirituality of Anishinaabeg.

Anishinaabeg. A particular nation of Indigenous people, often referred to as the Ojibwe, Ojibwa, or Ojibway. Dedibaayaanimanook's dadibaajim has also used this term in reference to all Indigenous peoples of the world.

Anishinaabewaadiziwin. Thinking as an Anishinaabe person; Anishinaabe-ness; the essence of being Anishinaabe. Dedibaayaanimanook uses the word "Anishinaabewiziwin" instead of Anishinaabewaadiziwin.

Anishinaabe-aajimodaa sa. Let us narrate in our language.

Anishinaabemowin. Language of the Anishinaabe people. How it is used can vary across regions, communities, and individuals within communities.

apisaabik. A type of rock or mineral with distinctive characteristics.

aweneniwiyang. (Who) we are; what our identity is; our subjectivity.

aweneniwiyang e'Anishinaabewiyang. Who we are as Anishinaabe people.

Baagwaashiwi-zaa'igan. Literally, Shallow Lake, now known as Pakwash Lake.

Baagwaashiwi-zaa'iganiins. Literally, Little Shallow Lake. This is now called Bruce Lake.

baamadaawe. Literally, he/she travels about, buying (furs); an independent trader, as distinct from one associated with the HBC. Namegosibii Anishinaabeg named George Swain Baamadaawe.

baawitig. Rapids; falls. People also used the term "gichi-baawitig" to refer to a falls. Evoking images and sounds of water as it comes flowing over rocks, Dedibaayaanimanook uses the expression "bimidaabikijiwan."

babaamiziwin. (Personal) affairs; (private) business. Consider yourself told to mind your own business if someone tells you, "Gaawiin giin gi babaamiziwin!"

biboon. Winter; a year. A child who is ten years old is described as "midaaso biboonwe"; literally, he or she is of ten winters.

Biigaanjigam(iing). The Anishinaabe community to the north of Namegosibiing, now referred to as the Pikangikum First Nation. Many of the Namegosibii Anishinaabe ancestors originate from Biigaanjigamiing.

binesiwag. The thunderers; thunderbirds. When we use the English word "thunder," we think in terms of insentient forces of compression, shock waves, heat, loud sounds, etc., but binesiwag defines animate beings who express their presence through rumbles, lightning bolts and strikes, masses of dark clouds, and so on. They were accorded special respect.

Bizhiwi Minis. Literally, Lynx Island. Today, the Bizhiwi Minis of Namegosibiing is called Cat Island; it is the largest island on the lake.

dagasa dawisijigedaa. Let us clear away a space.

dawisijigem. Act, process, or practice of clearing away the clutter.

debwemagak gakina gegoon. Everything in the natural world speaks truthfully. People thus looked to the natural environment around them for information, guidance, and truth.

debwetam. Agrees; belief.

debwewin. Knowledge as truth, usually based on a person's experiences and observations. Johnston (*Th!nk Indian*) uses the term "w'daeb-awe."

dewe'igan. Drum. Dedibaayaanimanook speaks of her mother's mitigwakik water drum.

diba'amaadim. Getting paid. This was the term for Treaty Time, when people gathered to receive their treaty annuity payments, usually five dollars per person.

dibiki-giizis. Literally, night sun. The moon.

ezhi-bimishinowaaj. Literally, where they lie at rest. A cemetery.

Gaa-dakwaasigej. Literally, the one who shines briefly, i.e., February.

Gaa-minisiwang. Literally, that has an island. This was the name of a lake with only one island, located close to where people gathered wild rice.

Gaa-minitigwashkiigaag. A marshy region where muskrats abound. An elongated bay along Namegosibiing's eastern shore was sheltered from prevailing wind; it is where the Namegosibii Anishinaabe community's senior elder, Dedibaayaanimanook, was born c. 1922.

gaaskiiwag. Dried (moose) meat. Included in this term is the crispiness of dried meat as indicated by the first part of the word, -gaask.

gego zhaaganaashiiyaadizisiidaa. Let us not be like the European people at the expense of being Anishinaabeg. Expressing the notion of decolonization, this saying is a call to become decolonized.

gete ya'ii. The old things, teachings, customs, and so on.

gichi. Large, big; grand.

gichi-Anishinaabeg. The senior people; the elders.

Gichi-baawitig. Big Falls on Trout Lake River where Namegosibii Anishinaabeg used a portage trail. In her dadibaajim, Dedibaayaanimanook indicates that the name was in reference to the lengthy trail people used to circumvent the falls and rapids in the same way she explains that the name Gichi-onigam denotes the long trail that travellers needed to negotiate in order to get around the tiny lake.

gichi-dewe'igan. The great ceremonial drum.

Gichi Manidoo. The Great Spirit.

giishkaatig. Cedar.

giiwanimo. She/he speaks untruthfully.

giiwedinong. In, at, towards the north.

giizhig. Day; sky.

Giizhigoog. The descendants of Giizhig. This is the term Oo'oons Kejick used in reference to all who have descended from his great-grandfather, Giizhig.

gikendaasowin. Knowledge.

gikendamaawiziwin. The ability to sense a pervasive attitude, atmosphere, undercurrent, character, and so forth.

gikinawaajichigan. A marker; signpost. To mark the location of a moose kill, a hunter would bend branches of nearby trees for future reference as a form of gikinawaajichigan (Dedibaayaanimanook, personal conversation, 2014).

Ginebigo-baawitig. Snake Falls, Ontario. Dedibaayaanimanook and her family once wintered at Snake Falls.

Gizhe Manidoo. Kind/loving spirit.

gojijiing. The source of a river; where a river flows through.

Gojijiwaawangaang. Literally, a sandy location where water begins to flow through. This was the location of the Namegosibii Anishinaabe community cemetery.

gookom. Your grandmother.

gookomens. Literally, your dear/little grandmother. Dedibaayaanimanook's aunt Gookomens was apparently small but energetic.

Gwiishkwa'oo. Robin.

Ikwewi-zaa'igan. Woman Lake. This was where several relatives of the Namegosibii Anishinaabeg made their home.

inaakonigem. Act of making a judgment; a law or rule; an agreement.

inaakwadabiigishing. She/he/it proceeds along (in the same way as the roots of a spruce tree).

ingichiniking. On/at/to/toward my right hand. This may also refer to the location or direction associated with my right.

ishkonigan. What is left over in the sense of unwanted, unacceptable, worthless, etc. It was evident that the land set aside for the Anishinaabe people as reserves was inferior to what the wemitigoozhiwag confiscated for themselves.

ishpiming. Above; the heavens.

izhibii'igaade. It is written.

izhibii'igem. Writing; the writing practice; text; the written record.

izhitwaawin. Cultural practices; cultural activity; culturality.

jiibay. Ghost.

Jiibayi-zaagiing. Now known as Jackfish Bay, this is where a creek empties into the bay in the northern region of Namegosibiing.

-kaan. A replica of; not real, genuine, or original. To illustrate, an elected chief is not of the original Anishinaabe system of leadership. Hence, he or she is an ogimaakaan, a replicated leader in the same way that natural teeth are wiibidan but a set of dentures is wiibidikaanan.

maadaawaang. Where two rivers converge.

Maadaawaang. Location where the English and Chukuni rivers converge. Historically, a Hudson's Bay outpost was located at Maadaawaang.

maamawichigewigamig(ong). Literally, (at) the building where everything is done. People could make purchases, trade, or even find employment at the HBC post.

madaawa'am. Travels down river, i.e., with the current.

madogaan. Lodge that is pointed at the top; a tipi.

maji manidoo. Evil spirit.

makamindô. Seized from them by force, fraud, duplicity, etc.; stolen from them.

Makoshkizh. The Bear Muzzle being who inhabited the night skies of the Namegosibii Anishinaabe boreal homelands.

manoominikem. The practice, product, or process of gathering wild rice.

mashkawiziiwin. Power; force; strength; influence; persuasiveness.

mawadishiwem. Act, process, or practice of visiting.

Memegweshiwi-zaa'igan. Mamakwash Lake (accessible to the Berens River), where Dedibaayaanimanook's father travelled for winter trapping.

mewinzha. A long time ago; time before memory; historically.

migizi(wag). Bald eagle(s).

Migiziwi-giizis. Bald Eagle Moon (February/March).

miiwishkaagewin. Notion of being in the way of, or being a hindrance to (as in the case of Red Lake) settlement, progress, development, and so on. Belief in this idea underpinned the Red Lake "frontier" mentality and drove efforts to be rid of Anishinaabe populations after the discovery of gold in the 1920s. I am grateful to Roger Roulette for bringing this term to my attention.

minikwewin. Alcoholism; alcohol consumption; alcohol. One of Dedibaayaanimanook's narratives states that individuals lost their treaty status when Indian agents found them with alcoholic beverages or in the local beer parlour.

minobimaadiziwin. (The practice of living) a healthy, balanced life.

mitigoog. Trees. Trees are appreciated and regarded with special recognition for the critical function they perform in the health of the earth and Anishinaabe populations.

namanjiniking. On/at/to/toward my left hand. This may also refer to the location or direction associated with my left.

namegos(ag). Trout. Namegosib's trout grew up to twenty-four kilograms under mishoomisag's stewardship.

Namegosi-ziibi. Trout (Lake) River.

Namegosibii Shishiing. This lake is now called Little Trout Lake.

Nengawi'-zaa'igan. Sandy Lake, Ontario.

neyaabikaang. Literally, where a slab of rock forms a point along the shoreline.

nigamon(an). Song(s).

nikag. Canada geese.

Niki-Giizis. Canada Goose Moon.

nitaa. Usually; in the habit of; adept at.

nitaa giiwanimo. He/she is in the habit of/adept at speaking untruthfully. The dadibaajim narratives of those who were in the habit of lying were regarded as unreliable.

nitam. First.

nitamibii'igem. Literally, what is written first; introduction.

nooka'igan. Dry meat pounded to a fine consistency. Dedibaayaanimanook mixed salt, fat, and berries into her nooka'igan.

nookomiban. My late grandmother.

noopimakamig. Boreal forest; places of the boreal forest, away from the lake.

Obizhigokaang. The Lac Seul community; Lac Seul First Nation. Dedibaayaanimanook's mother explained that Waabizhingwaakokaang, a reference to a channel flanked on both sides by white pines, was Lac Seul's original Anishinaabe name.

Obizhigokaawi-zaa'igan. Lac Seul Lake.

odaapinaawasom. The Anishinaabe health profession similar to obstetrics but practised from a midwifery perspective that focuses on a wholistic approach to childbirth.

odinaabanjiganiwaa. Information and knowledge people acquired through dreams, contemplation, and communication with the spirit beings.

odoodemiwin. A system of organizing kinship and identity; practice of the system.

ogichidaakwe. Dedibaayaanimanook indicates this to be the ceremonial dance of the great drum procession, performed by female members of the community.

ogwiimenzim. The practice of ceremonial naming.

Ojiiganang. One of the constellations Anishinaabe people interacted with.

omagakii(g). Frog(s); toad(s).

Omashkiigookwe. Literally, Swampy Cree woman. One of Dedibaayaanimanook's aunts was Omashkiigookwe Sarah, wife of her uncle Naadowe Robert.

omishoomisa'. His/her ancestors; his/her grandfathers.

onaabookaan. Homemade wine. As a component of Namegosibii Anishinaabe spiritual practice, onaabookaan was used in small quantities and with great care.

onjinem. A form of just punishment; receiving what is deserved.

oodenaa. Town.

oodenaang. To, in, into, from town. In certain contexts, this term is a figure of speech for the influences of wemitigoozhiiwaadiziwin colonialism that draw people from the ways of the ancestors and distract them from (the teachings of) the homelands.

Oshedinaa(ng). (At or in) the Trout Lake Ridge terminal moraine.

oshekamigaa. (It is) the height of land.

Oshekamigaawinini. The Man of the Height of Land. This was how Obizhigokaang Lac Seul people referred to Dedibaayaanimanook's grandfather, Giizhig. He was, as a band councillor, undoubtedly well known among Obizhigokaang's political leaders. The people of Obizhigokaang also spoke of the Namegosibii Anishinaabeg as Oshekamigaa Anishinaabeg.

osiganaanibimide. Bone fat that people used for making soup.

Otawagi-baawitig. Ear Falls, Ontario.

skaajimaniigin. Literally, the Scotsman's cloth; a tartan fabric. Namegosibii Anishinaabeg, as with other communities, were fond

of tartans. It was likely because many of the HBC traders were of
Scottish descent that this type of material was readily available at
the trading posts and outposts. Dedibaayaanimanook noted that
Gwiishkwa'oo's mother preferred the Buchanan green and yellow.

waabanong. The east. Associated with tomorrow, daybreak, and
the rising sun, the east is of great significance in Namegosibii
Anishinaabe ontology. One of Dedibaayaanimanook's ceremonial
names, Ekwaabanook, is a reference to the glow of dawn that
brightens the eastern skies. She received it from her paternal uncle,
Jiiyaan.

waabooz(oog). Rabbit(s). Rabbits were not regarded as a nuisance or
of inferior quality. Rather, they were valued as an important source
of fur and food, particularly when larger game animals were scarce.

Waaninaawangaang. Sioux Lookout, Ontario. This name refers to the
abundance of sand in the region.

waawiimbaajimowin. A type of speech strategy people use to avoid
certain topics. Language specialist Roger Roulette introduced this
word to me. It is not a term that is familiar to Dedibaayaanimanook.

wanamani. Red ochre.

Wanamani-zaa'igan. Red Lake, Ontario.

wanangosh(ag). Star(s).

wanii'igem. The practice, profession, and/or activity of trapping.

wazhashk. Muskrat. As with the waaboozoog rabbits, muskrats were
valued inhabitants of the boreal homelands.

Wazhashkonigam. Kenora, Ontario. When HBC reports wrote of "the
Rat," they were referring to Rat Portage, the latecomers' original
name for Kenora. Kenora itself derives from a combination of the
first two letters of the three place names, Keewatin (an anglicized
version of the word "giiwedin," north), Norman, and Rat Portage.

wemitigoozhi(wag). European settler man (men) or person(s).
The negative connotations this term evokes came about when
Anishinaabeg began to experience the foreigners' inimical attitudes
and behaviours. Also, but unrelatedly, "wemitigoozhi" refers to a

person-being who made brief appearances during a certain type of ceremonial.

wemitigoozhiiwaadiziwin. Thinking and acting as a European settler or descendant at the expense of Anishinaabewaadiziwin (see Geniusz, "Gego Wemitigoozhiiyaadizisiidaa"); colonialism; colonial thinking that includes capitalism and the pursuit of zhooniyaa.

wiikenzh. Sweet flag rhizome, used for its medical properties.

Wiikwedinong. Thunder Bay, Ontario.

wiin. A contrastive particle (see Nichols and Nyholm, *Concise Dictionary of Minnesota Ojibwe*). A person, to illustrate, stating "gaawiin wiin niin ingii'izhaasii" is underscoring the fact (s)he did not go there, even though others did.

wiisaakode. A person of mixed heritage. Dedibaayaanimanook was unsure of its derivation.

wiiyaabishkiiwej. Literally, having white or pale skin (indicating the distinctive physical feature of the Europeans as observed by Anishinaabeg). The term did not in and of itself carry negative connotations.

wiiyaasikewininiwag. Literally, men who deal with/in meat; game wardens.

zhaaganaashiimowin. (Use of) the English language.

Zhaawan. The being who inhabits the southern skies.

zhaawaninoodin. A south wind is blowing.

zhaawanong. Towards, from, or in the south.

zhawenjigem. Compassion. Dedibaayaanimanook's uncle Jiiyaan exemplified compassion when he gifted his infant niece with a ceremonial name. Itself a gift, zhawenjigem was attained through a process that began during the ando-bawaajigem dream quest journey.

zhooniyaa. Money, cash; the economic system based on the use of money.

Bibliography

Absolon, Kathleen. "Indigenous Wholistic Theory: A Knowledge Set for Practice." *First Peoples Child and Family Review* 5, no. 2 (2010): 74–87.

———. *Kaandossiwin: How We Come to Know.* Winnipeg: Fernwood Publishing, 2011.

Agger, Helen. *Following Nimishoomis: The Trout Lake History of Dedibaayaanimanook Sarah Keesick Olsen.* Penticton: Theytus Books, 2008.

Ahenakew, Freda. *Wâskahikaniwiyiniw-âcimowina: Stories of the House People.* Winnipeg: University of Manitoba Press, 1987.

Baca, Damián. "Te-ixtli: The 'Other Face' of the Americas." In *Rhetorics of the Americas: 3114 BCE to 2012 CE,* edited by Damián Baca and Victor Villanueva, 1–13. New York: Palgrave Macmillan, 2010.

Ballard, Myrle. "Flooding Sustainable Livelihoods of the Lake St. Martin First Nation: The Need to Enhance the Role of Gender and Language in Anishinaabe Knowledge Systems." PhD diss., University of Manitoba, 2012.

Bender, Margaret. "Reflections on What Writing Means, Beyond What It 'Says': The Political Economy and Semiotics of Graphic Pluralism in the Americas." *Ethnohistory* 57, no. 1 (2010): 175–82.

Bird, Louis. *Telling Our Stories: Omushkego Legends and Histories from Hudson Bay.* Toronto: University of Toronto Press, 2011.

Bishop, Charles. "The Emergence of the Northern Ojibwa: Social and Economic Consequences." *American Ethnologist* 3, no. 1 (1976): 39–54.

———. *The Northern Ojibwa and the Fur Trade: An Historical and Ecological Study.* Toronto: Holt, Rinehart & Winston of Canada, 1974.

Bohaker, Heidi. "Reading Anishinaabe Identities: Meanings and Metaphor in Nindoodem Pictographs." *Ethnohistory* 57, no. 1 (2010): 11–33.

Borrows, John. *Drawing Out Law: A Spirit's Guide.* Toronto: University of Toronto Press, 2010.

———. "Indian Agency: Forming First Nations Law in Canada." *PoLAR: Political and Legal Anthropology Review* 24, no. 2 (2001): 9–24.

———. "Listening for a Change: The Courts and Oral Tradition." *Osgoode Hall Law Journal* 39, no. 1 (2001): 1–38.

Brown, Alison, and Laura Peers. *Pictures Bring Us Messages / Sinaakssiiksi Aohtsimaahpihkookiya awa: Photographs and Histories from the Kainai Nation.* Toronto: University of Toronto Press, 2005.

Brown, Jennifer, and Susan Grey, eds. *Memories, Myths and Dreams of an Ojibwe Leader.* Kingston: McGill-Queen's University Press, 2009.

Brown, Jennifer, and Maureen Matthews. "Fair Wind: Medicine and Consolation on the Berens River." *Journal of the Canadian Historical Association* 4, no. 1 (1993): 55–74.

Butikofer, Gary. *The Butikofer Papers on Berens River Ojibwe History, Part II.2: Lac Seul Family Histories.* Winnipeg: Centre for Rupert's Land Studies, University of Winnipeg, 2009.

Clark, Jim. "Mawadishiwewin." In *Living Our Language,* edited by Anton Treuer, 74–76. St. Paul: Minnesota Historical Society Press, 2001.

Copway, George. *The Traditional History and Characteristic Sketches of the Ojibway Nation.* Boston: Benjamin B. Mussey, 1850.

Cruikshank, Julie. *Life Lived Like a Story: Life Stories of Three Yukon Native Elders.* Lincoln: University of Nebraska Press, 1997.

Cushman, Ellen. "New Media Scholarship and Teaching: Challenging the Hierarchy of Signs." *Pedagogy* 11, no. 1 (2011): 63–79.

Daniels-Fiss, Belinda. "Learning to Be a Nêhiyaw (Cree) Through Language." *Diaspora, Indigenous, and Minority Education: Studies of Migration, Integration, Equity, and Cultural Survival* 2, no. 3 (2008): 233–45.

Debassige, Brent. "Building on Conceptual Interpretations of Aboriginal Literacy in Anishinaabe Research: A Turtle Shaker Model." *Canadian Journal of Education / Revue Canadienne de l'Éducation* 36, no. 2 (2013): 4–33.

———. "Re-conceptualizing Anishinaabe Mino-bimaadiziwin (the Good Life) as Research Methodology: A Spirit-Centered Way in Anishinaabe Research." *Canadian Journal of Native Education* 33, no. 1 (2010): 11–28.

Dunning, Robert. *Social and Economic Change Among the Northern Ojibwa.* Toronto: University of Toronto Press, 1959.

Eagle, Melvin. "Wenji-ganawendamang gidakiiminaan." In *Living Our Language,* edited by Anton Treuer, 108–18. St Paul: Minnesota Historical Society Press, 2001.

Eastman, Charles. *From the Deep Woods to Civilization: Chapters in the Autobiography of an Indian.* 1916. Settler Literature Archive, 10. Lincoln: University of Nebraska Press, 1977.

Eigenbrod, Renate. *Travelling Knowledges: Positioning the Im/migrant Reader of Aboriginal Literatures in Canada.* Winnipeg: University of Manitoba Press, 2005.

Episkenew, Jo-Ann. *Taking Back Our Spirits: Indigenous Literature, Public Policy, and Healing.* Winnipeg: University of Manitoba Press, 2009.

Erdrich, Louise. *Books and Islands in Ojibwe Country.* Washington: National Geographic Society, 2003.

Gehl, Lynn. "Debwewin Journey: A Methodology and Model of Knowing." *AlterNative* 8 (2012): 53–65.

Geniusz, Wendy. "Gego Wemitigoozhiiyaadizisiidaa: The Decolonization Process." In *Anishinaabewin NISWI: Deep Roots, New Growth,* edited by The Ojibwe Cultural Foundation and Kenjgewin Teg Educational Institute, 3. M'Chigeeng, ON: The Ojibwe Cultural Foundation and Kenjgewin Teg Educational Institute, 2012.

————. *Our Knowledge Is Not Primitive: Decolonizing Botanical Anishinaabe Teachings.* Syracuse: Syracuse University Press, 2009.

Guédon, Marie-Françoise. "Dene Ways and the Ethnographer's Culture." In *Being Changed by Cross-Cultural Encounters: The Anthropology of Extraordinary Experience,* edited by David Young and Jean-Guy Goulet, 39–70. Peterborough: Broadview Press, 1994.

Hallowell, Alfred. "Bear Ceremonialism in the Northern Hemisphere." *American Anthropologist* 28, no. 1 (1926): 1–175.

————. "The Incidence, Character, and Decline of Polygyny Among the Lake Winnipeg Cree and Saulteaux." *American Anthropologist* 40, no. 2 (1938): 235–56.

————. "Some Empirical Aspects of Northern Saulteaux Religion." *American Anthropologist* 36, no. 3 (1934): 389–404.

————. "The Spirits of the Dead in Saulteaux Life and Thought." *Journal of the Royal Anthropological Institute of Great Britain and Ireland* 70, no. 1 (1940): 29–51.

Herzog, Benno. "Invisibilization and Silencing as an Ethical and Sociological Challenge." *Social Epistemology* 32, no.1 (2018): 13–23.

Hopkins, Susan. "Relational Flow Frames: Conducting Relationship-based Research in an Aboriginal Community." *Pimatisiwin: A Journal of Aboriginal and Indigenous Community Health* 10, no. 2 (2012): 177–90.

Jenness, Diamond. "The 'Blond' Eskimos." *American Anthropologist* 23, no. 3 (1921): 257–67.

Johnston, Basil. "One Generation from Extinction." *Canadian Literature* 124–25 (1990): 10–15.

————. *Th!nk Indian: Languages Are Beyond Price.* Cape Croker: Kegedonce Press, 2011.

Kovach, Margaret. "Conversational Method in Indigenous Research." *First Peoples Child and Family Review* 5, no. 1 (2010): 40–48.

Kulchyski, Peter. "and." *Postcolonial Studies* 18, no. 3 (2015): 320–25.

————. "Anthropology in the Service of the State: Diamond Jenness and Canadian Indian Policy." *Journal of Canadian Studies* 28, no. 2 (1993): 21–50.

————. "Bush Culture for a Bush Country: An Unfinished Manifesto." *Journal of Canadian Studies* 31, no. 3 (1996): 192–96.

LaCapra, Dominick. *Representing the Holocaust: History, Theory, Trauma.* Ithaca: Cornell University Press, 1994.

Landes, Ruth. *The Ojibwa Woman.* New York: Columbia University Press, 1938.

Matthews, Maureen. "Repatriating Agency: Animacy, Personhood and Agency in the Repatriation of Ojibwe Artefacts." PhD diss., University of Oxford, 2009.

Memmi, Albert. *The Colonizer and the Colonized.* Boston: Beacon Press, 1991.

Mignolo, Walter. *The Darker Side of the Renaissance: Literacy, Territoriality, and Colonization.* Ann Arbor: The University of Michigan Press, 1995.

————. "Delinking: The Rhetoric of Modernity, the Logic of Coloniality and the Grammar of De-coloniality." *Cultural Studies* 21, no. 2–3 (2007): 449–514.

Morris, Alexander. *The Treaties of Canada.* Toronto: Willing and Williamson, 1880.

Nicholas, George. "Decolonizing the Archaeological Landscape: The Practice and Politics of Archaeology in British Columbia." *American Indian Quarterly* 30, no. 3–4 (2006): 350–80.

Nichols, John, and Earl Nyholm. *A Concise Dictionary of Minnesota Ojibwe.* Minneapolis: University of Minnesota Press, 1995.

Peacock, Thomas. "Teaching as Story." In *Centering Anishinaabeg Studies*, edited by Jill Doerfler, Niigaanwewidam James Sinclair, and Heidi Kiiwetinepinesiik Stark, 103–16. East Lansing: Michigan State University Press, 2013.

Peers, Laura, and Jennifer Brown. "There Is No End to Relationship Among the Indians: Ojibwa Families and Kinship in Historical Perspective." *History of the Family* 4, no. 4 (1999): 529–55.

Peers, Laura, and Carolyn Podruchny. "Introduction: Complex Subjectivities, Multiple Ways of Knowing." In *Gathering Places: Aboriginal and Fur Trade Histories*, edited by Carolyn Podruchny and Laura Peers, 1–22. Vancouver: University of British Columbia Press, 2010.

Pitawanakwat, Brock. "Anishinaabemodaa Pane Oodenang: A Qualitative Study of Anishinaabe Language Revitalization as Self-Determination in Manitoba and Ontario." PhD diss., University of Victoria, 2009.

Promislow, Janna. "One Chief, Two Chiefs, Red Chiefs, Blue Chiefs: Newcomer Perspectives on Indigenous Leadership in Rupert's Land and the North-West Territories." In *The Grand Experiment: Law and Legal Culture in British Settler Societies*, edited by Hamar Foster, Benjamin Berger, and A. Buck, 55–77. Vancouver: University of British Columbia Press, 2008.

Richthammer, John. "Memento Mori: An Archival Strategy for Documenting Mortality on the Canadian Frontier at Red Lake, Ontario, before 1950." Master's thesis, University of Manitoba, 2007.

Rogers, Edward, and J. Garth Taylor. "Northern Ojibwa." In *Handbook of North American Indians 6*, edited by June Helm, 231–43. Washington: Smithsonian Institution, 1981.

Schultz, Emily, Robert Lavenda, and Roberta Dods. *Cultural Anthropology: A Perspective on the Human Condition*. Toronto: Oxford University Press, 2015.

Simpson, Leanne. "Anti-colonial Strategies for the Recovery and Maintenance of Indigenous Knowledge." *American Indian Quarterly* 28 (2004): 373–84.

———. "The Construction of Traditional Ecological Knowledge: Issues, Implications and Insights." PhD diss., University of Manitoba, 1999.

———. "Land as Pedagogy: Nishnaabeg Intelligence and Rebellious Transformation." *Decolonization: Indigeneity, Education and Society* 3, no. 3 (2014): 1–25.

Smallman, Shawn. "Spirit Beings, Mental Illness, and Murder: Fur Traders and the Windigo in Canada's Boreal Forest, 1774–1935." *Ethnohistory* 57, no. 4 (2010): 571–96.

Steinbring, Jack. "Saulteaux of Lake Winnipeg." In *Handbook of North American Indians 6*, edited by June Helm, 244–55. Washington: Smithsonian Institution, 1981.

Treuer, Anton. *Anton Treuer, a Linguist from Leech Lake, Speaks about the Ojibwe Language, the Importance of Indigenous Languages, Ways of Learning/teaching, the Last Battle at Sugar Point in Leech Lake and Personal Experiences of Learning the Language*, 1999. www.ojibwe.org/home/pdf/A_Treuer_Ojib_lang_Outtake.pdf.

———. "Ge-onji-aabadak Anishinaabe-inwewinan." *The American Indian Quarterly* 30, no. 1 (2006): 87–90.

Vizenor, Gerald. *Manifest Manners: Narratives on Postindian Survivance*. Lincoln: University of Nebraska Press, 1999.

Warren, William. *History of the Ojibway People*. St. Paul: Minnesota Historical Society Press, 1885, 2009.

Young, Mary. "Anishinabemowin: A Way of Seeing the World Reclaiming My Identity." *Canadian Journal of Native Education* 27, no. 1 (2003): 101–7.

Index

Relationships in parenthesis are in reference to Dedibaayaanimanook Sarah Keesick Olsen unless otherwise noted.